The Case of Literature

signale
modern german letters, cultures, and thought

Series editor: Peter Uwe Hohendahl, Cornell University

Signale: Modern German Letters, Cultures, and Thought publishes new English-language books in literary studies, criticism, cultural studies, and intellectual history pertaining to the German-speaking world, as well as translations of important German-language works. *Signale* construes "modern" in the broadest terms: the series covers topics ranging from the early modern period to the present. *Signale* books are published under a joint imprint of Cornell University Press and Cornell University Library in electronic and print formats. Please see http://signale.cornell.edu/.

THE CASE OF LITERATURE

*Forensic Narratives from
Goethe to Kafka*

ARNE HÖCKER

A Signale Book

CORNELL UNIVERSITY PRESS AND CORNELL UNIVERSITY LIBRARY
ITHACA AND LONDON

Cornell University Press and Cornell University Library gratefully
acknowledge the College of Arts & Sciences, Cornell University, for
support of the Signale series.

Copyright © 2020 by Cornell University

All rights reserved. Except for brief quotations in a review, this book, or
parts thereof, must not be reproduced in any form without permission in
writing from the publisher. For information, address Cornell University
Press, Sage House, 512 East State Street, Ithaca, New York 14850.

First published 2020 by Cornell University Press
and Cornell University Library

Librarians, a CIP data record is available from the Library of Congress
at https://lccn.loc.gov/2019032677

ISBN 978-1-5017-4935-3 (hardcover)
ISBN 978-1-5017-4936-0 (paperback)
ISBN 978-1-5017-4937-7 (epub)
ISBN 978-1-5017-4938-4 (pdf)

Contents

Acknowledgments   vii

Introduction   1

Part I Making the Case around 1800

1. The Case of Werther and the Institution of Literature   27

2. "Observe, Write!": Histories of Observation and the Psychological Novel *Anton Reiser*   49

3. Hot and Cold: History, Casuistry, and Literature in Schiller and Kleist   71

4. Conclusion: Literary Reference and Authorship   93

Part II The Case between Psychiatry, Law, and Literature

5. Schmolling, Hoffmann, Hitzig, and the Problem of Legal Responsibility   99

6. The Drama of the Case: Making the Case of Woyzeck   114

7. Drama, Anecdote, Case: Wedekind's *Lulu* 132

8. Conclusion: The Fiction of Authority 152

Part III Novelistic Casuistry

9. Freud's Cases 157

10. Fantasy of Facts: Döblin's Poetics of Uncertainty 174

11. The Man of Possibilities: Musil's Moosbrugger 190

12. Conclusion: The Function of Fiction 205

Bibliography 213

Index 229

Acknowledgments

For their support and friendship, I would like to thank my parents, Kirsten and Eitel Friedrich Höcker, and my friends and colleagues, whose encouragement has helped me to complete this book: Alison Cool, Rüdiger Campe, Marco Clausen, Kijan Espahangizi, Christiane Frey, Patrick Greaney, Jason Groves, Wolf Kittler, Andrea Krauß, Jörg Kreienbrock, David Martyn, Peri Mason, Ulrich Plass, Tom Roberts, Matthias Rothe, Ann Schmiesing, Jochen Steinbicker, Davide Stimilli, Elisabeth Strowick, Ellwood Wiggins, Meredith Miller and my friends from the RCC Boulder. I am, indeed, particularly grateful to Paul Fleming for his generous support and advice, and to Helmut Müller-Sievers for being a diligent, critical, and generous reader of my manuscript, and for having pushed me to make this book better. It would not have been the same book without his ingenious advice.

An earlier version of chapter 3 appeared under the title "In Citation: 'A Violation of the Law of Boundaries' in Schiller and Kleist," *Germanic Review: Literature, Culture, Theory* 89, no. 1: 60–75 (https://www.tandfonline.com). I am grateful to the press for allowing its reprinting here. I would also like to express my gratitude to the board and the editors of the Signale series at Cornell University Press, and to the two anonymous readers of my manuscript, whose advice and criticism has significantly contributed to its improvement.

The Case of Literature

Introduction

The Jerusalem Case

On October 29, 1772, Karl Wilhelm Jerusalem, a twenty-five-year-old lawyer in the town of Wetzlar, shot himself in the head in his apartment and died one day later.[1] Jerusalem, who came from a bourgeois background and had repeatedly come into conflict with the nobility and his superiors, did not find much satisfaction in his position as a legation secretary to the Principality of Brunswick-Wolfenbüttel. He was bullied, and his father had already arranged a new position for his son in Vienna when Jerusalem fell in love with the countess Elisabeth Herd, a married woman. Devastated and heartbroken after being rejected, Jerusalem decided to take

---

1. A collection of documents concerning the Jerusalem case can be found in Roger Paulin, *Der Fall Wilhelm Jerusalem: Zum Selbstmordproblem zwischen Aufklärung und Empfindsamkeit* (Göttingen: Wallstein, 1999).

his own life. Under false pretenses, he obtained a pistol from his acquaintance—Johann Christian Kestner, who was not aware of any of the unfortunate details—and shot himself. In a letter, Kestner told the story to his friend Johann Wolfgang Goethe, who had met Jerusalem as a student in Leipzig, and who also had settled in Wetzlar in May of the same year:

> As Jerusalem was now alone, he appears to have made all his preparations for this terrible deed. He wrote two letters. One to a relative, the other to H. After these preparations, around toward 1 o'clock, he shot himself in the forehead above his right eye. The bullet could not be found anywhere. No one in the house heard the shot except the Franciscan Father Guardian, who also saw the powder flash but because there was no further sound, paid no attention to it. The servant had hardly slept the night before and has his room far out at the back. It appears to have been done as he was sitting in his armchair in front of his desk. The back of the seat of the chair was bloody, as well as the armrests. Thereupon he slumped down from the chair. There was still a lot of blood on the floor. He was fully dressed, his boots on and wearing a blue coat with a yellow waistcoat.[2]

Jerusalem's body was found in the morning by one of the servants, and the doctor, who was called immediately, could not do anything for the young man, whose pulse was still beating. "The rumor of the event spread quickly," Kestner continues in his letter:

> The whole town was shocked and thrown into an uproar. I first heard about it at 9 o'clock, I remembered my pistols, and I don't know, in a short time I was so very shocked. I got dressed and went there. He had been laid on the bed, his brow covered, his face already that of a dead man.... Here and there lay books and some of his own written essays. "Emilia Galotti," its pages opened, lay on the desk at the window, next to it a manuscript, approximately the thickness of a finger, in quarto, of a philosophical nature. Part One or the first Letter had the title "On Freedom." He died at noon. In the evening at 10:45 he was buried in the common churchyard in stillness with 12 lanterns and several persons ac-

---

2. Johann Christian Kestner, "Letter to Goethe Reporting on Jerusalem's Suicide," in Johann Wolfgang von Goethe, *The Sufferings of Young Werther*, trans. and ed. Stanley Corngold (New York: W. W. Norton, 2012), 103.

companying him; barber's apprentices carried him; the cross was carried before him; no clergyman attended.³

The familiarity of these passages from Kestner's letter is not a coincidence: Goethe modeled his first novel, *The Sufferings of Young Werther* (1774), after the Jerusalem case, and the final pages borrow verbatim from Kestner's report on the suicide. The novel's famous last line—"no clergyman attended"—is a direct quote from the letter, as is Werther's signature dress, blue coat and yellow waistcoat.

The adaptation of an authentic case of suicide in Goethe's *Werther* shows that by the end of the eighteenth century, literary fiction has abandoned its moralizing and didactic purpose and has instead begun to reach toward the uncommented depiction of individual histories. *Werther* can no longer be understood as a moral example; as an individual case it is organized as a narrative so as to make accessible "the heart of a sick, youthful delusion."⁴ A "true depiction," Goethe writes in his autobiography regarding the *Werther* novel, does not have a didactic purpose, "it does not condone, it does not condemn; it develops sentiments and actions as they follow from one another, and in so doing it illuminates and instructs."⁵ In a conversation with the Swiss poet Johann Kaspar Lavater, Goethe is said to have labeled his first novel a *historia morbi*, a story of an illness, thereby implying that *Werther* belonged to the tradition of medical cases and their interest in psychopathology.⁶ The narrative presentation of an individual case based on contemporary events distinguishes Goethe's novel from other literary works of his time. It is telling that the novel, which appeared without a desig-

---
3. Kestner, "Letter," 103–104.
4. Johann Wolfgang von Goethe, "From My Life: Poetry and Truth," in *Werther*, 115.
5. Goethe, "From My Life," 118.
6. Hans Gerhard Gräf, "Nachträge zu Goethes Gesprächen, 1: Johann Kaspar Lavater," *Jahrbuch der Goethe-Gesellschaft* 6 (1919): 283–285. For a detailed discussion of Goethe's remark to Lavater, see Christiane Frey, "'Ist das nicht der Fall der Krankheit?' Der literarische Fall am Beispiel von Goethes *Werther*," *Zeitschrift für Germanistik* 19 (2009): 317–329.

nation of authorship, was initially not even perceived as literary fiction; the opening fiction of the editor and the epistolary form contributed to this perception.[7] That *Werther* could also be read as a documentation of a real case of suicide indicates a significant change in the status of literary fiction toward the end of the eighteenth century. It also shows the emergence of interest in psychological abnormalities and, just as important, in the ability of narrative fiction to present psychological cases. Insofar as it eliminates any external interpretative frame, *Werther* does not provide a general rule or principle to which the case relates, as was the custom in older traditions of casuistry, and it does not subscribe to an identifiable norm that the novel would champion. Goethe's novel absorbs the historical case into a narrative structure that retains the tension between the individual history and the general consequences that could be drawn from it. It is in reference to given cases that authors begin to display, to experiment, and to reflect on the conditions for the narrative appropriation of reality. The following pages will show that representing cases in fictional narrative became an important touchstone for the development of German literature.

What Is a Case?

The concept *case* refers to a particular way of thinking, administrating, and classifying that has gained epistemic relevance in various disciplinary and institutional settings.[8] In the most general terms, a case allows the making of connections between a specific, discrete incident that it reports and a general form of knowledge to

---

7. Regardless of the initial anonymous publication of the novel, *Werther* has been identified as the novel that inaugurates a new form of authorship, an author function, as Friedrich Kittler has argued, that regulates the hermeneutic interpretation of literary texts. (See Friedrich A. Kittler, "Autorschaft und Liebe," in *Austreibung des Geistes aus den Geisteswissenschaften*, ed. Friedrich A. Kittler [Paderborn: Verlag Ferdinand Schöningh, 1980], 142–173.)

8. Most prominently, John Forrester, "If P, Then What? Thinking in Cases," *History of the Human Sciences* 9, no. 3 (1996): 1–25.

which it contributes. The particular way a case fulfills its function depends on the disciplinary context in which it appears; criminal cases are used for purposes different from medical or psychological cases. To qualify as a case, the observation and record of a particular event requires a framework that attributes significance to it in regard to other possible cases, but not necessarily documented ones. Thus, a case can be defined as a distinctive set of references—even when it can be treated as a self-sufficient observation of a discrete and isolated event, it is functionally dependent.[9]

Historically, cases answer to a variety of moral, legal, and epistemic problems. They have been used to deduce general codes of conduct in moral theology, where they can also take on an illustrative and exemplary character. They can support legal arguments and become precedents against which other cases can be measured, evaluated, and used in legal processes of decision making. Finally, cases can be used to generate knowledge, such as in medical disciplines, where they were to be considered the primary method of informing therapeutic and—since the Renaissance—scientific practice.

The functional definition of the case varies with its disciplinary and institutional frame, whereas its formal definition is easier to apprehend: cases employ narrative—a sequential and coherently written account of events—as their principle of organization. Beyond this congruence, their form can vary significantly in focus, perspective, and length. Premodern collections of medical cases from the late sixteenth century onward, for example, were published as *consilia* or *observationes*; although they vary in focus, perspective, and narrative style, these collections were the first to make systematic use of cases and, therefore, are of particular relevance for the scientific formation of modern medical discourse.[10] *Consilia* were printed for practical educational purposes, and *observationes* are precursors to the modern concept of case that coincided with the birth of the clinic and the training of the medical gaze in

---

9. See Christiane Frey, "Fallgeschichte," in *Literatur und Wissen: Ein interdisziplinäres Handbuch*, ed. Roland Borgards, Harald Neumeyer, Nicolas Pethes, and Yvonne Wübben (Stuttgart: Metzler, 2013), 283.

10. See Robert Jütte, "Vom medizinischen Casus zur Krankengeschichte," *Berichte zur Wissenschaftsgeschichte* 15 (1992): 50–52.

the late eighteenth century.[11] In contrast to other forms of medical casuistry that often combine the description of symptoms with an anamnesis and diagnostic conclusions, *observationes* avoided any form of scholarly explanation and left open the relationship between an individual case and the sequence in which it appeared: "In the *observationes*, the hierarchy of case and commentary was reversed: no longer subordinate to the elucidation of doctrine, the case narrative became the primary object of attention."[12] *Observationes* form their own "epistemic genre" that is directed toward the production of knowledge based on individual cases.[13]

The premodern medical case remained an empirical genre with a decidedly pragmatic and practical orientation. Its popularity in the late sixteenth century was due to increasing frustration with the dominant Galenic medicine and its theoretical and speculative methods.[14] More generally speaking, cases often seem to become important when conventional paradigms of knowledge and knowledge production become obsolete or their general validity is questioned. Inversely, this means that no standard for their

---

11. See Michel Foucault, *The Birth of the Clinic: An Archaeology of Medical Perception*, trans. Alan Sheridan (New York: Pantheon, 1973). On *consilia* as a casuistic genre, see Michael Stollberg, "Formen und Funktionen medizinischer Fallgeschichten in der Frühen Neuzeit (1500–1800)," in *Fallstudien: Theorie, Geschichte, Methode*, ed. Johannes Süßmann, Susanne Scholz, and Gisela Engel (Berlin: Trafo Verlag, 2007), 81–95.

12. Gianna Pomata, "The Medical Case Narrative: Distant Reading of an Epistemic Genre," *Literature and Medicine* 32, no. 1 (2014): 15.

13. Gianna Pomata introduces the concept of *epistemic genre* to distinguish the case from literature and to characterize "those genres that are deliberately cognitive in purpose" (Pomata, "Medical Case Narrative," 15). Texts that can be affiliated with epistemic genres, Pomata specifies, develop in direct connection to scientific practices, and the knowledge they produce is not a cultural side effect, but the result intended by an author. Pomata distinguishes sharply between epistemic and literary genre: "Historians of knowledge should identify epistemic genres as that specific kind of genre whose function is fundamentally cognitive, not aesthetic or expressive—that kind of genre whose primary goal is not the production of *meaning* but the production of *knowledge*" (2). Pomata admits that this distinction can and should not be drawn rigidly and that historians of knowledge have indeed shown that poetics and epistemology are often interconnected. She believes, however, that the literary and the epistemic must be distinguished from one another in order to study and understand their specific effects.

14. See Stollberg, "Formen und Funktionen," 89.

composition exists and that one can attribute to them a liberating effect: "The adoption of case-related structures in literature as well as of narrative patterns in medical writing," Nicolas Pethes writes, "always serves as an attempt to leave behind standardized modes of representation in favor of new ones beyond established general categories. In short, writing case histories always means writing against genre—at least in the traditional sense of general typological schemes."[15]

The reference to the medical use of cases is particularly important in the following investigation because it differs significantly from casuistic practices in moral theology and jurisprudence: medical practitioners do not observe the individual case from the perspective of doctrine but instead proceed from an individual history. The narrative form of cases is sometimes considered sufficient evidence for the epistemic productivity of literary forms; this should not, however, lead to the easy conclusion that these cases can be fully understood in literary terms without reference to their disciplinary practices and institutional frames.[16] What is of interest in the following, rather, is the constitutive contribution of case narratives to the establishment of new scientific disciplines, in particular empirical psychology and, more important, the formation of an autonomous discourse of and about literary fiction from the late eighteenth century onward.

One of the earliest attempts to define the case as an essential mode of literary narrative, André Jolles's often-quoted *Simple Forms* (1930), is instructive here, although it is still heavily indebted to the tradition of casuistry in theology and jurisprudence. Jolles does not understand the case simply as a narrative illustration of a norm or

---

15. Nicolas Pethes, "Telling Cases: Writing against Genre in Medicine and Literature," *Literature and Medicine* 32, no. 1 (2014): 27.

16. Volker Hess strongly rejects any understanding of the case as a literary genre and instead proposes different perspectives on the form, organization, and function of the case. Hess does not see any generic uniformity of the case at all and instead focuses on the media techniques and social practices of notation, registration, and writing—which he calls *paper technology*. (Volker Hess, "Observation und Casus: Status und Funktion der medizinischen Fallgeschichte," in *Fall—Fallgeschichte—Fallstudie: Theorie und Geschichte einer Wissensform*, ed. Susanne Düwell and Nicolas Pethes [Frankfurt am Main: Campus Verlag, 2014], 37.)

a rule but as a negotiation of conflicts between norms. A case, he argues, raises a question without giving an answer; it is directed toward a decision without suggesting one.[17] Jolles defines the case by assigning it a specific "mental disposition" (*Geistesbeschäftigung*), in contrast to understanding the case as a genre. Considering the breadth in variation of narrative and epistemic forms of casuistic reasoning in medicine, jurisprudence, and literature, Jolles's definition of the case as a figure of thought rather than a set of narrative rules is indeed productive, as when he argues that the case has "a tendency to expand into an art form, . . . to become a novella."[18] Cases, in this view, precede the standardization of narrative forms and their solidification into genres. This opens up new perspectives on the exchange between literary and epistemic forms and on the constitutive potential of casuistic modes of representation for the development of literary forms: writing cases means not only writing against genre but also writing toward genre, toward theory, and toward applicable knowledge.

Dependent on their disciplinary focus, historical studies of cases have followed different traditions and trajectories. Interestingly, historians of science have emphasized continuities in which literary scholars, in reference to Foucault's history of modern biopolitics and the emergence of disciplinary and normalizing practices that center around the individual, have seen a paradigmatic shift.[19] Most prominently, John Forrester has argued for a tradition of "thinking in cases" that has shaped various scientific disciplines from antiquity to modernity.[20] In contrast to Foucault, Forrester does not see any decisive transformation or shift in the direction of casuistic think-

---

17. "The special character of the case lies in the fact that it asks the question, but cannot give the answer; that it imposes the duty of judgment upon us, but does not itself contain the judgment—what becomes manifest in it is the act of weighing, but not the result of the weighing." (André Jolles, *Simple Forms: Legend, Saga, Myth, Riddle, Saying, Case, Memorabile, Fairytale, Joke*, trans. Peter J. Schwartz [New York: Verso, 2017], 153.)
18. Jolles, *Simple Forms*, 153.
19. See Michel Foucault, *The Birth of Biopolitics: Lectures at the Collège de France, 1978–1979*, trans. Graham Burchell (New York: Picador, 2008).
20. See Forrester, "Thinking in Cases."

ing and reasoning.[21] Focusing on the development of narrative in cases, however, at the beginning of the eighteenth century we see medical case histories become increasingly more comprehensive in their description of individual circumstances.[22] With a special focus on psychological aspects, these cases also attribute more relevance to biographical details and thus become increasingly complex as narratives. Karl Philipp Moritz's *Magazin zur Erfahrungsseelenkunde* (1783–1793), often considered the birthplace of empirical psychology, is a decisive milestone in this tradition. Varying in length and narrative perspective, and following Moritz's rule to abstain from drawing conclusions, the cases published in the *Magazin* mix medical classification, pedagogical observation, and biographical narrative, thereby creating a dynamic ensemble of forms of writing in which literary effects and epistemic interest are indistinguishable from one another. As a result of this hybridization, case narratives in the late eighteenth century began to contribute to a new conception of literature that captured the problem of individuality by narrative means in order to create a general and empirical knowledge of the human. What Moritz was the first to call "the psychological novel" developed out of this context and contributed to the establishment of a novelistic form with an explicitly stated epistemic purpose.

But it is not only the tradition of medical cases that contributed to the development of narrative fiction in the second half of the eighteenth century. The *Causes célèbres et interessantes*, published by the French lawyer François Gayot de Pitaval in several volumes between 1734 and 1743, had an equally strong effect on German writers throughout the eighteenth and nineteenth centuries. In his footsteps, one of the leading legal scholars in the early nineteenth century, Anselm Ritter von Feuerbach, published a collection of criminal cases, *Merkwürdige Kriminal-Rechtsfälle in aktenmäßiger Darstellung* (1808–1829); Willibald Alexis and Eduard Hitzig

---

21. For a discussion of the case in Forester and Foucault, see Inka Mülder-Bach and Michael Ott, eds., "Einleitung," in *Was der Fall ist: Casus und Lapsus* (Paderborn: Wilhelm Fink Verlag, 2014), 9–31.
22. See also Frey, "Fallgeschichte," 285.

initiated a *Neue Pitaval* that appeared from 1842 to 1890. Friedrich Schiller had already recognized the literary potential of the collection of remarkable and interesting criminal cases based on verifiable historical events. He so appreciated *Pitaval* that he became the editor of a German translation published between 1790 and 1792, and contributed an introduction.

The examples of Karl Philipp Moritz and Friedrich Schiller show that in the German context, modern literature—its practice and its theory—emerged in reference to casuistic traditions. Authors around 1800, guided by an abiding interest in the human individual, combined their interest in legal cases with medical and psychological perspectives. Both the legal and medical traditions rely on casuistic forms of reasoning and record-keeping, but they differ in their use of casuistic reference. In contrast to the medical case, which is used to induce empirical knowledge of the human body, legal forms of casuistic reasoning were predominantly deductive—considering cases in their specific relation to the law and the general legal framework. Thus, a difference remains between the deductive use of legal cases in classifying and regulating behavior and the medical case as a set of empirically observed symptoms that in concert with other, similar sets yields knowledge of ever-greater generality. It is in the negotiation of this difference between singularity and generality that narrative literature finds its place.

This book, then, is concerned with understanding the contribution of narrative fiction to a "thinking in cases," and to the "history and philosophy of the case."[23] It shows that in the late eighteenth century, narrative literature begins to work out a mode of representing individual cases that exceeds singularity and novelty but stops short of generality and moral didacticism. Two questions guide my investigation: How does this new literature contribute to the establishment of casuistic forms of knowledge that have shaped the formation of psychological practices and legal decision making from the middle of the eighteenth century onward? And, inversely, how does the practice of casuistic writing contribute to the formation of a literary and aesthetic system commonly known as "German Litera-

---

23. Forrester, "If *P*, Then What?"

ture?" In seeking answers to these questions in the German-language canon, this book examines how we came to attribute to literature special formative and critical qualities that until today define our habits of reading, and more generally, our cultural self-conception.

A Case of Individuality

Endeavoring to contribute to a history of the literary case, this study builds on a solid foundation of recent scholarship that has discovered the case as an important genre for investigating the aesthetic and epistemological implications of narrative forms since the end of the eighteenth century. Particularly in German scholarship, the case has emerged as a prominent object for studying the intersections between literary forms and scientific knowledge. The larger context for this emergence is a reorientation of the humanities, which in recent decades have received important thematic and methodological impulses from institutional transformations of scientific cultures and knowledge production.[24] Literary studies in particular have begun to reevaluate forms of representation and procedures of communication, and to redefine the institutional status of literature, literary writing, and texts.

Much of the shift in literary studies toward nonliterary objects is owed to the influence of Michel Foucault's analysis of the human sciences and its general premise that societies from the 1750s onward established new disciplinary techniques for effectively controlling behavioral patterns and that they were able to do so based on knowledge derived from the observation of the individual. In a famous passage in *Discipline and Punish*, Foucault introduces the case as a new form of documentation by which an individual is made accessible as "an object for a branch of knowledge and as a hold for a branch of power."[25] In *Discipline and Punish*, the case appears

---

24. See also Arne Höcker, Jeannie Moser, and Philippe Weber, eds., *Wissen: Erzählen: Narrative der Humanwissenschaften* (Bielefeld: transcript, 2006), 11–16.
25. Michel Foucault, *Discipline and Punish: The Birth of the Prison*, trans. Alan Sheridan (New York: Vintage, 1977), 191.

at a crucial historical moment when disciplinary measures of control begin to replace the majestic rituals of sovereignty, resulting in a complete reorganization of a society that from then on centers around the individual. Equally important, the case emerges at the intersection of what Foucault identifies as the three primary disciplinary techniques: hierarchical observation, normalizing judgment, and the examination. The latter, Foucault explains, combines "the techniques of an observing hierarchy and those of normalizing judgment." It is accompanied by a complex system of registration and documentation, "a network of writing," as Foucault puts it, that allows for the "constitution of the individual as a describable, analyzable object," and at the same time, makes possible a comparative system for measuring the distance between individuals and the entirety of a population. Foucault refers to the specific form of the biographical reports and individual descriptions that dominate the new system of documentation as "a case": "The case . . . is the individual as he may be described, judged, measured, compared with others, in his very individuality; and it is also the individual who has to be trained or corrected, classified, normalized, excluded, etc."[26]

Foucault's remarks on the case as the unity of the notational system of individuality remained cursory. Although they suggest comprehending the case in relation to biographical modes of writing and even briefly invoke the transition from the epic to the novel as an indicator of the formation of a new model of individuality, they do not engage any further with the literary and narrative composition of the case or case history. Foucault does not attend to the case as a particular genre or textual form, although he considers the procedures of writing records an important element. In Foucault, the case appears as a concept or figure of thought that, within specific administrative settings, allows for the registration and coordination of individuals. In this context, Foucault introduces an important distinction that further complicates the attempt to give a coherent definition of the case. In contrast to premodern casuistry, Foucault points out, the modern case is no longer embedded in an already established system of classifications through which every single

---

26. Foucault, *Discipline*, 184, 189, 190, 191.

event will be attributed to a general rule. The modern case, rather, is utterly individual, and it is precisely as such that it finds its measure of comparability: the case is the individual in his or her individuality and this is what he or she has in common with other cases.

One would have thought that this new and modern concept of the case on which the human sciences rely—from psychology and pedagogy around 1800 to sexology and psychoanalysis around 1900—would develop into some kind of standardized model in order to direct the representation of individual cases toward a common goal and to make them comparable. As one sorts through cases and their collections toward the end of the eighteenth century, however, it soon becomes obvious how unsystematic the composition of cases turns out to be in regard to narrative form. One only needs to think of Karl Philipp Moritz's *Magazin zur Erfahrungsseelenkunde* as the most famous example from the late eighteenth century and consider the heterogeneity of its collected cases.[27] Moritz's very project of empirical psychology vitally depends on avoiding any restrictions regarding the composition of the solicited material. A full century later, sexological and criminological publications such as Richard von Krafft-Ebing's *Psychopathia sexualis* (1886) still exhibit no standards for the composition of cases and rely heavily on the collection of so-called *Beobachtungen* (observations). The only genre definition that Sigmund Freud will evoke to characterize his case histories is, famously, the literary novella.

Generally speaking, the narrative form of the case seems to support the case's individuality rather than providing a standardized framework for the purpose of scientific cognition. After all, one can only do justice to the absolute distinctiveness of an individual by making the individual's life the only standard for its representation.

---

27. Following Foucault's rendering of the case in *Discipline and Punish*, Andreas Gailus concludes his discussion of Karl Philipp Moritz and the *Magazin zur Erfahrungsseelenkunde*: "It is thus precisely Moritz's casuistic approach to the writing of the soul—his willingness, that is, to consider cases that are not yet exemplary cases of something—that opens up the conceptual space for a new notion of the 'individual': the individual, understood not as a member of a species but as a self shaped by a particular life-history." (Andreas Gailus, "A Case of Individuality: Karl Philipp Moritz and the Magazine for Empirical Psychology," *New German Critique* 79 [2000]: 79.)

There is a literary genre, however, that in the German context in the final decades of the eighteenth century, shares certain similarities with the case because it, too, centers on the representation of an individual biography: the novel. The novel attempts to depict an individual life by disregarding all the poetic rules and standards that had previously dominated literary writing and poetic discourse. It distinguishes itself from other genres by transgressing genre definitions altogether in order to depict life as a struggle between necessity and contingency. The modern novel marks a fundamental turning point in the relationship between literature and knowledge because it requires a mode of understanding no longer governed by the traditional discourses of poetics and rhetoric. The novel, instead, requires a theory, a completely new discourse able to capture the novel's critical potential and to make it accessible to aesthetics as the modern discourse concerned with artistic form in its relation to life.[28] By necessity, then, this book also contributes to the theory and history of the novel as the preeminent form of narrative in modernity.

The problem of the relation of the novel to the theory of literature has its corollary in the relation of the modern case to the theory of knowledge. The case does not exhibit any unity of form in the various and heterogeneous epistemic contexts in which it appears. A case, then, can hardly be defined in generic terms but must be understood as a relatively open process in which the mode of representation adapts to the epistemological context. Nicolas Pethes, to whose pioneering work on the literary case history my own study is greatly indebted, has suggested that the case be understood as a particular "mode of writing" that he calls, in reference to John Forrester's expression of "thinking in cases," a *writing in cases*. Rather than being defined by a set of readily available forms, an analysis of cases had to consider the specific mode of writing that defined each particular text.[29] The focus on "modes of writing" makes it possible to connect and align aesthetic and epistemological aspects

---

28. See Rüdiger Campe, "Form and Life in the Theory of the Novel," *Constellations* 18, no. 1 (2011): 53–66.

29. See Nicolas Pethes, *Literarische Fallgeschichten: Zur Poetik einer epistemischen Schreibweise* (Konstanz: Konstanz University Press, 2016), 15.

of cases and to disregard the distinction between literary and scientific texts in order to focus on the category of the case independent of its disciplinary and generic affiliation. This approach follows the theoretical-methodological assumptions of what Joseph Vogl has prominently termed a *poetology of knowledge,* which correlates the emergence of new objects and areas of knowledge with their modes of representation.[30] Vogl's *poetology,* however, refers to a particular historical period, the time "around 1800," during which the foundations of modernity were laid and anthropological knowledge emerged from a multiplicity of perspectives that did not yet show any disciplinary coherence.[31] At that time, however, the representation, mediation, and application of knowledge began to disperse and increasing specialization compelled administrative institutions to outsource some of their authority and decision-making power to experts. As Pethes and Susanne Düwell have argued, the development of specialized disciplines of the human sciences around 1800 was itself owed to the increasing importance of individual case histories.[32]

Literary Case Histories

As productive as the assumptions of a poetology of knowledge are for a history of the modern case around 1800, the exclusive focus on modes of writing has its historical limits. It works as long as the differentiation into specialized scientific disciplines has not yet completely succeeded and as long as there is not yet a positive concept of literary fiction that emerges around the same time to fulfill important cultural and societal functions such as the *Bildung* of middle-class citizens.

---

30. See Joseph Vogl, ed., "Einleitung," in *Poetologien des Wissens um 1800* (Munich: Fink, 1999), 7–16.
31. The literature on eighteenth-century anthropology is immense. An introductory survey is available in Alexander Kosenina, *Literarische Anthropologie: Die Neuentdeckung des Menschen* (Berlin: Akademie Verlag, 2008).
32. See Susanne Düwell and Nicolas Pethes, eds., "Fall, Wissen, Repräsentation: Epistemologie und Darstellungsästhetik von Fallnarrativen in den Wissenschaften vom Menschen," in *Fall—Fallgeschichte—Fallstudie,* 19.

In my own approach to what I call the *literary case history*, I understand a case not only as defined by particular modes of perception and observation but also as an important tool for administrative decision making; as a written document based on the knowledge of the individual within the biopolitical paradigm that, as Foucault has shown, emerges in the late eighteenth century. I am, therefore, not so much interested in what happens "underneath" the distinction between literature and science, but more in the particular status of literary writing in this science of the individual and in how literature positions itself to other casuistic modes of writing.

As the cultural, social, and epistemic function of literature itself is at stake in this exchange, this book explores the conditions under which literature performs a dual role as an object of theoretical reflection *and* as a dynamic ensemble of forms of writing that contributes to the formation of anthropological knowledge. By shifting the focus in this way, it is possible to read a surprisingly large part of the German literary canon since the eighteenth century as a sequence of cases. On the most fundamental level, this means that one can retrieve the historical cases on which literary texts are based. To take up the example from the beginning, Goethe's *The Sufferings of Young Werther* set new standards for the aesthetic depiction of subjectivity by adapting the case of Karl Wilhelm Jerusalem's suicide in Wetzlar. *Werther* was part of a lively exchange of cases that in the 1770s began to encompass medical, psychological, pedagogical, judicial, and literary writings. Lawmakers, physiologists, anthropologists, and political administrators were assembling the first systematic collections of cases with the explicit purpose of building general and actionable anthropological knowledge, while at the same time fictional narrative literature established itself as a privileged medium to portray the subjectivity, the inner motivation, and more generally, the psychology of its protagonists. Writers, increasingly invested in the interrogation of the "human heart,"[33] insisted that literature make genuine contributions to the knowledge of the

---

33. Friedrich Schiller, "The Criminal of Lost Honor: A True Story," in *Schiller's Literary Prose Works: New Translations and Critical Essays*, ed. Jeffrey L. High (Rochester, NY: Camden House, 2008), 39.

self; and they demonstrated this capacity of literary narrative by making use of documented, well-known cases. Friedrich Schiller's early crime novella *The Criminal of Lost Honor* (1786), to take another example, is based on a "true story"; and Heinrich von Kleist announces that his *Michael Kohlhaas* (1808–1810) is taken "from an old chronicle." For literary studies, the most dramatic consequence of this collaboration between narrative fiction and empirical anthropology is that as of the end of the eighteenth century, narrative literature can no longer be appreciated by means of a poetics—by a given set of established poetic forms—but by the way it contributes to the comprehension of psychological motivation. Taking into account that the authors of these canonical texts were not primarily literary writers, but often legally and medically trained experts, we can conclude that an autonomous discourse of literary fiction only developed as a by-product of negotiating the narrative modes for representing individual cases. Thus, the role of literary fiction changes: its understanding at a given time requires knowledge not only of its cultural and historical context but also of the narrative procedures and specific forms employed in the representation of cases. As the controversial and at times bewildered reactions to Goethe's *Werther* showed, an accepted interpretive framework for the reading of narrative fiction was still lacking. Contemporary critics of *Werther* struggled with the problem of how to read a text that presented an individual crisis without following any formal and linguistic rules and without invoking an institutional or moral framework in which its disturbing topic could be defused. In retrospect we can see that Goethe's *Werther* contributed to the establishment of a new mode of writing in which an individual's biography could be presented and interpreted as a case. At the same time, the novel initiated a critical discourse that redefined the particular status of literature and literary discourse distinct from other disciplinary and institutional forms. Literary case histories, therefore, operate on both levels, that of casuistry and that of literature.[34] The relationship between case and literature, however, is not static; it is renegotiated in each individual work. In certain contexts, a

---

34. See Frey, "Fallgeschichte," 287.

novel can be read as a case history, in other contexts, it proves to be critical of casuistic forms of reasoning. The literary, epistemic, and institutional contexts that define the respective meaning and thus the institutional standing of literary case histories from the end of the eighteenth to the early twentieth century will be the subject of the following pages.

Three Phases of Literary Fiction

In contradistinction to recent scholarship on the case, this book focuses specifically on the status of literature and literary discourse as it positioned itself in regard to psychology, or rather to the various forms of casuistry in which the individual is made accessible to psychological cognition. Instead of asking how medical, psychological, and forensic case histories developed by means of literary narrative, forms, and genres, I aim to show how references to authentic historical cases shaped literary discourse throughout the long nineteenth century and thereby contributed to establishing a modern conception of literary fiction. Not only around 1800, but throughout the nineteenth and early twentieth centuries, literary authors made use of historical cases as the subject matter for their artistic production and as a means for reflecting on the functions and forms of literary expression. Authors of the late eighteenth century were concerned with narrative primarily in regard to historical and poetic forms of storytelling: by making psychological introspection the prevalent literary perspective, they established the novel as a model of reflection on psychological development. The focus in nineteenth- and early twentieth-century literature changed with the epistemic and institutional circumstances in which cases were embedded. The three parts of this book will reflect these transformations by identifying three phases that define the particular status of literature in regard to: (1) psychological knowledge in the late eighteenth century; (2) legal and medical institutions in the nineteenth century; and (3) literature's own realist demands in the early twentieth century.

Although my selection of literary texts suggests a literary historical approach beyond epochal characterizations, it largely follows the German literary canon, considering this canon itself primarily as a collection of cases that appear to be singular in their cultural effects and formative for a notion of literature in general. Furthermore, my selection gives preference to literary texts dealing with cases that challenge existing norms, especially legal norms. When authors around 1800 set new literary standards by shifting their attention to the depiction of the psychological motivation of individuals who did not display the moral and rational features that Enlightenment philosophers had claimed to be natural human qualities, they focused on cases that challenged the unstated premises of the legal and civic order. Literary case histories in this tradition also always question the basis on which legal and moral decisions are made in modern society, a question encapsulated in the concept of legal responsibility that stirred up so much controversy throughout the nineteenth century and troubled authors from E. T. A. Hoffmann and Georg Büchner to Alfred Döblin and Robert Musil.

This focus on literary case histories that refer, in a broad sense, to the disputed realm between legal and medical-psychological authority, also explains the omission of a body of literary texts from the epoch that in German is called *bourgeois* or *poetic* realism. Although these texts often revolve around criminal cases—Annette von Droste-Hülshoff's *Die Judenbuche* (1842) and Theodor Fontane's *Unterm Birnbaum* (1885) are among the most prominent examples—they generally take a narrative direction different from that of the literary texts discussed in this book. Literary scholars from Georg Lukács to Franco Moretti have convincingly argued that nineteenth-century realism replaced the focus on the particular with a logic of the average and the quotidian.[35] This realism trades the specificity of the individual case for the general depiction of an average life, and thus, according to Lukács's

---

35. See Franco Moretti, "Serious Century," in *The Novel: History, Geography, and Culture*, ed. Franco Moretti (Princeton, NJ: Princeton University Press, 2007), 364–400.

ideological critique, mirrors the conception of bourgeois reality in its moral and legal legitimacy.[36] Newer studies on the epoch of realism have been more nuanced in showing that many of these texts display a poetic potential of undecidability underneath the surface level of representation and that they expose bourgeois reality itself to be linguistically and culturally constructed.[37] There have been attempts to approach realist texts from the perspective of *thinking in cases*, for example, by focusing on the realist novella as a literary reflection of the casuistic distinction between the particular and the general.[38] Following Moretti's discussion of nineteenth-century realism, Pethes argues that precisely by shifting from the focus on the individual and the particular to the depiction of an average everyday life, realist novellas approximate forms of casuistic reasoning. In Pethes's view, realist texts by Adalbert Stifter, Gottfried Keller, and others express the generalizing tendencies of cases in the archival and administrative culture of the nineteenth century.[39]

Such a broadening of perspective runs the risk of diluting the specificity of the case as discussed in this study: it could lead to labeling almost all narrative texts as case histories.[40] The omission of

---

36. See Georg Lukács, "Erzählen oder Beschreiben?" *Probleme des Realismus* (Berlin: Aufbau-Verlag, 1955), 101–145.

37. Among others, see Eva Geulen, *Worthörig wider Willen: Darstellungsproblematik und Sprachreflexion in der Prosa Adalbert Stifters* (Munich: Iudicium-Verlag, 1992); Christiane Arndt, *Abschied von der Wirklichkeit: Probleme bei der Darstellung von Realität im deutschsprachigen literarischen Realismus* (Freiburg im Breisgau: Rombach, 2009).

38. For example Daniela Gretz, "Von 'hässlichen Tazzelwürmern' und 'heiteren Blumenketten': Adalbert Stifters *Abdias* und Gottfried Kellers *Ursula* im Spannungsfeld von Fallgeschichte und Novelle," in Düwell and Pethes, *Fall—Fallgeschichte—Fallstudie*, 274–292.

39. "Die Erzählliteratur des 19. Jahrhunderts partizipiert nicht mehr nur an den Aspekten des Besonderen und Individuellen der Fallgeschichte, sondern scheint auch in der Lage zu sein, an die gegenläufigen Tendenzen des Genres im Rahmen der Verwaltungs- und Archivkultur des 19. Jahrhunderts—an Serialität, Normalität, Alltäglichkeit—anzuschließen." (Pethes, *Literarische Fallgeschichten*, 143.)

40. Paul Fleming suggests an interesting and compelling reading of Stifter's novellas that would indeed justify a discussion of these texts in the context of casuistic reasoning: "The ultimate ruse of Stifter's realism is not that unadorned ordinariness is worthy of art, but rather that the unusual is somehow usual, as gentle and normal as the law itself. By the narrator's own admission, the gentle law, the

texts from the canon of nineteenth-century realism, however, does not mean that realism as a literary problem is excluded from consideration. Quite the contrary, the question of realism—as a literary technique and as an epoch in the history of literature—informs all the works discussed in this book. It appears in Schiller's distinction between historical and literary forms of storytelling, which frames the life story of the *Criminal of Lost Honor*. In Georg Büchner's and Frank Wedekind's dramatic adaptations of casuistic materials, the problem of realism is inherently addressed in the transfer from narrative to dramatic modes of representation. Freud debates the problem when he compares his case histories with novellas to strategically contest their scientific status. Alfred Döblin calls into question the facticity of psychological storytelling to demand new forms of literary expression in alignment with the exact methods of the natural sciences, and his Austrian contemporary, Robert Musil, attempts to reform the culture of scientific rationality by establishing an essayistic mode driven by, what he calls, an *imaginary precision*.[41]

Finally, the problem of literary realism emerges in regard to the genre of the novel to which it is inextricably tied. The novel, according to Frederic Jameson, is "the final form of genre which it is virtually impossible for realism to dissolve without completely undoing itself in the process."[42] To some extent, the relation of realism and the novel frames this study on the literary case history and will guide the readings in the third and final part of this book, where

---

law of goodness finds a receptive audience in a small percentage of society, which means that it is not the norm that upholds and embodies the law; rather the rare, exceptional, and out of the ordinary do so. The law, in other words, is to be found not in the dead center and regular occurrences of society, but in its margins and in the minority." (Paul Fleming, *Exemplarity and Mediocrity: The Art of the Average from Bourgeois Tragedy to Realism* [Stanford, CA: Stanford University Press, 2009], 161–162.)

41. See Sigmund Freud and Josef Breuer, *Studies on Hysteria*, ed. and trans. James Strachey (New York: Basic Books, 1957); Alfred Döblin, "An Romanautoren und ihre Kritiker: Berliner Programm," *Schriften zu Ästhetik, Poetik und Literatur* (Olten: Walter Verlag, 1989); Robert Musil, *The Man without Qualities*, vol. 1, trans. Sophie Wilkins (New York: Vintage, 1995), 267.

42. Frederic Jameson, *The Antinomies of Realism* (London: Verso, 2015), 161.

Döblin's and Musil's engagement with cases and their contribution to a modern poetics of the novel are at issue.

Part I investigates the novel's engagement with the emerging discourses of pedagogy and psychology around 1800. Starting with a reading of Goethe's *Werther*, I argue that this novel not only created a new kind of hero with whom a whole generation of young readers could identify but also set up a narrative framework that made the history of Werther available to psychological interpretation. A few years later, Karl Philipp Moritz invoked the psychological productivity of novelistic storytelling in publishing the "psychological novel" *Anton Reiser* (1785–1790) as part of his project of empirical psychology or *Erfahrungsseelenkunde*. This use of fictional narrative for the representation of dispassionate observation, and the choice of engaging a literary genre for the production of psychological knowledge assigned irreducible cognitive qualities to literature. In Schiller and Kleist, finally, literature's contribution to what the former referred to as the natural "history of man"[43] becomes a matter of poetological concern when their novellas reflect on and challenge the narrative conditions of historical storytelling.

Whereas Part I is concerned with the emerging form of the literary case history, Part II deals with a matured relationship between literary and extraliterary discourses. Throughout the nineteenth century, the case history developed into an established epistemic genre that informed judicial institutions and lawmakers and played an important role in the process of legal decision making. More specifically, discussions about the problem of legal responsibility that dominated forensic debates from the 1820s to the birth of scientific criminology in the second half of the century were conducted with reference to case narratives. The three literary texts discussed in Part II do not engage with their cases on a psychological level but instead question the institutional authority of casuistic forms of representation. They do so, in part, by absorbing narration in more or less dramatic forms of staging, thereby opening up new perspectives on the aesthetic foundation of casuistic reasoning.

---

43. Schiller, "The Criminal of Lost Honor."

Through his legal involvement in the criminal case of Daniel Schmolling, E. T. A. Hoffmann develops a literary-philosophical perspective that informs his poetic program known as the Serapiontic principle, in which literature claims a position beyond the confines of reason. Based on an early case of legal responsibility, Georg Büchner's *Woyzeck* (1837) expounds the problem of judgment in the medical-legal context by staging the case as a dramatic ensemble of scenes of observation. Frank Wedekind's *Lulu* (1894), finally, presents cases from a sexological context as an arrangement of dramatic skits, exposing their anecdotal potential and staging sexual perversions as the reality of bourgeois fantasies and desires. All three texts discussed in Part II dissolve the narrative coherence of their cases, and by means of staging and symbolic representation successfully reclaim the singularity of the event.

When Sigmund Freud noticed that the case histories in his 1895 *Studies on Hysteria* read just like novellas, he could still pretend to be worried about the scientific status of his work. The psychoanalytic insight in the veracity of fiction, however, also affects the status of literature at the beginning of the twentieth century. Starting from a discussion of Freud's observation, Part III of this book focuses on texts that reference case histories in order to stake programmatic claims for a new form of literature: Alfred Döblin's program of a "fantasy of facts" will be discussed as well as Robert Musil's case-based concept of an "imaginary precision" in the novel *The Man without Qualities* (1930–1943).

Part I

Making the Case around 1800

1

THE CASE OF WERTHER AND THE INSTITUTION OF LITERATURE

Werther's Subjectivity

"How happy I am to be away!"[1] Ever since Goethe's young protagonist Werther opened his first letter to his friend Wilhelm with this statement, *being away* has become one of the key conditions for gaining subjectivity by objectifying oneself through writing.[2] Knowing oneself means to have succeeded in establishing a relation to oneself, and this complicated and difficult endeavor is not possible without a medium. Since Goethe's famous epistolary novel, this

---

1. Johann Wolfgang von Goethe, *The Sufferings of Young Werther*, trans. and ed. Stanley Corngold (New York: W. W. Norton, 2013), 5.
2. For a recent discussion of the novel's famous beginning, see Ansgar Mohnkern, "Woran leidet Werther eigentlich? Auch ein Beitrag zur Theorie des Romans," in *Genuss und Qual: Przyjemnosc i cierpiene: Aufsätze und Aufzeichnungen*, ed. Grzegorz Jaskiewicz and Jan Wolski (Rzeszów: Wydawnictwo Uniwersytetu Rzeszowskiego, 2014), 21–34.

medium, in a completely new and emphatically modern sense, has carried the name *literature*.

In Western literary history, *The Sufferings of Young Werther* is known as the novel with which a new form of individuality finds literary expression. Goethe's *Werther* is not a traditional epistolary novel as were its famous predecessors, Samuel Richardson's *Pamela* and Jean-Jacques Rousseau's *Julie*; it does not rely on a dramatic structure; Werther's letters are not supposed to elicit communication. Instead, these letters offer a series of snapshots, momentary and discrete impressions of their author's emotional state and subjective experience. The addressee—whether Wilhelm or Lotte does not make a difference—seems a mere excuse for Werther's relentlessly exhibited self-obsession.

Thus, to be away is not only the reason for Werther's initial happiness but also, in a twofold sense, the condition for his confessional discourse. *Being away* creates the distance that makes it necessary to write letters, and it simultaneously establishes a perspective from which self-observation becomes possible. The form of the epistolary novel serves as a vehicle, translating the discourse of the self into a seemingly communicative structure and successfully turning the incomprehensible individual monad into an apparently readable subject for a contemporary audience.

The beginning of *Werther*, however, leaves its readers with more questions than answers. The speaker is unknown. No time and place are given. And there must have been some kind of individual history that is yet unknown. It has been argued that the novel begins by stating an absence,[3] and thus it marks the impossible space from which the desired discourse of the self must originate. *Being away* at once highlights the possibility and the impossibility of the modern project of the auto-formation of the subject. It defines a condition of becoming rather than a particular place; it is a process in the course of which one is supposed to come to terms with oneself. That there is no happy ending for Werther could be understood according to the logic of Friedrich Schiller's antihero Franz

---

3. See Bernhard J. Dotzler, "Werthers Leser," *MLN* 114, no. 3 (1999): 445–470.

Moor a few years later: "Could respect for my person exist, when my person could only come into being through that for which it must be the condition?"[4]

Although Werther obviously fails on the level of the plot, he nevertheless succeeds in creating a discourse that is built on aesthetic expression rather than a language of reason. The readers of *Werther* did not relate to the protagonist by means of rational understanding but through empathy and identification. David Wellbery declared Werther to be the first romantic subject because he cannot be fully understood: Werther's speech renders subjectivity aesthetically but remains incomprehensible on the level of narrative discourse. That is why the novel cannot provide a final word for the moral or psychological understanding of the protagonist. Rather, it demonstrates the incommensurability of the two modes of discourse that it presents: the objective narrative of the editor and the emotional writing of the protagonist Werther.[5] In the discrepancy between these two discursive levels, the novel puts forward one of the central problems of modernity: the attempts of individuals to find their own ground within themselves, without relying on the order of the exterior world.

In this regard, the novel *Werther* marks and negotiates a historical threshold. It attempts to come to terms with a new form of individuality that differs from premodern understandings of the individual that were based on a socially specified status. According to the sociologist Niklas Luhmann, the eighteenth century successfully established a concept of individuality that was no longer the result of socialization but was tied to the notion of transcendental subjectivity.[6] Werther's struggle with the world results, at least partially, from his attempt to be a modern subject in a society that still upholds

---

4. Friedrich Schiller, *The Robbers*, trans. with an introduction by F. J. Lamport (London: Penguin, 1979), 34.

5. See David Wellbery, "Afterword to *The Sorrows of Young Werther*," in Goethe, *Werther*, 182–187.

6. See Niklas Luhmann, "Individuum, Individualität, Individualismus," *Gesellschaftsstruktur und Semantik: Studien zur Wissenssoziologie der modernen Gesellschaft* (Frankfurt am Main: Suhrkamp, 1993), 149–258.

the values of feudal hierarchy. Werther is introduced as a young man who tries not to be bothered by social boundaries, although his experiences make him painstakingly aware of them. Framed by the societal challenges of the late eighteenth century, the novel *Werther* negotiates the intrinsic value and worthiness (*Wert*) of the individual.[7] In his letter of November 30, Werther shows evidence of this conflict: "I shall, I shall not come to my senses [Ich soll, ich soll nicht zu mir selbst kommen]! Wherever I turn, I encounter an apparition that destroys my composure!"[8]

Who Tells the Story of Young Werther?

On the level of narrative, a similar conflict is carried between the two discursive modes on which *Werther* operates. The first is what one is accustomed to call the literary mode: the emotional letters of the protagonist who learns to relate to himself through writing. The second is the narrative frame that appears to have made possible the narrative of the protagonist in the first place. On the one hand, therefore, we encounter an emphatic notion of literary discourse; on the other hand, we seem to be presented with a case in the sense in which Michel Foucault referred to casuistic discourse, as the documentary techniques by which the individual—since the end of the eighteenth century—is constituted as "an object of a branch of knowledge and a hold for a branch of power."[9] But the novel does not take sides, or rather, it takes both sides. The editor appears twice in the novel, and his two different functions reveal a conflict that accompanied the novel's perception since its first publication and that, until today, informs its scholarly reception: it embodies a historical shift away from the didactic mode of exemplarity toward a

---

7. See Dirk Kemper, *Ineffabile: Goethe und die Individualitätsproblematik der Moderne* (Munich: Fink Verlag, 2004), 73–112.

8. Goethe, *Werther*, 69; Johann Wolfgang von Goethe, "Die Leiden des jungen Werther," in *Werke 6: Romane und Novellen I*, ed. Erich Trunz (München: C. H. Beck, 1996), 88.

9. Michel Foucault, *Discipline and Punish: The Birth of the Prison*, trans. Alan Sheridan (New York: Vintage, 1977), 191.

representation of singularity.[10] My discussion of *Werther* will be guided by this tension between exemplarity and singularity in the novel. I will show how this tension unfolds in the contemporary reception of the first version of the novel and how it influences Goethe's significant modifications for the second version of 1787, with which he reacts to the critical debate surrounding the novel's first publication.

The first appearance of the nameless editor in the 1774 version of *Werther* is easily overlooked, as it appears in the first edition on an unnumbered page and does not engage with the plot directly. It has the rhetorical function of emotionally preparing the reader for what is supposed to follow: "I have diligently collected everything I could discover about the story of poor Werther and set it before you here, knowing that you will thank me for it. You will not be able to withhold your admiration and love for his spirit and character or your tears for his fate. And you, good soul, who feels the same urgency as he, take comfort from his sufferings and let this

---

10. David Martyn has pointed out that such an interpretation must remain insufficient if it does not, at the same time, consider singularity itself just another variation of exemplarity. Following the contemporary reception of the novel from Lessing to Lenz, Blanckenburg, and Moritz, Martyn shows that the novel marks a historical transformation, not from exemplarity toward singularity, but "within the paradoxical dynamic of exemplarity itself." For Goethe's first novel, this means that "the more [its readers] insist on Werther's singularity, the more exemplary he becomes." (David Martyn, "The Temper of Exemplarity: Werther's Horse," in *Exemplarity and Singularity: Thinking in Particulars in Philosophy, Literature, and Law*, ed. Michèle Lowrie and Susanne Lüdemann [London: Routledge, 2015], 170.) Insofar as the novel maintains this tension between singularity and exemplarity without dissolving it, *Werther* must be understood as a case in the modern sense that furthermore embodies, as Susanne Lüdemann has put it, "the paradox structure of subjectivity in the bourgeois society itself." (Susanne Lüdemann, "Literarische Fallgeschichten: Schillers 'Verbrecher aus verlorener Ehre' und Kleists 'Michael Kohlhaas,'" in *Das Beispiel: Epistemologie des Exemplarischen*, ed. Jens Ruchatz, Stefan Willer, and Nicolas Pethes [Berlin: Kulturverlag Kadmos, 2007], 209.) For an in-depth discussion of exemplarity, from the rhetorical example to the exemplary function of the modern case, see Stefan Willer, Jens Ruchatz, and Nicolas Pethes, "Zur Systematik des Beispiels," in Ruchatz, Willer, and Pethes, *Das Beispiel*, 7–59; a discussion of the relation between case and example is included in Johannes Süßmann, "Einleitung: Perspektiven der Fallstudienforschung," in *Fallstudien: Theorie, Geschichte, Methode*, ed. Johannes Süßmann, Susanne Scholz, and Gisela Engel (Berlin: Trafo, 2007), 7–27.

little book be your friend if by fate or your own fault you can find none closer to you."[11]

Werther's life story is supposed to give comfort to those who suffer similar fates and are therefore susceptible to the sentimental language of his writing. With these editorial remarks, Werther's suffering is presented as an exemplary tale of a struggle that, although it is being experienced as a unique and individual fate by the protagonist, still provides its readers with a language suitable for the adequate expression of their own sufferings. *The Sufferings of Young Werther* has long figured as one of the most popular examples for the crisis of exemplarity at the end of the eighteenth century, not least because Werther himself is constantly searching for examples in which he can find some orientation for his own life.[12] In the famous letter of August 12, in which Werther reports his dispute with Albert on the justification of suicide, he refers in support of his claim of a "sickness to death," to the story of a girl "who had recently been found in the water, dead,"[13] and tells her story, which not only mirrors his own suffering but also foreshadows his own tragic fate. The story of a peasant boy, with whom Werther understandably sympathizes and whom Goethe added to the revised version of the novel from 1787, can be seen as another example and will be discussed in more detail later in this chapter.

The editor's first appearance frames Werther's story by emphasizing the potential to identify with the protagonist, but his second appearance creates a different relation to the reader.[14] At a crucial

---

11. Goethe, *Werther*, 3.
12. Paul Fleming, for example, discusses this crisis of exemplarity by analyzing the tension between exemplarity and mediocrity in regard to Werther's artistic attempts that are not blessed with the spark of genius but do not let him accept an average bourgeois life either. (See Paul Fleming, *Exemplarity and Mediocrity: The Art of the Average from Bourgeois Tragedy to Realism* [Stanford, CA: Stanford University Press, 2009], 3–7.)
13. Goethe, *Werther*, 36, 37.
14. For an in-depth analysis of the editor in *Werther*, see Jürgen Nelles, "Werthers Herausgeber oder die Rekonstruktion der 'Geschichte des armen Werthers,'" *Jahrbuch des freien deutschen Hochstifts* (Tübingen: Max Niemeyer Verlag, 1996), 1–37.

point in the novel, when Werther's emotional state rapidly worsens, the editor interrupts the stream of letters, addresses the reader directly, and takes over the narrative voice: "How devoutly I wish that enough documents in his own hand concerning the last remarkable days of our friend had been left to us so as to render it unnecessary for me to interpose my narrative in the sequence of remaining letters."[15]

As narrator, the editor is part of the text as a visible and active player in the novel's composition. It is now he who directs the reader's attention, he who interrupts not only the flow of letters but also the illusion of an intimate pact between the suffering protagonist and the susceptible reader. With this revelation, it dawns on the reader that from the very beginning, the apparently original journey of Werther had indeed been directed via some kind of outside force. With the appearance of the narrator as a figure of the text, the story of Werther is perceived differently. No longer are the readers in the position of accomplices who suffer with the protagonist, develop feelings of fear and pity, and passionately identify with him. Instead, they now take the perspective of an examining judge. It is here that Werther becomes a case to which the reader no longer relates by means of sympathy and compassion, but by approaching it from the perspective of a more general cognitive interest.[16] The narrator ceases to rely solely on Werther's letters, but refers to witness reports that he gathered from Lotte, Albert, his servants, and others:

> I have gone to great lengths to collect accurate reports from the lips of those in a position to be well acquainted with his history; it is a simple one, and all accounts of it are in agreement, barring a few insignificant details; it is only about the cast of mind of the persons closely involved that opinions differ and judgments diverge.

---

15. Goethe, *Werther*, 116.
16. See Marcus Krause, "Zu einer Poetologie literarischer Fallgeschichten," in *Fall—Fallgeschichte—Fallstudie: Theorie und Geschichte einer Wissensform*, ed. Susanne Düwell and Nicolas Pethes (Frankfurt am Main: Campus, 2014), 254; Rüdiger Campe, "Von Fall zu Fall: Goethes *Werther*, Büchners 'Lenz,'" in *Was der Fall ist: Casus und Lapsus*, ed. Inka Mülder-Bach and Michaela Ott (Paderborn: Wilhelm Fink, 2014), 44.

> What can we do but relate conscientiously all that we were able to glean after repeated efforts, intercalating the letters the departed left behind, never neglecting the slightest slip of paper we found, especially given the difficulty of discovering the truly genuine, the authentic motives behind even a single action when it is found among persons who are not of the common stamp.[17]

Not only does the representation of the life story of young Werther turn into an investigation that, given the novel's ending, has criminological dimensions, but the objective narrative of the editor also reframes and overwrites the initial "sympathetic" reading, when the letters were still the exclusive and unmediated material presented with an exemplary purpose.

It has been argued that the two discursive modes that intersect in Goethe's first novel stand for the historical transition from the traditional model of casuistry to a modern *thinking in cases*. The former presupposes a stable order of things as the common frame of reference while the latter connects the individual life story with a set of descriptive techniques.[18] According to this argument, Werther expresses in his writing the prevailing model of what is considered to be human and he attempts to align his own position with already determined moral principles. Although this interpretation may explain Werther's constant references to the notion of man, it attributes the innovative trait of the novel exclusively to the framework of social institutions and overlooks the self-empowering quality of Werther's own writing. I argue that the two seemingly conflicting discursive modes of writing are two sides of the same coin. Although Werther's letters are driven by the demand to realize his self without any reference to an outside order, the editor's intervention gives the institutional perspective that constitutively provides for this illusion.

Thus, the narrator in *Werther* has a function similar to that of the Society of the Tower in Goethe's second novel *Wilhelm Meister's Apprenticeship*, in which the two modes of discourse are already so intertwined that, following Friedrich Kittler's ingenious reading, the protagonist Wilhelm Meister can imagine himself as the

---

17. Goethe, *Werther*, 116.
18. See Krause, "Zu einer Poetologie literarischer Fallgeschichten," 254.

author of his own life, and his novel can become the archetype for the biographical form of the *Bildungsroman*.¹⁹ The Society of the Tower is the archive and the basic requirement of the novel, in which self-perception and public image correspond to one another and make it possible for Wilhelm to objectify his individual life by means of writing. In book eight of *Wilhelm Meister's Apprenticeship* one encounters the discursive rules that the Society of the Tower inaugurates and the status of which, as again Kittler writes, must be considered literary.²⁰ Jarno explains in Goethe's novel: "We wanted to make our own observations, and establish our own archive of knowledge. That is how the various confessions arose, written sometimes by ourselves and sometimes by others, from which the records of apprenticeship were subsequently put together."²¹

The Tower anchors the form of the novel, registers its biographical originality, integrates it into an archive of universal complexity, and conveys the contingencies of life in a new form of recording, to which the novel is the poetic equivalent.²² In other words, the Tower represents the institutional framework that creates the conditions for the individual to claim authorship and gain sovereignty over his own life story.²³ Before he dares to report on his own life, Wilhelm

---

19. "Erst ein Leser und Schreiber des eigenen Lebens, wie Wilhelm Meister es ist, kann zwischen seinem Bild von ihm, dem Bild Anderer von ihm und seinem Bild vom Bild Anderer von ihm trennen. Das Aufschreibesystem der Sekundärsozialisation überführt mithin den Helden, den seine Primärsozialisation zum Individuum machte, in ein Individuum-unter-Individuen. Literarische Positivität aber hat das Individuum als Autor. Dem Leser Wilhelm Meister erlaubt die Trennung der verschiedenen Perspektiven, an seinen Lehrjahren eine Funktion Autorschaft zu statuieren." (Friedrich Kittler, "Über die Sozialisation Wilhelm Meisters," in *Dichtung als Sozialisationsspiel*, ed. Gerhard Kaiser and Friedrich A. Kittler [Göttingen: Vandenhoeck & Ruprecht, 1978], 102.)

20. "Das paradoxe Tun des Turms . . . produziert eine neue Textsorte. Ihr Status ist literarisch." (Kittler, "Über die Sozialisation Wilhelm Meisters," 101.)

21. Johann Wolfgang von Goethe, *Wilhelm Meister's Apprenticeship*, ed. and trans. Eric A. Blackwell (Princeton, NJ: Princeton University Press, 1995), 336.

22. On the equivalence between institutional and poetological form in Goethe's *Wilhelm Meister's Apprenticeship*, see Joseph Vogl, "Lebende Anstalt," in *Für Alle und Keinen: Lektüre, Schrift und Leben bei Nietzsche und Kafka*, ed. Friedrich Balke, Joseph Vogl, and Benno Wagner (Zurich: Diaphanes, 2008), 21–33.

23. In this regard, Goethe's novel can be understood as a first step toward the genesis of what Rüdiger Campe has described as the novel of the institution.

Meister requests to take a look into the Tower's recording of his "apprenticeship."[24]

In contrast to Wilhelm Meister, Werther does not yet have access to his *files*. The biographical and institutional modes of discourse still confront each other as separate narrative entities that do not yet inform each other. What is at stake, then, is not just a new approach to the notion of individuality under the auspices of casuistry but, even more, it is the institutional status of literary discourse. Goethe's *Werther* turns into a case of literature because it claims that literature plays a constitutive role in the institutional framework for the presentation of cases.[25] The novel does this by maintaining the tension between the two discursive modes—that of Werther and that of the editor. *The Sufferings of Young Werther* emphasizes the incommensurability of literary narrative with the knowledge it provides; it stages the perspectives from which Werther can appear as a modern individual on the one hand, and as a case on the other.

Campe subsumes a number of novels from the early twentieth century under this term, among them Robert Walser's *Jakob von Gunten* and Kafka's novels *Der Proceß* and *Das Schloss*. He argues, however, that the novel of the institution had already been built into the *Bildungsroman* from its very beginning in *Wilhelm Meister's Apprenticeship* in the form of the Society of the Tower. (See Rüdiger Campe, "Kafkas Institutionenroman: *Der Proceß, Das Schloss*," in *Gesetz: Ironie: Festschrift für Manfred Schneider*, ed. Rüdiger Campe and Michael Niehaus [Heidelberg: Synchron, 2004], 197–208.)

24. "Having reasoned with himself for some time, he finally decided to tell her as much as he knew about himself. She should get to know him as well as he knew her, and he began to work over his own life story; but it seemed so totally lacking in events of any significance, and anything he would have to report was so little to his advantage that more than once he was tempted to give up the whole idea. Finally he decided to ask Jarno for the scroll of his apprenticeship from the tower, and Jarno said this was just the right time. So Wilhelm got possession of it." (Goethe, *Wilhelm Meister's Apprenticeship*, 309.)

25. Christiane Frey makes a similar argument when she writes: "Der Roman *Werther* kann also nicht nur als Fallgeschichte gelten, sondern er handelt von Fallgeschichten, die wiederum auf den Romanfall verweisen. Diese Logik, der der Roman hier zu folgen scheint, ist also durchaus kasuistisch zu nennen, wenn man darunter ein Denken in Fällen versteht." (Christiane Frey, "'Ist das nicht der Fall der Krankheit?' Der literarische Fall am Beispiel von Goethes *Werther*," *Zeitschrift für Germanistik* 19 [2009]: 317–329.)

The Case of Literature

The frame of reference that guarantees the success of this operation is, to say it once again, literature. It is only by means of literary language that the question of identity finds a positive answer, and all other attempts to establish firm ground for Werther's project of self-realization are doomed to fail. The kind of individuality that Werther tries to accomplish is based on notions of uniqueness, singularity, and the conviction that the individual's relation to the world must be accomplished within that individual. Thus, Werther's search for identity can hardly rely on society.[26] But the other two options that Werther explores remain equally unsuccessful. His attempt to align himself with nature fails when he recognizes destruction as its primary principle and begins to understand that the price for being in accordance with nature eventually means not to be at all.[27] The most promising option—to overcome his conflicted

---

26. This is Niklas Luhmann's argument on modern individuality: "Hier konnte einerseits ein neuartiger politischer Moralismus einsetzen, der sich selbst das Recht zu allen Mitteln zuspricht. Als Reaktion darauf suchte die Restauration nach neuen Formen der Institutionalisierung von Freiheit, fast könnte man sagen: der Institutionalisierung von Individualität. Was 'Individuum' eigentlich heißt, mußte dabei politisch unbestimmt bleiben. Der Deutsche Idealismus liefert dafür die philosophische Formulierung: Das Individuum wird als einmaliges, einzigartiges, am Ich bewußt werdendes, als Mensch realisiertes Weltverhältnis begriffen; und Welt (oder sozial gesehen: Menschheit) ist eben das, was im Individuum 'selbsttätig' zur Darstellung gebracht wird. Seitdem ist es unmöglich (obwohl viele das nicht einsehen!), das Individuum als Teil eines Ganzen, als Teil der Gesellschaft aufzufassen. Was immer das Individuum aus sich selbst macht und wie immer Gesellschaft dabei mitspielt: es hat seinen Standort in sich selbst und außerhalb der Gesellschaft. Nichts anderes wird mit der Formel 'Subjekt' symbolisiert." (Luhmann, "Individuum, Individualität, Individualismus," 212.)

27. One hundred years later, the Goethe-reader Friedrich Nietzsche wrote about the desire that also guides Werther through his experience with nature: "'According to nature' you want to *live*? O you noble Stoics, what deceptive words these are! Imagine a being like nature, wasteful beyond measure, indifferent beyond measure, without purposes and consideration, without mercy and justice, fertile and desolate and uncertain at the same time; imagine indifference itself as a power—how *could* you *live* according to this indifference? Living—is that not precisely wanting to be other than this nature? Is not living—estimating, preferring, being unjust, being limited, wanting to be different? And supposing your imperative 'live

self by making love the center of everything—must also fail because unconditional love requires self-abandonment.[28] Only literature appears as a successful guide for establishing a foundation for the project of subjectivity. The famous episode in which Werther and Lotte recognize each other as kindred spirits, merely by pronouncing the name of the author Klopstock, can be, and indeed has been, interpreted in this way.[29] The reference to *Emilia Galotti* at the end of the novel is further evidence that Goethe's *Werther* places itself in the context of literary discourse, although Gotthold Ephraim Lessing's bourgeois tragedy highlights the irreconcilable distance by which the novel separates itself from the literary tradition of tragedy. Werther is no longer a tragic hero, however much he likes to depict himself as such. He is not subject to a tragic fate from which there is no escape. Instead, Werther attempts to claim authorship over his own life under the conditions of a discursive network called literature. His letters are no longer deeds within a dramatic play that must end tragically, but testimonies of his innermost desires inspired by his readings of "my Homer" and *his* Ossian.[30]

Friedrich Kittler has pointed out the important link between writing and reading for Werther as the modern hero who would

---

according to nature' meant at bottom as much as 'live according to life'—how could you *not* do that? Why make a principle of what you yourselves are and must be?" (Friedrich Nietzsche, "Beyond Good and Evil," in *Basic Writings of Nietzsche*, trans. and ed. Walter Kaufmann [New York: Modern Library, 2000], 205.)

28. For an in-depth discussion of Werther's attempts to correlate his self with society, nature, and love see Dirk von Petersdorff, "'I Shall Not Come to My Senses!' *Werther*, Goethe, and the Formation of Modern Subjectivity," in Goethe, *Werther*, 202–217; Kemper, *Ineffabile*.

29. "We walked over to the window. Thunder rumbled in the distance, a splendid rain was falling on the land, and the most refreshing scent rose up to us in the fullness of a rush of warm air. She stood leaning on her elbows, her gaze penetrating the scene; she looked up at the sky and at me, I could see tears in her eyes, she put her hand on mine and said, Klopstock!—I immediately recalled the splendid ode that was in her thoughts, and I sank into the flood of feelings that she poured over me with this byword" (Goethe, *Werther*, 20). (For close scholarly analysis of this episode, see Richard Alewyn, "Klopstock!" *Euphorion* 73 [1979]: 357–364; and Friedrich A. Kittler, "Autorschaft und Liebe," in *Austreibung des Geistes aus den Geisteswissenschaften*, ed. Friedrich A. Kittler [Paderborn: Verlag Ferdinand Schöningh, 1980], 142–173.)

30. Goethe, *Werther*, 7.

claim authorship over the representation of his life by omitting the poet as a third agent.[31] But this third agent is indeed still present in the form of the editor. In contrast to Wilhelm Meister, Werther is not a reader of his own story who has already learned to distinguish between his self-perception and others' perceptions of him. Self-observation is not one of Werther's strengths, in spite of his endless musings about his place in nature and society. To attribute consistency and continuity to Werther's life story, the novel requires an editor who collects what Werther writes in order to compare it to the reports of others. The "author function" has not yet completely developed;[32] the discourse of the self does not yet master the knowledge it conveys. But the archives of institutions like the Society of the Tower in Goethe's *Wilhelm Meister's Apprenticeship* will be made up of texts like *The Sufferings of Young Werther* to teach heroes like Wilhelm Meister how to claim authorship for their own biographies.

It is well-known that initially Goethe's *Werther* had quite a different effect. Apparently, the editor was hardly recognized and readers instead identified almost unconditionally with their hero. "The publication triggered nothing short of a 'Werther-mania,'" Christiane Frey and David Martyn write: "Readers dressed like Werther, read what Werther reads, speaking like Werther in his signature emphatic and sentimental style; and, yes, in a few reported instances, purportedly went so far as to imitate suicide."[33] In his autobiography, *Poetry and Truth*, Goethe himself remembered the effect of the publication of his first novel:

> The effect of this little book was great, indeed enormous, mainly because it struck at precisely the right moment.... One cannot require the public to receive an intellectual work intellectually. In fact, readers paid

---

31. See Kittler, "Autorschaft und Liebe," 152.
32. See Michel Foucault, "What Is an Author," in *Aesthetics, Method, and Epistemology*, ed. James D. Faubion and Paul Rabinow (New York: New Press, 1998), 205–222.
33. Christiane Frey and David Martyn, "Doubling Werther (1774/1787)," in Goethe, *Werther*, 218; an in-depth discussion of the effects of the publication of Goethe's *Werther* can be found in Martin Andree, *Wenn Texte töten: Über Werther, Medienwirkung und Mediengewalt* (Munich: Fink Verlag, 2006).

attention only to the subject matter, the content, something I'd experience with my friends; and along with this the old prejudice set in, arising from the dignity of a published book: that it must have a didactic purpose. But a true depiction does not have one. It does not condone, it does not condemn; it develops sentiments and actions as they follow from one another, and in so doing it illuminates and instructs.[34]

Frey and Martyn have pointed out the revolutionary aspect of this statement, which denies that literature has a didactic purpose or fulfills a primarily moral function.[35] This does not mean, however, that the novel could not have a didactic effect, which for Goethe was made possible by the realistic depiction of young Werther's story and by the causality with which events and emotions arose from one another. But in fact, Goethe's *Werther* was not very successful in finding such informed readers. Instead of learning from Werther's story, his readers either identified with him and thus failed to establish an objective distance or they simply disapproved of the novel's lack of moral positioning against Werther's immoral decision to commit suicide. Both of these readings belong to the same order of discourse that expects literature to present exemplary heroes as models worth imitating. For *Werther*, a new audience had to be educated that would be able to read novels critically before the "intellectual work" could be received "intellectually."

Causality and Exemplarity (Blanckenburg)

This is one of the tasks that Friedrich von Blanckenburg set before himself in his 1775 review of Goethe's novel. Blanckenburg had published his book-length *Versuch über den Roman* in the very same year that *The Sufferings of Young Werther* appeared and he had found Goethe's novel in line with his theory of the genre that was still widely considered trivial and not worthy of serious aesthetic consideration. For Blanckenburg, the novel was not supposed to

---

34. Johann Wolfgang von Goethe, "From My Life: Poetry and Truth," in Goethe, *Werther*, 118.
35. Frey and Martyn, "Doubling Werther," 219.

be judged by the moral exemplarity of its characters, but by the causality with which the poet had linked actions and events. "At the least," he claims, "the novelist must show possible characters in the real world."[36] Blanckenburg argued that in real life the inner development of man interrelates with his outer circumstances, so that the novelist must present a tight-knit web of causes and effects.[37] The kinds of characters he envisioned for the novel were not supposed to be modeled after certain typical traits. The poet should rather "individualize his characters" to clearly attribute their actions and deeds to their individual features.[38]

In Goethe's *Werther* Blanckenburg believes he has found an exemplary novel in light of his theory, and his review is meant as an extension and continuation of his *Versuch über den Roman*.[39] For Blanckenburg, *Werther* is an exemplary novel not because it presents an exemplary character worth imitating, but because it demonstrates the causal relations between the protagonist's inner constitution and his outer circumstances.[40] Goethe "wanted to give us the inner history of a man and set out to demonstrate how his fate arose from the basis of his individuality."[41]

Even Werther's suicide, as morally problematic as it may be, does not upset Blanckenburg. It is not in his interest to justify Werther and his deeds, but to discover "poetic truth."[42] From the perspective of moral exemplarity, *The Sufferings of Young Werther* could hardly be seen as a praiseworthy piece of literature. From the perspective of narrative composition, however, the novel appears as an

---

36. Friedrich von Blanckenburg, *Versuch über den Roman: Faksimiledruck der Originalausgabe von 1774. Mit einem Nachwort von Eberhard Lämmert* (Stuttgart: J. B. Metzler, 1965), 257.
37. See Blanckenburg, *Versuch*, 263–266.
38. See Blanckenburg, *Versuch*, 277.
39. See Robert Ellis Dye, "Blanckenburgs *Werther*-Rezeption," in *Goethezeit: Studien zur Erkenntnis und Rezeption Goethes und seiner Zeitgenossen (Festschrift für Stuart Atkins)*, ed. Gerhard Hoffmeister (Bern: Francke, 1981), 67.
40. See Martyn, "Temper of Exemplarity," 169–170.
41. Friedrich von Blanckenburg, "Die Leiden des jungen Werthers," in *Texte zur Romantheorie II (1732–1780), mit Anmerkungen, Nachwort und Bibliographie von Ernst Weber* (Munich: Fink Verlag, 1981), 396.
42. Blanckenburg, "Die Leiden," 403.

ideal work of art. "The poet," Blanckenburg writes about Goethe, "only seen as a poet, has fulfilled his obligation by providing in this story an altogether poetic ideal, i.e. a perfectly intertwined and developing whole."[43] Thus, for Blanckenburg it is the correlation of the presented events and circumstances with the emotions of the protagonist that lead to his final deed and make it comprehensible. He does not share the concern of all-too-eager defenders of moral standards that the novel could invite its readers to follow in Werther's footsteps. Rather than perceiving the novel as running the risk of promoting suicide as a solution, Blanckenburg understands it as a case history in the modern sense. In his reading, Werther's story does not reflect back on an already existing law of general moral validity and truth, but instead presents an individual case as a demonstration of possibility. The lesson one should draw from Werther's life story, then, does not pertain to the realm of traditional casuistry and truth anymore, but to that of possibility and probability.

Blanckenburg specifically emphasizes the uniqueness and singularity of the novel's events and keeps highlighting the individuality of the protagonist, but it is the causal motivation of the plot, the form of the novel, that lets him present the novel as an instructive example for young and future novelists, and *Werther* as a case from which one can derive useful insights into the human heart. As the novel illustrates the saddening path of young Werther, it teaches its readers to become attentive and alert observers of their fellow human beings. Indeed, Blanckenburg argues that Goethe's novel is a practical pedagogical tool to foster awareness in parents and educators and to teach them how to better observe their children's behavior and emotional development:

> And parents, teachers, you who have children and subordinates in whom you observe this higher sensitivity develop, do not take the force from this tender soul to move forward and to be strengthened by practicing. Do not constrain this force! Do not kill it! But learn from poor Werther the path it can take; and learn, with the knowledge of its power over him, to guide it more effectively and securely. Who can be a better

---

43. Blanckenburg, "Die Leiden," 427.

guide than those who know all the missteps? If you pay attention even to the tiniest movements, as you should, you will now become aware of the smallest disorientation and can detect the first step on the road to ruin.[44]

Following Blanckenburg, Goethe's novel should not be evaluated according to the moral standards it conveys but in regard to the knowledge it provides. In his reading, *Werther* becomes a case by means of its form, which makes possible for the individual what Aristotle thought to be unfeasible: to become the object of knowledge. Indeed, Michel Foucault's definition of the modern case accurately applies to Blanckenburg's review of *Werther*: "The case is no longer, as in casuistry or jurisprudence, a set of circumstances defining an act and capable of modifying the application of a rule; it is the individual as he may be described, judged, measured, compared with others, in his very individuality; and it is also the individual who has to be trained or corrected, classified, normalized, excluded, etc."[45]

But when literature does not content itself anymore with giving examples for morally good behavior, when it does not confine itself to evoking feelings of fear and pity, and instead presents individual cases as real occurrences in the world, a literary theory becomes necessary that teaches novelists how to write and readers what to make of that writing. This is the reason for Blanckenburg's request to add a lesson to general education on how to read the poets.[46] At the end of Blanckenburg's reading of Goethe's *Werther* as a case, one finds an appeal for literary education and literary theory, for which Blanckenburg himself had already provided the textbook with his *Versuch über den Roman*. Goethe's *Werther* and Blanckenburg's *Versuch über den Roman* not only appear in the same year of 1774, but in combination, they pave the way to a new understanding of literature as the framework in which individuality can be documented, objectified, and examined for real-world applications.

---

44. Blanckenburg, "Die Leiden," 438.
45. Foucault, *Discipline*, 191.
46. See Blanckenburg, "Die Leiden," 430.

A Psychological Case

There is no evidence that Goethe took notice of Blanckenburg's review. Considering his emphasis on the novel's intended realism in the passage from his autobiography quoted above, however, one can assume that he would have applauded Blanckenburg's discussion of his novel as an "intellectual" work of art. Blanckenburg responded to the agitated reception of the novel with a theory, but Goethe himself responded by means of literature. Since 1781, Goethe had considered revising his novel and he finally began to execute his plan in 1786 when his publisher Göschen planned an edition of his collected works with *Werther* as the first volume. As Hannelore Schlaffer has pointed out, it was by no means the development of his own poetic proficiency that spurred him on, but the desire to react to the public reception of his work.[47] Three main alterations contribute to a complete reorientation of the 1787 version of the novel. First, the charismatic idiom of Werther's letters is erased and replaced by the standard High German. Second, the editor now functions as a much more withdrawn, distanced, and omniscient narrator. And finally, Goethe has added the episode of the peasant boy whose story presages that of Werther, and whom his protagonist defends passionately against criminal charges. These three changes serve one main purpose: to distance the perspective of the narrative from that of the novel's characters in order to make it more difficult for the reader to identify with them. By further strengthening the position of the editor, Goethe transforms *Werther* into a psychological case, and Schlaffer thus concludes that the second version of the novel is effectively the cure for the Werther-disease that the first version had spread.[48]

A psychological case requires a perspective that only the second version of the novel provides. In the 1774 version, the editor inter-

---

47. See Hannelore Schlaffer, "Leiden des jungen Werthers (Zweite Fassung)," in Johann Wolfgang von Goethe, *Sämtliche Werke nach Epochen seines Schaffens* (Münchner Ausgabe), Bd. 2.2., ed. Hannelore Schlaffer, Hans J. Becker, and Gerhard H. Müller (Munich: Hanser, 1987), 844.

48. See Schlaffer, "Leiden," 846.

rupts Werther's meditation at the climactic moment in which crisis leads to the decision of suicide: "Around this time, the decision to leave this world had developed in the soul of the young man."[49] Preceding this moment, the editor had reported the increasing distrust between Albert and Werther that also affects the trust of their beloved Lotte. Werther's decision to commit suicide, one must conclude, directly results from the development of the liaison with his married friends. As they are cited as witnesses for the editor's narrative, the events are described through their perspective. This changes in the version of 1787. If there had ever been any mistrust between Werther and Albert, the narrator does not leave any doubt that this was solely due to Werther's psychological condition:

> Indignation and displeasure became more and more deeply rooted in Werther's soul, growing ever more tightly entangled and gradually taking possession of his entire being. The harmony of his mind was completely devastated, an internal heat and violence, which labored to confuse all his natural powers, produced the most repellent effects and finally left him with nothing but an exhaustion from which he sought to rise with even greater anxiety than when he had struggled with all the woes of his past. The dread in his heart sapped his remaining intellectual strength, his vivacity, his wit; he became a sorry companion, always more unhappy, and always more unfair the unhappier he grew.[50]

By focusing on the internal life of the protagonist and choosing a more psychological perspective, the function of the editor's narrative changes in the novel in general. The editor's interference no longer appears as an interruption in which the internal meditation of Werther is confronted with the reports of witnesses; instead, the editor's narrative now appears as the continuation of a distanced reading of the letters, which was driven by a psychological interest from the very beginning. Instead of presenting Werther's decision for suicide as a sudden incident triggered by outer circumstances, the novel now depicts his story as the gradual development of his

---

49. Johann Wolfgang von Goethe, *Sämtliche Werke. Briefe, Tagebücher und Gespräche*, section I, vol. 8: *Die Leiden des jungen Werther, Die Wahlverwandschaften, Kleine Prosa, Epen*, ed. Waltraut Wiethölter (Frankfurt am Main: Deutscher Klassiker Verlag, 1994), 208.

50. Goethe, *Werther*, 72.

psychological condition almost inexorably running toward the final deed of suicide.[51] Not only does the second version of the novel disambiguate the story of Werther as a psychological case, it also deals with other cases that refer back to the case of the novel.[52] To remove any doubt as to how the story of young Werther should be read, Goethe added the case of the peasant boy, with whom Werther identifies almost as unconditionally as the readers of the 1774 edition of the novel had identified with him. Werther mentions the peasant boy for the first time in his letter to Wilhelm of May 30, near the beginning of the novel. The boy who fell in love with the mature widow represents Werther's ideal of innocence, truth, and pure love: "Never in my life have I seen urgent desire and hot, ardent craving in such purity: indeed I can say, a purity such as I have never conceived or dreamed of. Do not scold me if I tell you that when I remember this innocence and truth, my innermost soul glows and that the image of his loyalty and tenderness pursues me everywhere and that, as if I myself had caught its fire, I yearn and languish."[53]

More than a year later, the story finds a continuation. Werther, who had just returned to Wahlheim from his disastrous attempt to escape the unhappy situation caused by his feelings for Lotte, inquires about the peasant boy and learns that the story had taken an unfortunate turn. Driven by his love and an uncontrollably heightened desire, the boy had attempted to rape the widow, "to take her by force."[54] Following this incident, he was dismissed and replaced by another chap, to whom, as rumor has it, she would soon be married. Despite his violent behavior, Werther admires the boy even more enthusiastically for the untempered force of "this love, this loyalty, this passion" that was still alive in an "uncultivated"

---

51. I am following Rüdiger Campe's argument, who writes: "Die Erzählung ist nicht mehr durch den harten Takt des Falls und den Einschnitt der Tat zwischen Krise und Entschluss gekennzeichnet. Sie schildert stattdessen die fortlaufende Sequenz des Falls ab, die wesentlich eine sich zur Tat hin entwickelnde Geschichte ist." (Campe, "Von Fall zu Fall," 46.)
52. See Frey, "Ist das nicht," 321.
53. Goethe, *Werther*, 14.
54. Goethe, *Werther*, 60.

class of people where it had not yet been restrained by the restrictive forces of civilization.[55] What Werther here considers an expression of the most pristine inner life is otherwise called a criminal act.[56] It is this discrepancy that is further accentuated in the final episode of the case. Still madly in love with the widow, the boy murders her new boyfriend and alleged rival. Still convinced of the purity of his motives, Werther comes to the boy's defense and advocates for him: "He felt him to be so unlucky, found him so innocent even as a criminal, and put himself so completely in his place that he fully believed he could persuade others as well. He wished he were able to speak at once in the man's defense, the most vivid speech was already rushing to his lips."[57]

It hardly comes as a surprise that Werther's commitment is not rewarded. His defense of the murderer, however, anticipates the debates about legal responsibility that will inform the judicial and criminological discussions of the nineteenth century by means of case narratives. But Werther does not approach his defense legally, just as he dismisses rhetorical speech altogether throughout the novel.[58] When he speaks for the boy, he speaks for himself. Although in telling young Werther's story the editor speaks for him, Werther speaks not only for the young boy but also, by proxy, for himself. The perspective of the narrator shows how identification and distance are being played against each other. The narrator can take the perspective of the individual Werther and in the next moment fall back into the anonymous position of a merely neutral

---

55. Goethe, *Werther*, 61.
56. Campe, "Von Fall zu Fall," 47.
57. Goethe, *Werther*, 74.
58. An example of Werther's dismissal of rhetoric can be found in the letter of May 26, where he rejects the idea of rules for artistic production that should solely be guided by nature: "Much can be said in favor of the rules, about the same that can be said in praise of bourgeois society. A man formed by them will never produce anything vapid or in poor taste, just as someone shaped by the laws and decorum can never become an unbearable neighbor or a notorious villain; on the other hand, say what you will, rules will destroy the true feeling of nature and the genuine expression thereof" (Goethe, *Werther*, 11). A few days later, in the letter of May 30, Werther points out that this "holds true for poetry as well" (Goethe, *Werther*, 13), which is then followed by the story of the peasant boy.

narrative mode. This is what distinguishes modern case narratives from mere moral examples: they tell individual life stories in such a way that they disclose the inner motivation behind actions while still guaranteeing a distance that makes it possible to integrate the story into a general system of knowledge. In the first version, one can already speak of *Werther* as a case; in the second version, the novel also shows the conditions necessary to narrate individual life stories as cases.

As Friedrich von Blanckenburg's reading of Goethe's novel shows, his contemporaries read *Werther* as more than a model worth imitating. The novel was also perceived as a case narrative by which observations could be made that could easily be deployed for educational purposes. Goethe's novel takes part in a pedagogical discourse that by the end of the eighteenth century had organized itself around experience and observation. The revisions Goethe made in the 1787 version in preparation for his collected works only underscore this affiliation. The change in perspective and the newly established sovereignty of the narrator document a new standard for the novelistic rendering of observations that had just been introduced by Karl Philipp Moritz in his psychological novel *Anton Reiser*. In fact, Goethe had met Moritz—the editor of the *Magazin zur Erfahrungsseelenkunde*—in 1786 during his Italian journey, and a letter to his pen pal Charlotte von Stein from the same year gives evidence that he knew and admired the first books of Moritz's novel. We can confidently assume that the Roman conversations with Moritz and his reading of Moritz's novel influenced Goethe in the revisions of *The Sufferings of Young Werther* and were responsible for the psychological focus of the 1787 version. In contrast to Goethe's *Werther*, however, Moritz had placed his own novel explicitly in the context of empirical psychology and had based it on a rigorous regime of self-observation, which chapter 2 will examine more closely.

2

"Observe, Write!"

Histories of Observation and the Psychological Novel Anton Reiser

Anton Reiser Reads *Werther*

While we can only assume the extent to which Goethe's revisions to the second edition of *The Sufferings of Young Werther* had been influenced by his reading of the first two books of Karl Philipp Moritz's *Anton Reiser*, we know that Moritz admired Goethe's *Werther*. The autobiographical hero of his psychological novel, Anton Reiser, proves to be a—rather naive—admirer of Goethe's first novel, in which he recognizes his "idea about the *near* and the *far*" and "a continuation of his reflections on life and existence." However, he has no real understanding of "Werther's actual sufferings": "In short, Reiser recognized in Werther all his own thoughts and feelings, except for the item of love."[1]

---

1. Karl Philipp Moritz, *Anton Reiser: A Psychological Novel*, trans. Ritchie Robertson (London: Penguin, 1997), 204–206.

But even before Anton discovers Goethe's *Werther*, it has left its mark on the third book of the psychological novel, when the narrator reports on Anton's advancing attempts to keep a diary: "The need to share his thoughts and feelings gave him the idea of again keeping a kind of diary, in which, however, he no longer wanted, as formerly, to record trivial external events, but rather the internal history of his mind, and to send what he recorded to his friend in the form of a letter."[2]

It is not difficult to recognize the epistolary form of Goethe's novel in Anton's attempt to find an appropriate way of observing his own life by means of written records, and barely hidden is the reference to Friedrich von Blanckenburg's *Versuch über den Roman* with its psychological requirement to focus on the inner history of man. Moritz's genre designation "psychological novel" is the conscious attempt to follow up on the contemporary theory of the novel and its epistemological rather than poetological claims.[3] It is interesting that Moritz combines both the theoretical and practical approach to the novel and that he does so in regard to Goethe's *Werther*.[4] Although Anton reads *Werther* in a clearly identificatory

---

2. Moritz, *Anton Reiser*, 187.

3. Dörr dedicates a whole chapter of his book *Reminiscenzien* to *Anton Reiser* and *Werther* and pays particular attention to the two discursive areas of *Erfahrungsseelenkunde* and the theory of the novel combined in the new genre definition "psychological novel." (See Volker C. Dörr, *Reminiscenzien: Goethe und Karl Philipp Moritz in intertextuellen Lektüren* [Würzburg: Königshausen & Neumann, 1999], 49–115.)

4. Elliott Schreiber pointed out the importance of *Werther* for Anton's emotional and intellectual development. In his discussion of Moritz's reading of *Werther*, Schreiber focuses on the aesthetics of the autonomous artwork by confronting Anton Reiser's engagement with Werther's letter dated August 18 with Moritz's close reading of Werther's letter dated May 10 in a published piece titled *Über ein Gemählde von Goethe*. In regard to the psychological novel, Schreiber shows how Anton's identification with Werther is tied to a transformative experience of reading that reciprocally affects the reader and the text. "In *Anton Reiser*," Schreiber concludes, "Moritz provides a vivid and complex account of how the escalating production and reception of sentimental literature in the late eighteenth century contributed to the sense of perpetual change that marks modernity." (Elliott Schreiber, *The Topography of Modernity: Karl Philipp Moritz and the Space of Autonomy* [Ithaca, NY: Cornell University Press, 2012], 23.)

way, the novel *Anton Reiser* presents *Werther* as a model of observation that successfully implements the demand for a psychological perspective. Even before Goethe establishes, in the second version of his novel, the narrative mode that enables such a psychological perspective, Moritz presents *Werther* as a model of self-observation suitable for young people like Anton Reiser.

Moritz's psychological novel has often been read in the context of the *Magazin zur Erfahrungsseelenkunde*, the first psychological journal in Germany: a collection of psychological reports that Moritz had initiated, compiled, and edited in collaboration with Karl Friedrich Pockels and Salomon Maimon between 1783 and 1793.[5] The close connection between Moritz's psychological novel and the *Magazin* is unquestionable and has received a good amount of scholarly attention, but subordinating the novel to the category of *Erfahrungsseelenkunde* fails to recognize its literary potential and its epistemological effects on the development of empirical psychology.[6] *Anton Reiser* is not only another case of Moritz's extensive psychological project but also a paradigmatic case for the importance of literary form in the observation and recording of psychic phenomena.[7] The institutional framework of the novel is

---

5. I will continue using the German term *Erfahrungsseelenkunde* as well as the German title of Moritz's journal. Anthony Krupp has pointed out that the translation of *Erfahrungsseelenkunde* as "empirical psychology" could be misleading and would be "more accurately rendered as 'experiential science of the soul,'" to avoid "the rationalist associations evoked by the term *psychologia*." (Anthony Krupp, "Observing Children in an Early Journal of Psychology: Karl Philipp Moritz's *Gnothi sauton* (*Know Thyself*)," in *Fashioning Childhood in the Eighteenth Century: Age and Identity*, ed. Anja Müller [Aldershot: Ashgate, 2006], 34.) Considering the methodological premises of *Erfahrungsseelenkunde*, the term *Magazin* would not be sufficiently understood by translating it as "journal," but refers to a storage device and filing system that makes available observations and cases to future interpretation.

6. This connection is discussed most substantially in Lothar Müller, *Die kranke Seele und das Licht der Erkenntnis: Karl Philipp Moritz' Anton Reiser* (Frankfurt am Main: Athenaum, 1987).

7. Closely following Lothar Müller's claim that the novel must be understood as a pathological case history, Christiane Frey asks what is needed to turn a case history into a psychological novel and argues that *Anton Reiser* contributes to psychology by means of its literary, and, more specifically, "romanhafte," presentation

not just the *Magazin zur Erfahrungsseelenkunde*, but literary discourse as an epistemological rather than aesthetic enterprise.⁸ This is why the novel's references to Goethe's *Werther* uncover two different ways of reading: one emphatically and unconditionally identifies with Werther, and the other distances the reader from the sufferings of the protagonist by emphasizing the novel's exemplary character and by recognizing the epistolary form as an appropriate means of self-observation. Moritz's psychological novel is itself not an epistolary novel, and Anton's readings are always already framed and presented in a psychological discourse that does not focus on the biographical development of Anton's character but on the emotional effects of his experiences. In this, the psychological novel differs significantly from *The Sufferings of Young Werther*, where the fiction of the editor still provides the reader with the pleasure of taking Werther's letters as authentic documents.⁹ By contrast, *Anton Reiser* makes use of a particular narrative voice to create the distance necessary for psychological observation and self-observation. *Anton Reiser*, as I argue later in this chapter, is a literary exercise in establishing a perspective from which self-observation becomes possible. More than being just a case of *Erfahrungsseelenkunde*, the psychological novel experiments with the narrative conditions of observation as an essential requirement for practicing empirical psychology.

---

of psychic material. (See Christiane Frey, "Der Fall *Anton Reiser*: Vom Paratext zum Paradigma," in *Signaturen des Denkens: Karl Philipp Moritz*, ed. Anthony Krupp [Amsterdam: Rodopi, 2010], 19–41.)

8. Moritz is known for his radical formulation of the autonomy of the artwork. (See Helmut Pfotenhauer, "'Die Signatur des Schönen' oder 'In wie fern Kunstwerke beschrieben werden können?': Zu Karl Philipp Moritz und seiner italienischen Ästhetik," in *Kunstliteratur als Italienerfahrung*, ed. Helmut Pfotenhauer [Tübingen: Niemeyer, 1991], 67–83.)

9. In this context, Volker C. Dörr argues that the psychological novel can be read as "Kontrafaktur des Briefromans": "Der Text des 'Anton Reiser' diskutiert emphatische Fehllektüren und führt sie zugleich im narrativen Binnentext vor—exemplarisch an einem Text, der Fehllektüren nur vorführt und (deswegen) seinerseits anregen konnte" (Dörr, *Reminiscenzien*, 115).

Beobachtungsgeschichten: *Erfahrungsseelenkunde* and the Method of Observation

The fact that Moritz published excerpts from *Anton Reiser* in the *Magazin* would suggest that the novel was to be understood as a case among others in the context of *Erfahrungsseelenkunde*. But the connection between *Erfahrungsseelenkunde* and the psychological novel is far more complex. To begin with, it has often been noted that the *Magazin zur Erfahrungsseelenkunde* consists of a wide array of textual forms and genres that cover a vast field of disparate themes and topics.[10] According to Andreas Gailus, this is one of the most notable accomplishments of the *Magazin*:

> Whereas anthropology is concerned with establishing itself as an institutional discipline with clear methodology and borders, Moritz untiringly emphasizes the status of *Erfahrungsseelenkunde* as an emergent science still in the process of defining its object, methods, and disciplinary boundaries. This attitude is reflected in the highly eclectic and unusually loose structure of Moritz's journal, which brought together excerpts from novels and character sketches of school pupils, detailed descriptions of aphasias and gory narratives of murderers, the stale reasoning of rationalist know-alls like Moritz's co-editor Pockels and a piece of mad writing—a kind of Dadaist writing *avant la lettre*—that pokes fun at the belief in social progress through medicine.[11]

Whereas the epistemological project of the *Magazin zur Erfahrungsseelenkunde* essentially depends on the variety of representation, *Anton Reiser* attempts to align psychological observation with

---

10. See Nicolas Pethes, "Vom Einzelfall zur Menschheit: Die Fallgeschichte als Medium der Wissenspopularisierung zwischen Recht, Medizin und Literatur," in *Popularisierung und Popularität*, ed. Gereon Blaseio, Hedwig Pompe, and Nicolas Pethes (Cologne: Dumont, 2005), 70; and Yvonne Wübben, "Vom Gutachten zum Fall: Die Ordnung des Wissens in Karl-Philipp Moritz *Magazin zur Erfahrungsseelenkunde*," in *"Fakta, und kein moralisches Geschwätz": Zu den Fallgeschichten im "Magazin zur Erfahrungsseelenkunde" (1783–1793)*, ed. Sheila Dickson, Stefan Goldmann, and Christof Wingertszahn (Göttingen: Wallstein), 140.
11. Andreas Gailus, "A Case of Individuality: Karl Philipp Moritz and the Magazine for Empirical Psychology," *New German Critique* 79 (2000): 78.

the genre of the novel. To understand the context and implications of this attempt requires an understanding of Moritz's use of the novel: he interconnects observation with a particular form of narrative recording so as to allow for the psychological understanding of individual experiences.

The relevance of the *Magazin zur Erfahrungsseelenkunde* in regard to the development and establishment of a discipline of empirical psychology is well-known.[12] The epistemological contribution of Moritz's novel to this psychological project exceeds its being a case among others, by establishing a connection between observation and writing that is essential for the success of any scientific operation. Empirical observation alone does not suffice to produce general anthropological knowledge, a goal to which *Erfahrungsseelenkunde* explicitly subscribes. Observations need to be recorded, documented, collected, arranged, and made accessible in order to be of more than just individual value. The eighteenth century saw the publication of numerous scholarly treatises on the method of observation, but the problem of recording observations in writing did not seem of particular concern.[13] In 1778, however, the author and Enlightenment pedagogue, Johann Karl Wezel, concluded an essay, published in Johann Bernhard Basedow's and Joachim Heinrich Campe's journal, *Pädagogische Unterhandlungen*, with the appeal: "And now, you pedagogues, tutors, informants, kindergarten teachers, principals, vice-principals, schoolmasters, and professors!—*Observe*, write!"[14]

Wezel's essay "Über die Erziehungsgeschichten" anticipates by four years Moritz's much more famous "Vorschlag für ein Magazin zur Erfahrungsseelenkunde" in the renowned journal *Deutsches*

---

12. See Dickson, Goldmann, and Wingertszahn, *"Fakta, und kein moralisches Geschwätz."*

13. The method, art, and spirit of observation in eighteenth-century medical discourse is presented and discussed in the chapter "Observieren" in Nicolas Pethes, *Zöglinge der Natur: Der literarische Menschenversuch des 18. Jahrhunderts* (Göttingen: Wallstein, 2007), 201–257.

14. Johann Karl Wezel, "Über die Erziehungsgeschichten," in *Gesamtausgabe in acht Bänden*, vol. 7, ed. Jutta Heinz and Cathrin Blöss (Heidelberg: Mattis Verlag, 2001), 430.

Museum. Moritz's proposal for a collection of psychological cases in a *Magazin*, and his essential innovation to carefully distinguish between facts and moral judgments,[15] can already be found in Wezel's essay, which is concerned with the composition of what he first calls "Erziehungsgeschichten," and later, "Beobachtungsgeschichten," histories of observation. Although Wezel does not explain this change from education to observation, it is clearly related to the methodological problem he aims to address. The essay reacts to an unsuccessful call for "Erziehungsgeschichten" by the editors of the journal: "One did not comply with their demand. Maybe some of those who would have had the strength shied away from the difficulties; others maybe did not see the difficulties, wanted to write, but could not, because they did not know how to direct their attention. I will say a few words about the *difficulties* and *composition* of such a history."[16]

Wezel's main concern is the attempt to connect pedagogical observation with its written recording in order to contribute to a general pedagogical science. As the greatest danger for such an endeavor he identifies man's inclination to theorize, to classify, and to jump to conclusions. And he explains that nowhere else would this human tendency cause more harm than in the art of education, which must strictly limit itself to unbiased observation: "For a long time, it [the art of education] must content itself with the *collection of individual experiences*, from which we can sometimes abstract and register a small general rule, and then deliberately wait to see whether sooner or later the opposite experience will nullify it" (Wezel, 436).

To this effect, Wezel suggests a kind of empirical survey, a collection of histories of observation that would not attempt to systematize and would be based on unprejudiced observation. But even if the human urge to theorize, to summarize, and to conclude were to be successfully eliminated, observation needs to overcome other, equally challenging obstacles. Most notably, how should one choose

---

15. Here, I refer to Moritz's famous exclamation "Fakta, und kein moralisches Geschwätz," in his "Vorrede zum 'Magazin zur Erfahrungsseelenkunde,'" in Karl Philipp Moritz, *Dichtungen und Schriften zur Erfahrungsseelenkunde*, ed. Heide Hollmer and Albert Meier (Frankfurt am Main; Deutscher Klassiker Verlag, 2006), 811.

16. Wezel, "Über die Erziehungsgeschichten," 430.

a focus without any experience? A successful observation requires "extensive psychological knowledge," as Wezel argues: "Wherefrom should a young man, who dedicates himself to the task of education, acquire such skills?" (Wezel, 431). Wezel considers history, biographies, novels, comedies, and tragedies to be valuable in this regard, "as long as one could be certain that the composer of true histories and the author of fictional events would have followed the model of nature" (Wezel, 432). As long as there is no guarantee of this, however, the best method is to rely on one's own experiences and to learn from the observation of oneself. Here, Wezel encounters another problem that will later become central to Karl Philipp Moritz's program of *Erfahrungsseelenkunde* and will significantly inform the narrative structure of the psychological novel *Anton Reiser*: "Self-observation requires its own talent, a specific acuteness of the inner sense, of consciousness; a faculty to carefully listen to our feelings, drives, passions, a faculty to become almost two people, one who observes while the other acts, and the former inwardly reflects after each revolution *what* could be caused by the latter, and how" (Wezel, 432). A few pages later, Wezel characterizes this observation as "cold" (Wezel, 438), a metaphor that will leave its mark on Moritz's method of self-observation, and, as I show in chapter 3, will essentially inform Friedrich Schiller's poetological reflections in his "true story," *The Criminal of Lost Honor*.

In sum, Wezel argues that general anthropological knowledge must first be accomplished on the basis of thorough and unrestricted observation before application-oriented histories of pedagogical value can be successfully composed. And the method of observation he envisages is not to leave anything out. The observer has to inform himself about every single detail in the life of his pupil, whether by means of his own observations or by the interrogation of his predecessors: "All this information he shall store in his memory as if it were a magazine, and he shall not make any selection other than parting facts from judgments and speculations" (Wezel, 437).

Just as important as this procedure of observation, however, is its written recording. After having discussed the obstacles and challenges of the method of observation in general, Wezel gives detailed instructions on how to compose histories of observation.

Besides a report of the facts and a detailed description of the individual, such a history must also pay attention to the observation itself; to contribute to a general knowledge of pedagogical practice, it must document its circumstances and arrangements. Histories of observation, therefore, must record observations as well as take into account the following three aspects regarding method: "(1) *How* did one proceed? (2) *Why* did one proceed in this manner? and (3) *What* followed from this procedure?" (Wezel, 441). Thus, these histories not only contribute to an archive of observations but also develop a complex technique of documentation, in which observing and writing directly correspond to each other by reflecting and conveying their methodological objectives.

A few years after Wezel published his account on histories of observation, and with a similarly emphatic notion of the observational method, Karl Philipp Moritz wrote his famous "Vorschlag für ein Magazin zur Erfahrungsseelenkunde" and successfully initiated a new field of psychological inquiry. Under the motto "Gnothi seauton"—*know thyself*—and for the ten years between 1783 and 1793, the *Magazin* was a place to publish empirical observations and became an archive of heterogeneous materials such as diaries, anecdotes, biographies, letters, and autobiographies. Because the *Magazin* marked the beginning of a new field of study, and its contributors could not refer back to an already existing psychological system, the editors had to content themselves with the mere collection of materials from which they hoped to derive a true and complete system of psychological knowledge: "In the beginning, all these observations must be collected in a magazine under certain rubrics, without any reflection until a sufficient quantity of facts are there, and then at the end all of this must be ordered into a purposeful whole. What an important work for humanity this could be!"[17]

It was one of the outstanding innovations of Moritz's project that it did not require any specific expertise, that not only scientifically educated doctors and pedagogues but also uneducated laymen

---

17. Karl Philipp Moritz, "Vorschlag zu einem Magazin einer Erfahrungs-Seelenkunde," in *Werke I: Dichtungen und Schriften zur Erfahrungsseelenkunde*, ed. Heide Hollmer and Albert Meier (Frankfurt am Main: Suhrkamp, 1999), 796–797.

could make valuable contributions to the *Magazin*'s collection of observations and self-observations. Due to its preliminary character and "theoretical dilettantism,"[18] the *Magazin* became a largely heterogeneous archive that eschewed the consistency of medical collections of cases.[19] Although the *Magazin* did not subscribe to a particular order of knowledge, Moritz reports that he followed the advice of Moses Mendelsohn, namely, to apply a system of medical classification drafted by Marcus Herz in his *Grundriß aller medizinischer Wissenschaften* in 1782.[20] As a result, the *Magazin* strongly focused on mental pathologies and moral aberrations of the soul (*Seelenkrankheitskunde*), and the observations collected under this rubric were often taken from juridical contexts. Andreas Gailus has emphasized the importance of forensic practices for *Erfahrungsseelenkunde* that did not emerge solely from "the simple extension of medical discourse to mental problems but from the complex crossings of medical thought, (auto)biographical traditions, and juridical narratives."[21] According to Gailus, Moritz's *Erfahrungsseelenkunde* is a successor of François Gayot de Pitaval's *Causes célèbres et intéressantes* and a precursor of nineteenth-century criminology.[22] Indeed, in his "Vorschlag," Moritz

---

18. Müller, *Die kranke Seele*, 77.
19. The lack of a consistent form of the contributions and the importance of interpretive restrictions for the success of the entire project might have been the reason for Moritz, as Monika Class speculates, to solely speak of observations instead of cases. (See Monika Class, "K. P. Moritz's Case Poetics: Aesthetic Autonomy Reconsidered," in *Literature and Medicine* 32 [2014], 50.)
20. See Moritz, "Vorschlag," 809. The reference to the *philosophical doctor*, Marcus Herz, further shows, as Lothar Müller argues, the proximity of *Erfahrungsseelenkunde* to Enlightenment anthropology and a developing medical psychology. It also shows the extent to which Moritz applied medical categories to the investigation of the soul and how much the *moral doctor* owed to the medical sciences. For a detailed discussion of Marcus Herz's influence on Moritz and the *Magazin*, see the chapter, "Porträt eines philosophischen Arztes: Marcus Herz," in Müller, *Die kranke Seele*, 48–75.
21. Gailus, "Case of Individuality," 73.
22. "Edited by Karl Philipp Moritz, the *Magazin zur Erfahrungsseelenkunde* might be said to anticipate nineteenth-century developments in pedagogy, psychiatry, and criminology Foucault has convincingly analyzed in terms of micropower and biopolitics. Moritz urged his readers to make public 'the secret history of [their] own thoughts,' record the behavior of neighbors, students, and friends, publish their

emphasizes the usefulness of *Erfahrungsseelenkunde* for the purpose of social control and, by considering the criminal a worthy object of study, suggests that it could develop into a valuable tool in support of the legal system:

> We witnessed the execution of a thousand criminals, without considering worthy of analysis the moral damage of these limbs, which were cut off from the social body. But these limbs are as important for the moral doctor as they are for the judge, who must perform the sad operation. How did the inflammation of the damaged limbs slowly increase? Was it possible to prevent the growth of the evil, to cure the damage? What negligence in inspecting or dressing the wound caused it to spread until all antidotes were ineffective? On which thorn did the healthy finger scratch itself? Which little unnoticed splinter remained in it, inflamed, and gave rise to such a dangerous tumor?[23]

Although Moritz strategically begins his "Vorschlag" with the social malady of crime, *Erfahrungsseelenkunde* did not attempt to establish itself as a psychological discourse by focusing on monstrosities and particularly spectacular and dreadful cases of capital crimes. In fact, Moritz took the opposite path when drawing "attention to the seemingly little," which can nevertheless have significant effects, as the above quoted passage strikingly shows.[24] Instead of evoking great social effects, Moritz is initially concerned with observation as the basic requirement for objective analysis. *Erfahrungsseelenkunde*, thus, constituted itself as a strict regime of meticulous observation considering nothing too small, nothing too insignificant to escape the scrutiny of the attentive observer.[25] And like Wezel,

---

earliest childhood memories, and write case histories of criminals, madmen, and other misfits" (Gailus, "Case of Individuality," 69).

23. Moritz, "Vorschlag," 793.
24. Moritz, "Vorschlag," 801.
25. "Attention to the seemingly little" not only puts emphasis on detailed observation but must furthermore be taken literally as the importance that Moritz attributed to childhood for the moral development of man. For a detailed discussion of the *Philanthropinum*, see Pethes, *Zöglinge der Natur*, 234–243. On Moritz's critique of philantropism and in particular of Basedow's Dessau school, see Elliott Schreiber, "Thinking inside the Box: Moritz's Critique of the Philanthropist Project of a Non-Coercive Pedagogy," in Krupp, *Signaturen des Denkens*, 103–130.

Moritz, too, is aware that proper observation requires a disciplined practice of self-observation:

> The proper observer of man must begin with himself: at first, he must meticulously draft the history of his own heart from his earliest childhood on; he must pay attention to all of his childhood memories, and he must not consider unworthy anything that had ever made a strong enough impression on him so that it still occupies his thoughts. [H]e must take the time to describe the history of his thoughts, and to make himself the object of his continuing observation. He does not need to be without any passion, but he must understand the art of momentarily stepping out of the turbulences of his desires in order to play the cold observer for a while without caring the slightest about himself.[26]

This instruction for self-observation and successfully becoming a "cold" observer is an accurate description of what Moritz forcefully implemented in his psychological novel *Anton Reiser*.[27] Even the insights into the difficulties of self-observation in Moritz's "Vorschlag" are owed to the autobiographical experiences on which his novel is built. One encounters in the "Vorschlag" the dangerous addiction to novels and dramas that will lead Anton Reiser astray.[28]

---

26. Moritz, "Vorschlag," 799.

27. The connection of Moritz's concept of self-observation with the pietist assumption that certainty of faith required constant observation of one's spiritual condition, has often been noticed, and *Erfahrungsseelenkunde* has been interpreted as a secular version of Pietism. (See Fritz Stemme, "Die Säkularisierung des Pietismus zur Erfahrungsseelenkunde," *Zeitschrift für deutsche Philologie* 72 [1953]: 144–158.) More recent studies have argued that *Erfahrungsseelkunde* should not be reduced to the religious tradition of Pietism alone and that it must rather be understood as a distinct secular discipline of anthropology that follows philosophical as well as medical traditions. Raimund Bezold discusses this connection in the chapter "Innenschau und Selbsttäuschung," in his book *Popularphilosophie und Erfahrungsseelenkunde im Werk von Karl Philipp Moritz* (Würzburg: Königshausen & Neumann, 1984), 152–166. Hans-Jürgen Schings rejects the claim that *Erfahrungsseelenkunde* could be reduced to pietist traditions in his discussion of *Anton Reiser* in *Melancholie und Aufklärung: Melancholiker und ihre Kritiker in Erfahrungsseelenkunde und Literatur des 18. Jahrhunderts* (Stuttgart: Metzlersche Verlagsbuchhandlung, 1977), 226–234.

28. "Die Nachahmungssucht erstreckt sich gar so weit, daß man Ideale aus Büchern in sein Leben hinüber trägt. Ja nichts macht die Menschen wohl mehr unwahr, als eben die vielen Bücher. Wie schwer wird es dem Beobachter, unter alle dem, was durch das Lesen von Romanen und Schauspielen in den Karakter gekom-

Surely Moritz had his own crisis-ridden life in mind when he presented self-observation as self-elevation from feeling oppressed by an implacable fate: "As soon as my own state becomes a burden to myself," he writes, "I desist from being too interested in myself, and I begin to look at myself as an object of my own observation, as if I were a stranger whose fortune and misfortune I listen to with cold-blooded attention."[29]

Remarkably absent from Moritz's "Vorschlag," and the *Magazin* in general is a discussion of the written recording of observations and the techniques of documentation necessary for their collection. Moritz himself seemed to have employed a system of recording that, akin to that of medical *observationes*, was based on extensive written documentation. In his "Vorschlag," he mentions a combination of recording techniques that accompany the process of observation: note keeping and tabulation.[30] But how does one proceed from these notes and tables to a coherent report? Remarkably, no guidance is given regarding the composition of a contribution to the *Magazin*, even though precise instructions for the composition of medical case histories were customary in medical textbooks, professional and popular journals, and in pedagogical contexts such as Wezel's instructions for the composition of histories of observation.[31]

The analogies between Wezel's essay and Moritz's "Vorschlag" are striking. Both propose an anthropological project based on empirical observation and archival collection; both share a belief in the importance of self-observation for the development of the observer; and both adopt the metaphor of the *cold* observer who reaches for objectivity in service of knowledge of the human soul.

---

men ist, das Eigne und Originelle wieder hervorzusuchen! Anstatt Menschen, oh Wunder! hört man jetzt Bücher reden, und siehet Bücher handeln. Leute, die wenig Romane gelesen haben, sind noch immer der leichteste Gegenstand für den Menschenbeobachter. Man lebt und webt jetzt in der Bücherwelt, und nur so wenige Bücher führen uns noch auf unsere wirkliche Welt zurück" (Moritz, "Vorschlag," 804).

29. Moritz, "Vorschlag," 802.
30. See Moritz, "Vorschlag," 805.
31. See Stefan Goldmann, "Kasus—Krankengeschichte—Novelle," in Dickson, Goldmann, and Wingertszahn, *"Fakta, und kein moralisches Geschwätz,"* 33–65.

But for Wezel, proceeding from individual observation to general knowledge is enabled by a particular form of writing and recording that aligns the transmission of information with the method by which it is processed. The essential innovation of his *histories of observation* is combining the clinical method of observation with a technique of written recording that pays particular attention to observation itself. Moritz, to the contrary, does not give any instructions for the transcription of observations or seem interested in developing a more standardized procedure. With the psychological novel, *Anton Reiser*, however, he aligns the theoretical reflections from the "Vorschlag" with a particular form that implements the ambitious program of self-observation on the level of narrative.

The Psychological Novel (Moritz)

Although the *Magazin zur Erfahrungsseelenkunde* did not depend on a particular form or directly contribute to the formation of a specific genre, Moritz approached his own self-observation in the form of the novel. *Anton Reiser: A Psychological Novel* is largely based on Moritz's childhood and appeared in four individual volumes between 1785 and 1790; short excerpts were also published in the *Magazin*.[32] Indeed, Moritz attributed special importance to the novel and explicitly so in regard to the project of *Erfahrungsseelenkunde*. In his comments to the first three volumes of the *Magazin*, he wrote: "A book that I edited under the title *Anton Reiser, a psychological novel*, and of which I have disclosed some fragments in this Magazin, comprised a lot of observations concerning this matter: the memories of Anton Reiser's earliest childhood were particularly important to determine his character and, to a certain extent, also his future fate. There will be many occasions in the future that I will refer to this *psychological novel*, as it

---

32. For a detailed discussion of the excerpts of *Anton Reiser* published in the *Magazin zur Erfahrungsseelenkunde*, see Frey, "Der Fall *Anton Reiser*."

contains the strongest collection of observations of the human soul that I had the opportunity to compile."[33]

In Moritz's assessment of *Anton Reiser*, the novel as a genre is of exemplary importance for the project of *Erfahrungsseelenkunde*. It allows for a particular form of observation that is supposed to provide insights into an individual's life and thus to meet the basic requirements of empirical psychology. Moritz's project of a psychological novel, however, takes *Erfahrungsseelenkunde* to a different level. Whereas the *Magazin* is based on the experiences and observations of its contributors and holds on to its unconditional methodological empiricism, the psychological novel replaces the experiential principle of immediacy with a literary narrative that establishes a critical distance to the life story of Anton Reiser. The protagonist himself does not have a say in the entire novel; instead, an omnipresent narrator discloses Reiser's childhood experiences from the perspective of a critical observer who is unhesitant to interrupt the narrative for his uncompromising psychological conclusions. A passage from the novel's second volume, in which the narrator reports on one of Anton's many, often awkward attempts to find recognition, illustrates this dominating narrative voice:

> Reiser also sought by all possible means to confirm the precentor's good opinion of him. This went so far that he walked up and down with an open book in his hand in a public place where the precentor often went, in order to attract his teacher's attention and be considered such a model of diligence that he even studied while out walking.—Although Reiser did actually enjoy the book he was reading, the pleasure of being noticed in this pose by the precentor was much greater, and from this trait one may see his inclination towards vanity. The appearance meant more to him than the substance, though the substance was not unimportant either.[34]

---

33. Karl Philipp Moritz, "Fortsetzung der Revision der drei ersten Bände dieses Magazins," in *Magazin zur Erfahrungsseelenkunde als ein Lesebuch für Gelehrte und Ungelehrte: Mit Unterstützung mehrerer Wahrheitsfreunde herausgegeben von Karl Philipp Moritz*, ed. Petra and Uwe Nettelbeck (Nördlingen: Franz Grelo, 1986), 195.

34. Moritz, *Anton Reiser*, 116.

Although even contemporary readers were aware of the autobiographical traits that Anton Reiser shared with Karl Philipp Moritz, the novel should not be mistaken for the private case of its author. Rather than following the practice of confession, it displays a particular narrative as the appropriate form of observation. In the context of the psychological novel, psychology refers to a specific mode of observation: cold. Moritz's novel establishes by means of narrative what *Erfahrungsseelenkunde* had requested from its contributors: to momentarily play the cold observer by stepping out of the turbulences of one's desires and by not worrying in the least about oneself. In the context of the psychological novel, the request for cold observation is implemented by means of cold narration. The autonomous sovereignty of the psychological perspective is established by means of the sovereignty of the narrator who marks the cognitive threshold of the novel.

From the very beginning, the narrator's presence can hardly be overlooked. In the prefaces with which each of the four volumes opens, he positions himself as the cognitive authority who guarantees the general importance of Anton Reiser's individual history. These prefaces reflect on the genre of the psychological novel itself and help its readers to distinguish it from the genre of the popular novel, which in the eighteenth century had the reputation of serving those with morally weak and seducible personalities. Anton Reiser's own reading mania and book addiction testifies to this: "Reading had become as much a necessity to him as opium is for Orientals, who use it to attain a pleasant state of insensibility."[35] In contrast to the novels that Anton Reiser consumes to escape the miseries of his young life, Moritz's psychological novel opens with the promise of realism when it reveals that the novel's "observations are for the most part taken from real life."[36]

Although Moritz holds on to the designation *novel*, he pursues a redefinition of the genre. As a psychological novel, *Anton Reiser* would not entertain with stories of adventure and romance; its

---

35. Moritz, *Anton Reiser*, 142.
36. Moritz, *Anton Reiser*, 3.

"main purpose is to describe man's internal history."[37] With this remark, Moritz places the novel in the context of the theory initiated by Friedrich von Blanckenburg's *Versuch über den Roman* and its famous dictum that the novel should depict "the inner history of man."[38] While Moritz's novel shares some of the central features of Blanckenburg's ideal novel—such as the biographical storyline, the narrative distance, and the causally arranged structure of the plot—it differs from Blanckenburg's teleological concept. Blanckenburg explicitly distinguishes between the biographer and the novelist:

> The poet shall be and wants to be more than the mere biographer of his characters. The biographer . . . records what he sees and knows; but he does not know the angle from which he shall look at it, and this angle will only know those who oversee the entirety of this one individual character. He does not know the relations and connections between what he records and what his characters shall or can become. He cannot see the point in which all individual streams meet and concur. . . . It is different with the poet. He is at the same time both the creator and historiographer of his characters, and he stands on such high ground that he sees the final purpose of it all.[39]

The two most emphasized guidelines of Blanckenburg's conception of the novel contradict each other: the novel's plot must be

---

37. Moritz, *Anton Reiser*, 3.

38. Josef Fürnkäs emphasizes the importance of Blanckenburg's *Versuch über den Roman* for the historical-philosophical analysis of the psychological novel: "Wichtig für die Analyse des Einzelwerks *Anton Reiser* als Ursprung des geschichtsphilosophischen Formtypus psychologischer Roman ist Blanckenburgs *Versuch* insofern, als er die Bedingungen der Möglichkeit eines idealen bürgerlichen Romans, gedacht als 'innere Geschichte' eines Menschen programmatisch formuliert." (Josef Fürnkäs, *Der Ursprung des psychologischen Romans: Karl Philipp Moritz' Anton Reiser* [Stuttgart: J. B. Metzlersche Verlagsbuchhandlung, 1977], 6.) Fürnkäs later emphasizes the twofold function of the "innere Mensch" for Blanckenburg's ideal novel: "Der innere Mensch hat für den Roman, der die innere Geschichte eines Menschen sein soll, einen doppelten logischen Status. Einmal ist er konkreter Inhalt bzw. Gegenstand des Romans. . . . Zum anderen ist der innere Mensch transzendentale Bedingung der Möglichkeit des idealen Romans." (Fürnkäs, *Der Ursprung*, 17.)

39. Friedrich von Blanckenburg, *Versuch über den Roman: Faksimiledruck der Originalausgabe von 1774. Mit einem Nachwort von Eberhard Lämmert* (Stuttgart: J. B. Metzler, 1965), 379–380.

causally arranged within a realist setting, but it is supposed to eventuate toward an ending determined to show the ideal completion of its characters. The possibilities of the novel are therefore dogmatically limited in regard to its content.[40] Eberhart Lämmert, the editor of Blanckenburg's treatise, has further pointed out that Blanckenburg attempts to use the great contemporary and public interest in novels to direct it toward more serious goals.[41] He adheres to an Enlightenment concept of *Bildung* to which he attributes—as his review of Goethe's *Werther* shows—an important educational function.

In contrast to Blanckenburg's pedagogical approach to the novel, Karl Philipp Moritz's psychological novel is driven by an epistemological question. This difference must be taken into account when comparing their respective references to the "inner" history as the guiding principle of Blanckenburg's ideal and Moritz's psychological novel. For Blanckenburg, the inner history of the hero must be the organizational principle for novelistic composition. The adventure to be told is the development and conversion of the hero's ethos, and by no means the exterior history of his life. While Moritz, too, focuses his psychological novel on the inner history of the protagonist, Anton's life is not told as a story of conversion from which a refined individual arises, ready to take responsibility for himself and, thus, for others. In the context of Blanckenburg's theory of the novel, the focus on the inner history holds a moral function. In Moritz's novel, the moral perspective is replaced by a psychological one that is directed toward cognition.

Thus, Moritz's psychological novel *Anton Reiser* differs from Blanckenburg's orientation toward perfection. But it also differs from an autobiography that answers the question of how its author became what he is.[42] *Anton Reiser* is not written toward an ending and it does not follow the idealist narrative of the completion of a

---

40. See Kurt Wölffel, "Friedrich von Blanckenburgs *Versuch über den Roman*," in *Deutsche Romantheorie: Beiträge zu einer historischen Poetik des Romans in Deutschland*, ed. Reinhold Grimm (Frankfurt am Main: Athenäum 1968), 58.

41. See Eberhart Lämmert, "Nachwort," in Blanckenburg, *Versuch*, 554.

42. For a discussion of the problem of autobiography in regard to its linguistic form, the situation of its author, and the position of the narrator, see Philippe

sovereign individual. In contrast to Blanckenburg's ideal novel, the psychological novel does not result in a *Bildungsroman*, but is—as Lothar Müller concludes in his book-length study of *Anton Reiser*— more closely related to the model of the medical case history.[43] Müller argues for placing the novel in close proximity to the contemporary boom of anthropology and medicine rather than in the context of the novel. Its methodological core is the casuistic approach of *Erfahrungsseelenkunde*, and the search for a general knowledge of the human soul.

In his call for contributions to the *Magazin* in 1782, Moritz had explicitly emphasized the importance of *Erfahrungsseelenkunde* for the novelist, who would find it necessary to study *Erfahrungsseelenkunde* before even daring to begin a literary composition.[44] To that effect, Moritz's novel must be read not only as the inner history of its protagonist Anton Reiser but also as a programmatic attempt to engage the genre of the novel for the project of *Erfahrungsseelenkunde*. *Anton Reiser* is a contribution to the theory of the novel: it sets out to demonstrate what the novel can accomplish within the larger framework of literary anthropology.

It is obvious that Moritz's psychological novel stands in a rather complex referential context, and its generic definition causes particular problems. *Anton Reiser* can be, and has indeed been, read as literary novel, biography, autobiography, medical case history, and a case narrative in the context of the *Magazin zur Erfahrungsseelenkunde*. The psychological novel transgresses generic boundaries almost purposefully. It is worth recalling the first sentence of the novel's preface: "This psychological novel could equally well be called a biography, since its observations are for the most part taken from real life."[45] The readers of *Anton Reiser* must have been confused concerning the kind of text that they were about to read. Every

---

Lejeune, *On Autobiography*, trans. Katherine Leary (Minneapolis: University of Minnesota Press, 1989).

43. "Blanckenburgs idealer Roman tendiert zum Bildungsroman, Moritzens psychologischer Roman ist aufs engste mit dem Modell der Krankengeschichte verknüpft" (Müller, *Die kranke Seele*, 42).

44. See Moritz, "Vorschlag," 798.

45. Moritz, *Anton Reiser*, 3.

genre designation is immediately replaced by reference to another: from novel to biography to observation. Surely, this is not an arbitrary list; it is directed toward the depiction of *real life* that would not have to bother with questions of genre. In view of *real life*, the laws of genre and its limits can be suspended.

Thus, the psychological novel does not have to follow a given form, and Moritz counters the criticism that he loses himself in details that do not seem to directly contribute to the big picture with reference to real life: "Anyone who values such a faithful portrayal will not be offended by what initially seems trivial and insignificant, but will bear in mind that the intricate texture of a human life consists of an infinite number of trifles, all of which assume great importance when interwoven, however insignificant they may seem in themselves."[46]

As a genre, the novel offered itself to *Erfahrungsseelenkunde* precisely because it did not have to subject itself to any poetic restrictions. It gains form by means of reference to its object through the depiction of life. The novel can claim to meet its only requirement of causality not through artistry, but by following the causality of life, where every detail has important biographical effects: "Anyone who examines his past life will, at a first glance, perceive nothing but futility, loose ends, confusion, obscurity, and darkness; but the more firmly his gaze is fixed, the more the darkness disappears, the futility gradually vanishes, the loose ends join again, confusion and disorder form a pattern—and discord is imperceptibly resolved into concord and harmony."[47] A fixed gaze in combination with attention to detail, therefore, is supposed to reveal the consistency of life. A careful reading of *Anton Reiser*, however, shows that the conception of a life that proceeds according to recognizable causal principles while keeping the semblance of its unique individuality is made possible by the sovereign perspective of a narrator. Only a few pages into the second book and thus almost immediately following the cited passages from its preface, the narrator interrupts the story

---

46. Moritz, *Anton Reiser*, 87.
47. Moritz, *Anton Reiser*, 87.

of Reiser's life so as to reveal this secret: "Here I have unavoidably had to recapitulate and anticipate some points in Reiser's life, in order to juxtapose matters that, according to my plan, belong together. I shall do this many more times; and anyone who apprehends my plan will require no apology for these seeming digressions."[48]

As Josef Fürnkäs argues in his study on the origin of the psychological novel, the narrator of *Anton Reiser* can do both: he can enter the inner world of Reiser's thoughts and emotions and he can back out anytime into an analytic and schematic perspective. By substituting an epic with an analytic position, the narrator lends consistency to Reiser's life story, and thus establishes the protagonist's identity.[49] And as the psychological novel proceeds on the assumption of the protagonist's pathology and thereby eliminates any subjective perspective, it does not leave much room for interpretation. Instead of merely presenting the story of Anton Reiser's suffering, the novel uses narrative as a diagnostic tool for the representation of observations and hence combines the depiction of the inner history of the protagonist with an analytic perspective that exceeds the individual and moves toward general cognition. In this regard, Moritz's psychological novel is more than just the individual history of Anton Reiser. The narrator of the novel claims an elevated perspective from which he can reflect on the conditions of possibility for the inner history of the protagonist and on the difficulties of self-observation. On every level, the novel appears to be an exercise in "cold" observation: the narrator successfully establishes an aesthetic distance from the life and miseries of the protagonist, but the plot presents a series of Anton's failed attempts to establish such a sovereign perspective toward his own life. The psychological novel, therefore, deals with obstacles to self-observation while successfully establishing such a perspective by means of a distanced and "cold" narrative. Anton's own attempts to gain control over his life stand in stark contrast to the sovereignty with which the narrator positions himself as the psychological authority.

---

48. Moritz, *Anton Reiser*, 91.
49. See Fürnkäs, *Der Ursprung*, 50–53.

The critical innovation of Moritz's psychological novel is to be found in this discrepancy between a protagonist—who keeps failing because he cannot distinguish his reading from his world, the fiction he reads from the reality in which he lives—and a narrator, who by means of sociopsychological analysis exposes Anton's attitude from the perspective of a cold observer. The novel's plot is completely subordinated to a rigorous regime of observation. Although Blanckenburg's ideal novel could still be understood as a moral example of a life well pursued, the meaning of the psychological novel does not simply emerge from the hero's life story but results from the relation between the protagonist's story and the critical perspective by which the narrator claims analytic and interpretive sovereignty. Thus, *Anton Reiser* accomplishes much more than being just an individual case in the context of *Erfahrungsseelenkunde*: by aligning the narrative of an individual life story with general psychological cognition, it establishes a model for writing about cases. At the same time, the use of narrative for the representation of observation and the choice to engage a literary genre for the production of psychological knowledge give new meaning to literary discourse and assign to literature essential cognitive qualities.

3

Hot and Cold

History, Casuistry, and Literature in Schiller and Kleist

The epistemological standard for the practice of observation at the end of the eighteenth century is for the observer to be *cold*. The subject shall speak for itself and must be protected from hasty conclusions and prejudices. Johann Karl Wezel advised the pedagogical observer to remain a "cold spectator" and not to interfere with the object of observation,[1] and Karl Philipp Moritz repeatedly emphasized the importance of cold self-observation as a basic requirement for the project of *Erfahrungsseelenkunde*. The observer of man must begin with himself before being able to observe others. Know thyself—*gnothi seauton*—is the most important requirement for becoming a successful observer and contributor to empirical psychology. He must observe everything that happens "as if

---

1. Johann Karl Wezel, "Über die Erziehungsgeschichten," in *Gesamtausgabe in acht Bänden*, vol.7, ed. Jutta Heinz and Cathrin Blöss (Heidelberg: Mattis Verlag, 2001), 438.

it were a play" and the people "as if they were actors." And he himself must become part of this observation "as if he were a stranger" whose stories of fortune and misfortune he needed to hear with "coldblooded attentiveness."[2] In his novel *Anton Reiser* Moritz had implemented his "Versuch für ein Magazin zur Erfahrungsseelenkunde." The novel is a literal translation of the program of cold observation into storytelling: under the name Anton Reiser, the author Karl Philipp Moritz objectifies his own biography and tells his own story from the distance of an impartial spectator. Although awareness of the autobiographical nature of the material contributes to an understanding of the novel as a programmatic attempt to implement the demands of *Erfahrungsseelenkunde*, *Anton Reiser* is more than a mere autobiography.

Moritz's psychological novel implements the coldness of observation by means of cold narration, and thus develops a model for telling individual histories that can both claim historical truth and have value for general psychological cognition. Telling true stories that contribute to a knowledge of human nature without interfering with the object is the task of Moritz's *Erfahrungsseelenkunde* as well as that of literary authors who are no longer content with merely entertaining an audience. They hear the call to contribute to the anthropological project of the eighteenth century.

In this context, Friedrich Schiller published his novella *The Criminal of Lost Honor* in 1786. In the spirit and tradition of the French *Pitaval*, a collection of legal cases published by the French lawyer, François Gayot de Pitaval, in several volumes between 1734 and 1743, the German translation of which Schiller would edit in 1792, his novella intervened in the debate of historical storytelling by framing the story of a criminal with a discussion of its narrative conditions. The preface of Schiller's novella shows a certain proximity to Moritz's project when the errors of man are declared to be most instructive for psychology. In difference to Moritz's *Erfahrungsseelenkunde*, however, Schiller explicitly addresses the problem of

---

2. Karl Philipp Moritz, "Vorschlag zu einem Magazin einer Erfahrungs-Seelenkunde," in *Werke I: Dichtungen und Schriften zur Erfahrungsseelenkunde*, ed. Heide Hollmer and Albert Meier (Frankfurt am Main: Suhrkamp, 1999), 802.

observation in conjunction with its representation. The request for cold *observation* in Moritz now turns into the request for cold *narration* and is thus treated as a problem of poetological dimensions. Although Heinrich von Kleist did not explicitly address the poetological questions that Schiller's novella had posed, Kleist's novella *Michael Kohlhaas* is also best understood as a contribution to the discussion of the poetics of cases.[3]

In the following, I argue that Schiller's *Criminal of Lost Honor* and Kleist's *Michael Kohlhaas* are not only two literary case histories but also, moreover, two cases that comprise what will become distinctions of literature itself: the distinctions between history and story, between history and case, and between case and story. These distinctions are at stake wherever literary texts cite historical material to produce case histories. Rather than merely citing the historical case, these stories refer to the case in history as an instance of storytelling.

A Tear on a Letter

My reading of the two literary cases starts with an episode from Kleist's *Michael Kohlhaas* that functions as the peripeteia of the novella. During his stay in Brandenburg, Michael Kohlhaas, who is trying to avail himself of all legal possibilities in order to settle his

---

3. Both novellas have been the object of countless interpretations and have also been discussed in the context of the history of psychology and with reference to the genre of the case. Bernd Hamacher sees Kleist's *Michael Kohlhaas* as a critical commentary on Schiller's famous novella and argues that Kleist exposes the limits of the emerging criminal psychology in Schiller's *Criminal of Lost Honor*. (See Bernd Hamacher, "Geschichte und Psychologie der Moderne um 1800 (Schiller, Kleist, Goethe): 'Gegensätzische' Überlegungen zum 'Verbrecher aus Infamie' und zu 'Michael Kohlhaas,'" in *Kleist-Jahrbuch*, ed. Günter Blamberger, et al. [Stuttgart: J. B. Metzler, 2006], 60–74.) Susanne Lüdemann explicitly discusses both novellas in the context of the emergence of case history, and argues that literature distinguishes itself from other—particularly judicial and medical—discourses by purposefully undermining directive distinctions. (Susanne Lüdemann, "Literarische Fallgeschichten: Schillers 'Verbrecher aus verlorener Ehre' und Kleists 'Michael Kohlhaas,'" in *Das Beispiel: Epistemologie des Exemplarischen*, ed. Jens Ruchatz, Stefan Willer, and Nicolas Pethes [Berlin: Kulturverlag Kadmos, 2007], 208–223.)

conflict with the junker Wenzel von Tronka, receives a letter from his lawyer in Dresden with bad news. The message reports the denial of his legal dispute against the junker, and causes Kohlhaas to let a tear drop onto the letter. The mayor, who notices this reaction, approaches Kohlhaas to ask the reason for this surprising emotion, and promises to help him in this matter of obvious injustice. But the mayor's advocacy is without success; the court issues a resolution to vilify Kohlhaas as a troublemaker and orders him to refrain from bothering the Chancellery "with such paltry and pitiful affairs."[4] This second dismissal of his legal request leaves Kohlhaas devoid of any hope of finding justice via the law, and this time his reaction is much less controlled: "Having read the letter, Kohlhaas ... seethed with anger."[5] With his trust in the law deeply injured, Kohlhaas decides to claim justice for himself by taking the law into his own hands, and thus enters the path that will turn him into "one of the most upright and at the same time terrible men of his time."[6]

In more than one way, this episode is important for Kleist's narrative of the horse dealer Kohlhaas, whose sense of justice is irreparably shattered.[7] On the one hand, in precisely this passage Kohlhaas loses his confidence in the law and sees no alternative but to seek justice for himself. On the other hand, the description of Kohlhaas's emotions and affects clearly has psychological inten-

---

4. Heinrich von Kleist, "Michael Kohlhaas," in *Selected Prose of Heinrich von Kleist*, trans. Peter Wortsman (Brooklyn: Archipelago, 2010), 161. (All English quotations are from this translation.)
5. Kleist, "Michael Kohlhaas," 161.
6. Kleist, "Michael Kohlhaas," 143.
7. Joachim Rückert has rightly pointed out that Kleist uses the word *Rechtgefühl* instead of *Rechtsgefühl* in his *Kohlhaas*. In this small semantic shift, Rückert sees a manifestation of an ethical law and a moral sense that runs parallel to the positive law and guarantees its abidance. See Joachim Rückert, "'... der Welt in der Pflicht verfallen ...' Kleists 'Kohlhaas' als moral- und rechtsphilosophische Stellungnahme," in *Kleist-Jahrbuch*, ed. Hans Joachim Kreutzer (Berlin: Erich Schmidt Verlag, 1988/1989), 357–403. An important contribution to this discussion can be found in Dania Hückmann, "Unrechtes und Ungerechtes: Rache bei Kleist," in *Heinrich von Kleist: Konstruktive und destruktive Funktionen von Gewalt*, ed. Ricarda Schmitt, Séan Allan, and Steven Howe (Würzburg: Königshausen & Neumann, 2012), 231–246.

tions and offers insights into his emotional state that make his subsequent actions comprehensible on this level. In the following, I argue that this sequence, proceeding from a tear on a letter to an outburst of fury, has specific relevance for the story and its narrative structure.

It is telling that the original version of *Michael Kohlhaas* Kleist published in the journal *Phöbus* in 1808 shows certain omissions in this passage: the whole episode of the first letter onto which Kohlhaas sheds a tear is missing. Instead, Kohlhaas only receives one negative message, and it is this letter that causes him to burst into rage and triggers his crusade for justice.[8] Only in the revised version of the book in 1810 is this initial moment further delayed. What could have been the reason for Kleist to revise precisely this passage and to defer Kohlhaas's furious outburst?

Anthony Stephens, who briefly discusses this passage, emphasizes the psychological expedience of this later addition.[9] Indeed, there is no plot-related relevance that would have made this addition necessary. Since the unsuccessful attempt of the mayor to advocate for Kohlhaas adds nothing new to the overall plot, it is a compelling conclusion that Kleist wanted to highlight the psychological development of his protagonist in more detail and depth.

This circumstance brings up the question that has dominated the scholarly discussion of *Michael Kohlhaas* in the past three decades: the question of the relation between literary and historical narrative, which the novella's title addresses with the subtitle "From an Old Chronicle."[10] With the episode of the tear that Kohlhaas lets fall onto the letter, Kleist has, purposefully or not, inserted a reference to a text, in which the question of historical narrative is

---

8. Heinrich von Kleist, "Michael Kohlhaas [Phöbus-Fassung]," in *Sämtliche Werke und Briefe*, vol. 2, ed. Helmut Sembdner (Munich: dtv, 1993), 292.
9. See Anthony Stephens, "'Eine Träne auf den Brief': Zum Status der Ausdrucksformen in Kleists Erzählungen," in *Kleist: Sprache und Gewalt* (Freiburg: Rombach, 1999), 160.
10. See Carol Jacobs, *Uncontainable Romanticism: Shelley, Brontë, Kleist* (Baltimore: Johns Hopkins University Press, 1989); and Rüdiger Campe, *The Game of Probability: Literature and Calculation from Pascal to Kleist*, trans. Ellwood H. Wiggins Jr. (Stanford, CA: Stanford University Press, 2013).

programmatically discussed on a poetological level: Schiller's 1786 novella *The Criminal of Lost Honor*.¹¹ Prevented from crossing the border because of bad luck and misunderstanding, the wanted robber and murderer Christian Wolf, now at the end of his attempt to escape from the authorities, surrenders and turns himself in to the judge with the following words: "You still have no idea?—Write to your prince how you found me, and that I betrayed myself of my own free will—and that God will have mercy on him some day, as he will have on me now—plead for me, old man, and shed a tear on your report: I am the Innkeeper of the Sun."¹²

But there is more evidence that Kleist referenced Schiller's novella in *Michael Kohlhaas*. After the death of Kohlhaas's wife, as a result of her desperate attempts to prevent the looming disaster, Kohlhaas answers her last wish that he would forgive his enemies by quietly promising to himself: "Let God never forgive me if I forgive the Junker!" [so möge mir Gott nie vergeben, wie ich dem Junker vergebe!]."¹³ Both Anthony Stephens and Bernd Hamacher have identified this promise as another reference to Schiller's "Host of the Sun," Christian Wolf, who in the passage quoted above uses a similar phrase to ask for forgiveness, "that God will have mercy on him some day, as he will have on me know." And yet, although the intention of the clemency plea to the Prince would be unmistakably clear, the analogous passage in Kleist's *Kohlhaas* lacks this decisiveness because the German "vergeben" (to forgive) can also be read as "vergelten" (to repay).¹⁴ Hamacher concludes that Kleist is

---

11. Although I am not the first reader to identify a connection between the two novellas in regard to the motif of a tear on a legal letter (most prominently, see Stephens, "Eine Träne auf den Brief"), my overall argument in regard to casuistic forms of writing does not depend on whether or not Kleist consciously refers to Schiller's text.

12. Friedrich Schiller, "The Criminal of Lost Honor: A True Story," in *Schiller's Literary Prose Works: New Translations and Critical Essays*, ed. Jeffrey L. High (Rochester, NY: Camden House, 2008), 55.

13. Kleist, "Michael Kohlhaas," 168.

14. "'Vergeben' kann hier im Sinne von 'vergelten' gelesen werden, so dass konträre Paraphrasen möglich sind: 'Ich hoffe, dass Gott mir meine Taten nicht in gleicher Weise vergilt, wie ich die Taten des Junkers vergelte,' oder auch: 'Gott möge mir gnädiger sein, als ich es dem Junker gegenüber bin,' aber auch ganz im

systematically attempting to dissolve clarity where Schiller attempts to produce it. This also applies to the motif of the tear on the letter that Kleist uses almost conversely to its reference to Schiller. First of all, Kohlhaas himself lets a tear fall onto the letter, while Schiller's protagonist Christian Wolf asks the superior to do him the favor of writing on his behalf and to sign the letter with a tear. Whereas in Schiller's lachrymose scene we witness the criminal's effort to obtain advocacy, in Kleist's we see the loss of support. The letter that Kohlhaas receives and wets with his bodily fluid makes him understand that his lawyer cannot do anything for him, and that he is left to his own devices in his quest for justice. In both cases, the tear on the letter has a certifying function; it indicates an immediate testimony that the writing in documents can only ever produce through mediation. But in Schiller the tear on the letter remains a fictitious testimony, as Christian Wolf's request appears to be nothing other than the rhetorical instruction for his advocate to get in the right mood to appeal convincingly for the criminal's amnesty, and finally to drop a tear on the letter as evidence of the request's authenticity and pureness. In Kleist's novella the tear on the letter fulfills a very different task. The motif does not appear at the end of the novella as in Schiller. Instead, it appears at the very point in the novella when the plot turns around, at its peripeteia. The tear that Kohlhaas drops onto the letter conveys new insight into the story that had so far been contained by framing the novella as having been taken from an "old chronicle" and by the immense use of documents. More than ninety of these documents can be counted in Kleist's novella, among them the prophecy of a gypsy woman that remains secret throughout the novella and that the end of the text proclaims must be read about in history.[15] I argue that there is a

---

Gegenteil: 'Gott möge mir nie vergeben, falls ich dem Junker vergebe.'" (Hamacher, "Geschichte und Psychologie," 69.)

15. See Stephens, "Eine Thräne auf den Brief." More recent studies on the traffic of documents in *Michael Kohlhaas* can be found in Friedrich Balke, "Kohlhaas und K. Zur Prozessführung bei Kleist und Kafka," *Zeitschrift für Deutsche Philologie* 130, no. 4 (2011): 503–530, and Rupert Gaderer, "Michael Kohlhaas (1808/10): Schriftverkehr–Bürokratie–Querulanz," *Zeitschrift für Deutsche Philologie* 130, no. 4 (2011): 531–544.

connection between this prophetic note that Kohlhaas will eventually swallow, which turns him into the mute witness and keeper of history, and the tear that he drops onto the disappointing letter from his lawyer. To convincingly make this argument, it is necessary to follow the reference to Schiller's *Criminal of Lost Honor* in more detail.

Cold (Schiller)

It is not surprising that Kleist's *Kohlhaas* references Schiller's novella. Beyond the motif of the tear, the two texts share a number of references. Both novellas refer to historically documented cases and position themselves in a popular contemporary tradition tracing back to the collections of remarkable and interesting criminal cases collected and published by the French lawyer François Gayot de Pitaval in the mid-eighteenth century. *Pitaval* stories, as they are metonymically called, were generally understood to be presentations of legal cases that presented psychological complexities in conjunction with judicial proceedings. They aimed to entertain and educate an audience consisting of academics and laymen alike. Friedrich Schiller showed his appreciation for the value of this work, when he agreed to be the editor of the 1792 German edition, translated by Carl Wilhelm Franz and Friedrich Immanuel Niethammer, and published under the title *Merkwürdige Rechtsfälle als ein Beitrag zur Geschichte des Menschen*. In the preface to his edition, Schiller begins with a lament about the unfortunate state of popular literature: "Insipid novels destructive of taste and morality, dramatized stories, so-called ladies' books, and the like, constitute to this day the staple of our circulating libraries, and ruin the remnant of sound principles which our stage-poets have not yet destroyed."[16] This complaint targets the popular genre of love and adventure novels that was so vigorously dismissed by literary critics in the eighteenth

---

16. Friedrich Schiller, "Preface to the First Part of the Celebrated Causes of Pitaval," in *Schiller's Complete Works*, vol. 2, ed. Charles J. Hempel (Philadelphia: I. Kohler, 1861), 458.

century. The new literature that Schiller, Moritz and others demanded sought to be of educational use, a literature of *Bildung* that would foster critical thought and direct it toward worthy aims. Schiller was convinced that the collection of Pitaval's criminal cases would be of such use when he agreed to lend his name to the German edition. This honorable commitment had poetic as well as anthropological reasons:

> [The present work] contains a number of judicial cases which, in point of interest, complication, and variety of objects, almost rival a romance [*Roman*] and have moreover the advantage of being historically true. Man is here seen in the most complicated situations exciting our expectation to the utmost, and keeping the reader agreeably employed in exercising his powers of divination in the unraveling of the plot. The secret play of passion is here unfolded to our sight, and many rays of truth are shed over the secret machinations of intrigue, and of spiritual as well as temporal frauds. Motives, which in common life, are hidden from the eye of the observer, become more manifest, where life, liberty, and property are at stake, and in this way the criminal judge is able to cast a deeper look into the human heart. . . . This important gain which is of itself sufficient to justify the commendations bestowed upon this work, is still greatly enhanced by the legal knowledge with which the relation of these cases is interspersed, and which is rendered lucid and intelligible by the individuality of the case to which the legal technicalities apply.[17]

According to Schiller, *Pitaval* accomplished what literature had thus far failed to do: to offer insight into the inner history of man, to vividly depict human passion and drives, to artfully arrange the plot, and to guarantee historical truth. Only a few years earlier, Schiller had published his *Criminal of Lost Honor* as an attempt to accomplish this poetic agenda.

Similar to the stories of *Pitaval*, Schiller's novella is based on a historical case. *The Criminal of Lost Honor* refers to the life story of the robber and murderer Friedrich Schwan, who was executed in 1760 and whose case had elicited a lot of public attention. Schiller's historical source was his philosophy teacher Jacob Friedrich Abel, whose father Konrad Ludwig Abel had been the judge

---

17. Schiller, "Preface," 459.

responsible for the murderer's arrest. But even before Schiller proceeds to the actual story, he takes the case as an opportunity for poetic reflections that echo Aristotle's *Poetics*, particularly the distinction between history, philosophy, and poetry. In his introductory remarks to the novella, just as in his later preface to the German edition of *Pitaval*, Schiller clearly follows an Enlightenment notion of *Bildung* that aims for a general knowledge of human nature by means of the exact observation of the individual; an aim closely related to Johann Karl Wezel and Karl Philipp Moritz's concurrent pedagogical and psychological projects. Schiller writes:

> The human heart is something so simple and yet so multifaceted. One and the same capacity or desire can play out in thousands of shapes and directions, can cause thousands of contradictory phenomena, can appear in different combinations in thousands of characters, and thousands of dissimilar characters and events can be spun from the one and the same impulse, even if the individual in question never recognizes the relationship of his actions to those of the rest. If a new Linnaeus were to appear and classify humankind into genus and species according to drives and inclinations, how astonished we would be to find those whose vice must now suffocate in a constricted bourgeois sphere and the narrow confines of the law, together in one and the same species with a monster like Cesare Borgia.[18]

Against this background, the "conventional treatment of this story," which contents itself with following the mere judicial facts and details, would not be suited to the study of "the everyday bourgeois sphere" (Schiller, 39). The distance between the historical subject and the reader would be too great to provide an understanding or even a vague sense of the manifold relations between the actions of the individual human being and the intensity of his emotions: "A gulf separates the historical subject at hand and the reader that preempts any possibility of self-comparison or practical usefulness, and, instead of inspiring a therapeutic sense of terror, which could serve as a warning to an egotistical sense of normalcy, the story

---

18. Schiller, "Criminal of Lost Honor," 39.

elicits only a distant, disapproving shake of the head. . . . Lost with the relation is the lesson; and the story, instead of serving as an institution of learning, must make do with the meager accomplishment of satisfying our curiosity" (Schiller, 39–40). In order to contribute to the education of the reader and not to degenerate into some kind of light fiction, the narrative must close the historical gap. This enables the reader to come to an understanding of the historical subject and to learn from the story. The author can choose between two possibilities with which to master this difficult task: "Either the reader must become as heated as the protagonist, or the protagonist must become as cold as the reader" (Schiller, 40).

This is where the mediation between the historical subject and the reader turns into a poetological concern. And yet, as a historian the author does not have a real choice, as Schiller elaborates:

> I know that many of the best storytellers of our own time and from antiquity have employed the former method and have appealed to the heart of the reader through a captivating rendering. But this approach is a usurpation on the part of the author and violates the republican freedom of the reading public, who have the right to judge for themselves. At the same time, the method is a transgression of genre boundaries, for it is the exclusive and characteristic domain of the rhetorician and the poet. The historian has no choice but the latter method. (Schiller, 40)

That is to say that the protagonist must cool down to the emotional temperature of the reader, and this must have an immediate effect on the narrative depiction of the historical case. If he wants to become the historiographer of the human soul, and if he wants to meet the standards of historical objectivity, the narrator must abstain from any poetic effort and rhetorical manipulation. Or, to carry forward Schiller's famous anatomical metaphor of the "autopsy of his depravity" (Schiller, 41), the pen must be turned into a scalpel in the hands of the historical author.

In this context, literary scholars have rightly pointed out that Schiller's poetological remarks would be nothing more than a programmatic statement, and Schiller himself does not seem to match up to them in his depiction of the story of the *Criminal of Lost*

Honor.[19] With regard to the form and content of the story, the narrative of Schiller's novella contradicts his claim to poetic abstinence, and furthermore, his refusal of rhetoric is itself rhetorical. The exposition of the novella quite closely follows the precepts of the principium or exordium, introduced by Quintilian as a means to prepare audiences for the purpose of the speech and to secure their sympathy.[20] Rhetoric is most effective when it succeeds in being persuasive by not being rhetorical. Schiller's novella is not a true story simply because it is based on historical facts, but rather because it narrates on the assumption that the story is true. The novella itself treats historical truth not in regard to verifiable external facts, but as an effect of narrative. And Christian Wolf's request to the judge to petition for him, by letting a tear fall onto the letter, underscores Schiller's poetic agenda. The tear would be a witness of the true feelings of the criminal, it would testify to his remorse, contribute to the authenticity of his plea, and thus, to the truth of his story.[21]

Hot (Kleist)

When Kleist refers to Schiller's *Criminal of Lost Honor* with the motif of the tear on the letter, he simultaneously references the problem of historiographic objectivity at stake in Schiller's novella. Kleist

---

19. See Harald Neumeyer, "Unkalkulierbar unbewußt: Zur Seele des Verbrechers um 1800," in *Romantische Wissenspoetik: Die Künste und die Wissenschaften um 1800*, ed. Gabriele Brandstetter and Gerhard Neumann (Würzburg: Könighausen & Neumann, 2004), 157; and Viktor Lau, "'Hier muß die ganze Gegend aufgeboten werden, als wenn ein Wolf sich hätte blicken lassen': Zur Interaktion von Jurisprudenz und Literatur in der Spätaufklärung am Beispiel von Friedrich Schillers Erzählung 'Der Verbrecher aus verlorener Ehre,'" *Scientia poetica* 4 (2000): 95.

20. See Lau, "Hier muß die ganze Gegend," 96.

21. Here, I am following the line of argument of Bernd Hamacher, who writes that the tear "soll eine Wahrhaftigkeit herstellen, die der bloßen Schrift nicht zukommt. Analog auf die Ebene des Textes der Erzählung übertragen, hieße das: Wenn dieser von einer Träne benetzt würde—sei es des Erzählers, sei es des Lesers—, dann wäre der Untertitel nach dieser Vorstellung berechtigt, und es handelte sich um eine 'wahre Geschichte'" (Hamacher, "Geschichte und Psychologie," 68).

also bases his novella *Michael Kohlhaas* on a historically documented case, and he, too, claims historical authenticity for the story, even in its title. While Schiller's novella identifies itself as "true story," Kleist's *Michael Kohlhaas* pretends to be taken from an old chronicle.[22] But in Kleist, it is Kohlhaas himself who sheds a tear on the saddening letter. It is his own fate to be abandoned by the law that triggers this bodily affect and that heralds the following acts of terror. Schiller's *Criminal of Lost Honor* ends with the motif of the tear as a call for a narrative that his preface rhetorically rejected as a violation of "the republican freedom of the reading public." In Kleist's text, the same motif marks the very moment of the story's reversal into tragedy.

One might suspect that Kleist is purposefully citing the motif from Schiller so as to deconstruct his poetic dictum. To use Schiller's poetological metaphor: the hero of Kleist's story is effectively heating up in this passage. First, it is only a tear that blurs his vision, but soon the second negative notice will lead to a full outburst of rage and to his violent battle, at once against and in favor of the law. Kleist's Kohlhaas itself has been the subject of heated debates. To some, such as the lawyer Rudolf von Ihering, he was a fighter for justice;[23] to others, such as the philosopher Ernst Bloch, he was only a "Paragraphenreiter," a stickler for the letter of the law;[24] and to still others, he was a pathologically deranged personality, an opinion to which Goethe's assessment of the horse dealer

---

22. "Aus einer alten Chronik." In his book *Passions of the Sign*, Andreas Gailus points out Kleist's use of the preposition "aus" instead of the more common preposition "nach" and draws conclusions regarding the relation between history and story: "Unlike the much more common *nach*, which would have constructed a rather loose relation of similarity between the novella and the chronicle, *aus* qualifies this relation in two additional ways: First, in pointing to an act that separates, and hence isolates, the novella from its source; and second, by emphasizing the uneven size of the two texts, implying that the novella is only part of the chronicle. The preposition thus calls attention to the fact that Kohlhaas's story derives from another narrative dealing with a broader and more general subject." (Andreas Gailus, *Passions of the Sign: Revolution and Language in Kant, Goethe, and Kleist* [Baltimore: Johns Hopkins University Press, 2006], 109.)

23. Rudolf von Ihering, *Der Kampf ums Recht* (Vienna: Propyläen, 1900).

24. Ernst Bloch, *Naturrecht und menschliche Würde* (Frankfurt am Main: Suhrkamp, 1961), 93.

as hypochondriac also contributed. One thing is certain: Kleist's *Michael Kohlhaas* did not leave its readers cold.[25]

Could one therefore claim that Kleist chose the second possible way of storytelling that Schiller dismissed in his novella's preface for the benefit of historical narrative? And if the episode of the tear attests to the author's intention for the reader to warm up just as the hero does, what is the effect on the "republican freedom of the reading public," the violation of which Schiller suspected to be the consequence of this kind of narrative?

Kleist addresses the freedom of the reading public in a passage that has often been the center of scholarly attention. The Elector of Saxony tries by all means to bring into his possession the prophecy concerning his future fate, which Kohlhaas had received from an old gypsy woman and had carried with him in a leaden capsule ever since. In the name of the Elector, his chamberlain pays an old peddler who resembles the woman who originally gave the note to Kohlhaas, tasking her with getting hold of the paper. "Chance" has it, however, that the peddler woman chosen by the chamberlain because of her resemblance is the gypsy woman herself. In good romantic manner, the narrator rises to speak: "And since probability is not always on the side of truth, it so happened that something occurred here which we will report, but which we are duty-bound to permit any reader so inclined to doubt."[26]

In his book *The Game of Probability*, Rüdiger Campe claims that readers will not be able to profit much from their freedom. If they do not believe in the identity of the women, they will not be able to understand the rest of the novella. And if the women were in fact not identical, the reader would face an even more severe inexplicability.[27] At the same time, Campe continues, this episode is not simply the end of the story, but marks the distinction between a novella and a historical transcript "from an old chronicle" as literature:

---

25. A summary of the debates on morality and constitutional law triggered by the novella can be found in David Ratmoko, "Das Vorbild im Nachbild des Terrors: Eine Untersuchung des gespenstischen Nachlebens von 'Michael Kohlhaas,'" in Blamberger et al., *Kleist-Jahrbuch*, 218–231.

26. Kleist, "Michael Kohlhaas," 246.

27. See Campe, *Game of Probability*, 388.

"The paradoxical poetical formula signals the ending of *Kohlhaas* therefore as the moment when Aristotle's distinction between poetry, philosophy, and history—and hence the text's fictional status—is at stake."[28]

This distinction of poetry is further supported when Kohlhaas finally swallows the paper with the prophecy that carries the knowledge of Saxony's future fate and gives the horse dealer the opportunity to take a last and lasting revenge on the Elector of Saxony who has come to witness Kohlhaas's execution:

> The Elector cried out: "Now then, Kohlhaas, the horse trader, you to whom justice has been done, prepare yourself to give your due to His Imperial Majesty, whose legal counselor stands here, and to pay the price for your cross-border disruptions of the peace!" Removing his hat and flinging it to the ground, Kohlhaas said he was ready, and after once again picking up his children and pressing them to his breast, he handed them to the magistrate of Kohlhaasenbrück; and while the latter led them away, quietly weeping, he strode toward the execution block. No sooner had he unwound the kerchief from his neck and opened the pouch, then, with a fleeting glance at the circle of people that surrounded him, he spotted, in close proximity, the gentleman with the blue and white feathers in his hat standing between two knights who half-hid him from view. Taking a sudden stride forward, in a manner alarming to the guards, Kohlhaas untied the tube from around his neck; he removed the slip of paper, unsealed it, and read it through; and with his steady gaze glued to the man with the blue and white feathers in his hat, the latter looking on hopefully, he stuffed the paper in his mouth and swallowed it. At that very moment the man with the blue-and-white-feathered hat trembled and collapsed unconscious. But as his stunned companions bent down to him and lifted him up off the ground, Kohlhaas leaned over the block, where his head fell to the executioner's axe. Here ends the story of Kohlhaas.[29]

Not only for the Elector of Saxony but also for the readers of Kleist's novella, the content of the paper that Kohlhaas swallows remains a mystery. Other than the Elector, however, the readers of Kohlhaas's story will have access to it in the chronicles of Saxony. For after the end of the story of Kohlhaas has been announced, the reader is advised to look up the rest of the story in history books:

---

28. Campe, *Game of Probability*, 374.
29. Kleist, "Michael Kohlhaas," 253–254.

"Soon thereafter, torn in body and soul, the Elector of Saxony returned to Dresden, where chronicles can be found that relate the rest of his story."[30] This ending directly corresponds to the subtitle of the novella disclosing that it has been taken from an old chronicle. One possible interpretation is that here history appears to be the guarantor of poetic truth. In return, this would mean that history had to rely on facts established by means of poetry. One must therefore understand history and poetry to be mutually supportive; one cannot do without the other. The radical distinction between poetry and history, for which Schiller argues in *The Criminal of Lost Honor*, is impossible. Although Kleist's novella can be read in such a way that it attributes prophetic agency to poetry, it appears to be much more plausible that Kleist's novella emphasizes the importance of narrative fiction for history. What Kleist's novella demonstrates in regard to Schiller's claimed priority of history over poetry is that the (republican) freedom of the reading public is nothing but an empty formula, and the distinction between poetry and history nothing more than a (rhetorical) deception of the reader.

Case and History

The conflict over the distinction between history and story in Schiller and Kleist is framed by the presentation of their novellas as cases that use the narrative of an individual story to reference the more general problem of historical truth. The historicity of a case is necessary neither to support its individuality nor to verify its truthfulness; but it constitutes the circumstances under which the particular case can happen again.

This makes it necessary to further distinguish between case and history, between their specific modes of reference and the particular ways in which they relate to their source. Whereas historical writing is supposed to make available past events based on the unaltered and accurate presentation of original documents, the case presents its source material in reference to an order of knowledge,

---

30. Kleist, "Michael Kohlhaas," 254.

to the formation of which it will itself contribute.[31] One could, therefore, distinguish history and case as two different forms of cognition. Whereas history claims access to a documented truth, the case presents knowledge in an emerging form, pending verification by the very possibility of its repetition.

To this binary distinction of history and case, literature appears to be a third mode. It can be found on neither site of the distinction, since for literature the difference between source and citation is not essential, but rather located on the same ontological level.[32] Kleist's references to Schiller in *Michael Kohlhaas* leading to the confusion of history and story are witness to this quality of literature. When Kleist references Schiller, literature is marked as a particular practice of writing that enables reference to the distinction between history and case and at the same time displays their literary means and conditions. To further strengthen this claim, I once again return to Kleist.

The gypsy episode at the end of *Michael Kohlhaas* contains another—albeit indirect—reference to Schiller. In a short anecdote titled "Improbable Veracities" that Kleist wrote only half a year after the novella, he once again uses the formula of probability not always being on the same side as truth. In this anecdote, an old army officer promises to tell three improbable stories that he introduces as follows: "For people demand of truth, as its primary requirement, that it be probable. And yet probability, as experience teaches us, is not always on the side of truth."[33] At the end of the anecdote and after the audience has listened with astonishment and disbelief, one of the listeners reveals the source of the third story: "The story

---

31. Hans Lipps gives a similar definition of the case: "Das Besondere eines Falles ist etwas anderes als die dem Begriff einfach entzogene Individualität eines existierenden Gegenstandes. Ein Fall wird auf den Begriff *zu*, aber nicht—wie ein Gegenstand—von dem Begriff *her* nur eben weiterbestimmt. Fälle werden auf einen Begriff *hin* erkannt." (Hans Lipps, *Die Verbindlichkeit der Sprache* [Frankfurt am Main: Klostermann, 1958], 51.)

32. For a discussion of the logic of literary reference, see Rüdiger Campe and Arne Höcker, "Introduction: The Case of Citation: On Literary and Pragmatic Reference," in *Germanic Review: Literature, Culture, Theory* 88, no. 1 (2014): 40–43.

33. Heinrich von Kleist, "Improbable Veracities," trans. Carol Jacobs, *Diacritics* 9, no. 4 (Winter 1979): 45.

[*Geschichte*] is in the appendix to Schiller's *History of the Revolt of the United Netherlands*, and the author notes expressly that a poet should not make use of this fact, the history writer [*Geschichtsschreiber*], however, because of the irreproachable nature [*Unverwerflichkeit*] of the sources and the agreement of the witnesses, is compelled to take it up."[34]

The irreproachable nature of the source clearly marks the referential stakes of historical discourse. A text qualifies as history when referring to a source that antecedes it. However, if one follows the link to the source of the third story that Kleist's officer tells, one finds a very different presentation of the unlikely event. In Kleist's anecdote, the story is about an ensign who, by the enormous power of an explosion, is transported from one side of the French river Scheldt to the other. Without being harmed and still carrying banner and baggage, nothing but his position seems to have changed. In Schiller's *History of the Revolt of the United Netherlands*, a similar incident is reported in a series of events dealing with a devastating explosion at the river Scheldt and cases of miraculous survival by several people, including the protagonist of Schiller's history, the Duke of Parma himself:

> Many had escaped in the most wonderful manner. An officer named Tucci was carried by the whirlwind like a feather high into the air, where he was for a moment suspended, and then dropped into the river, where he saved himself by swimming. Another was taken up by the force of the blast from the Flanders shore and deposited on that of Brabant, incurring merely a slight contusion on the shoulder. He felt, as he afterwards said, during this rapid aerial transit, just as if he had been fired out of a cannon. The Prince of Parma himself had never been so near death as at that moment, when half a minute saved his life.[35]

The difference in presentation of the same case is remarkable, particularly in regard to the logic of historical storytelling. Kleist's officer presents the event as an isolated and individual case, and,

---

34. Kleist, "Improbable Veracities," 46.
35. Friedrich Schiller, *History of the Revolt of the United Netherlands*, trans. Lieut. E. B. Eastwick and Rev. A. J. W. Morrison (London: Anthological Society, 1901), 316.

thus, emphasizes its improbability, but Schiller embeds the incident in a series of similar cases with the opposite effect: the story appears less fantastic and more probable. Here, it is not historical truth that justifies the story to be told by the historiographer. Instead, it is the similarity of this event to the event that is important to the overall historical context: the lucky and miraculous survival of the Duke of Parma. Therefore, it is surprising that, according to Kleist, Schiller refers to the Aristotelian distinction between history and poetry in this context. It is even more surprising to find that he in fact fails to do so. Although the source of the third story in Kleist's anecdote can indeed be found in Schiller's *History of the Revolt of the United Netherlands*, Kleist's reference to Schiller's citation of the Aristotelian distinction is a fake.[36] When following this fictitious reference concerning the singularity of the historically certified event, one instead finds not a single event but a series of events. Under the premises of the questioned identity of truth and probability, the fake citation reverses the distinction of history and poetry from the *Poetics* just as the ensign in the story switches from one riverbank to the other.

Schiller also uses the Aristotelian distinction between history and poetry to frame the story of *The Criminal of Lost Honor*. In

---

36. In *Uncontainable Romanticism*, Carol Jacobs presents a reading of this constellation that alludes to the fictitious quote in Kleist's anecdote, and with reference to the problem of the source she concludes: "The single citation we are offered from this source [Schiller's *Geschichte des Abfalls der vereinigten Niederlande*], however, is not, by way of verification, about the siege but about the way in which stories and histories differ in their relationship to their sources: 'that a poet should not make use of this fact; the history writer, however, because of the irreproachable nature of the sources and the agreement of the witnesses is compelled to take it up.' . . . Let us forget for a moment that this citation is nowhere to be found in Schiller. . . . What defines history is that its relationship to its sources is *unverwerflich* ('irrefutable'); they are literally incapable of being dislocated. The text of history is founded upon an 'agreement of the witnesses' to which it simply adds its voice by way of corroboration. History's repetition of its sources verifies their authenticity, as though they were the necessary cause of history, but with the writer's repetition of the text of history all that is shot to pieces. What better proof do we have of this than the passage cited above, which misrepresents its historical source? For Schiller's history, as we have seen, preaches not the valorization of historical truth but the naiveté of believing possible a repair of the rupture his history has just described" (Jacobs, *Uncontainable Romanticism*, 191).

contrast to the series of events that supports the historical case of the lucky survival of the Duke of Parma, it is a single case of an individual that is supposed to carry the weight of the "history of humankind."[37] The claimed truth of the story—or rather its importance as a contribution to the establishment of a future understanding of the human soul—is not guaranteed by a collection of cases, as it was, for example, in Moritz's *Erfahrungsseelenkunde* and Pitaval's *Causes célèbres*. Instead, the individual life story of Christian Wolf is supposed to stand in for the general truth of humankind and must therefore certify this truth by means other than historical precision. This might have been the reason that Schiller did not follow the path of historical and *cold* storytelling that he presented as the only valid alternative for not patronizing the reader. Indeed, Schiller does not show much accuracy in regard to the historical case, so that it is possible to conclude that he invented the case *against* its historical sources.[38] In contrast to the criminal Friedrich Schwan in Jacob Friedrich Abel's historical report of the case, Schiller's criminal is marked by an unfortunate physiognomy, he is socially shunned by women—in short, he appears to be a naturally disadvantaged human being, an outsider of society. Thus, his natural disposition and his subsequent social marginalization hurt his innermost feelings and, fueled by emotions of rage and revenge, drive him further toward a criminal career. In Schiller's adaptation of the historical case, these insights into the psychological causality of the unfortunate protagonist are responsible for turning the story into a modern case that not only informs our understanding of the motivation of the criminal individual but also intends to establish an understanding of humankind in general. The framework of the story announces its strict following of the historical sources, but the framed story of the criminal's life authenticates psychological truth by means of poetic imagination and literary empathy. In her discussion of the problem

---

37. Schiller, "Criminal of Lost Honor," 39.

38. Here, I closely follow the conclusions from Johannes F. Lehmann, "Erfinden, was der Fall ist: Fallgeschichte und Rahmen bei Schiller, Büchner und Musil," *Zeitschrift für Germanistik* N. F. 19 (2009): 380.

of truth in Schiller's novella, Gail K. Hart thus argues that in "Schiller's rendering, the choice between evoking either literary empathy or historical understanding seems to fall with literary warmth."[39] And similarly, Susanne Lüdemann concludes that the subtitle, "A True Story," would rather refer to poetic, and not so much to historical truth.[40] Both Hart and Lüdemann make reference to a letter from Schiller to Caroline von Beulwitz in December 1788, in which Schiller specifies the advantage of *inner* over historical truth:

> What you say of *history* is certainly right and the advantage of *truth* that history has over novels, could alone elevate it above them. The question is, however, whether the *inner truth*, which I call philosophical and artistic truth ... does not have as much value as historical truth. That a person in *such* situations feels, acts, and expresses himself in *such a way* is a great, significant fact for humanity and the novelist or dramatist has to get that across. The inner correspondence, the truth, will be felt and acknowledged without the actual occurrence of the event. The usefulness is not to be missed: this way one comes to know *mankind* and not simply *one man*, the human race and not the easily unrepresentative individual.[41]

By means of literary empathy, and hence contrary to the dismissal of the poet in the preface of Schiller's novella, the story of Christian Wolf's life exceeds the scope of the individual case and claims universal exemplarity. To convey the internal history of the protagonist, the historical perspective has to be complemented by a different form of observation that is ready to sacrifice historical accuracy for psychological understanding.

Schiller's programmatic preface to *The Criminal of Lost Honor* not only sets up a mode of representation that he then violates in the narrative of the actual story but also sets up a guiding distinction

---

39. Gail K. Hart, "True Crime and Criminal Truth: Schiller's 'The Criminal of Lost Honor,'" in High, *Schiller's Literary Prose Works*, 229.

40. "Und wenn Schiller seine Novelle im Untertitel 'Eine wahre Geschichte' nennt, so ist damit offenbar die 'poetische', und nicht (oder nicht nur) die historische Wahrheit gemeint" (Lüdemann, "Literarische Fallgeschichten," 216).

41. "Friedrich Schiller an Caroline von Beulwitz (14.12.1788)," in Friedrich Schiller, *Kritische Gesamtausgabe, Bd.2: Schillers Briefe*, ed. Fritz Jonas (Stuttgart: DVA, 1893), 172. (Translation by Hart, "True Crime and Criminal Truth," 228.)

for the reading and interpretation of the entire novella. Not the individual case of Christian Wolf and not even the exemplary case of a criminal must be considered the overarching theme of the novella, but the question of how to tell an individual story in light of general psychological cognition and truth. When Schiller employs literary fiction to complement the historical facts of the story in order to arrive at psychological understanding, it means that the mediation between the particular and the general cannot be accomplished solely on the basis of history but must rely on literary imagination.

This conflict is addressed once again at the very end of the story when Christian Wolf turns himself in and asks the judge for an emotional sign of his sympathy by letting a tear fall onto the report that contains his confession. The guiding poetological distinction between history and poetry that frames the novella is not resolved or even decided by the end of the story. The tension between these two modes of narrative cognition remains intact and the decision regarding how to judge the criminal Christian Wolf is left to the judge and to the reader.

As I argued earlier in this chapter, reading Kleist's *Michael Kohlhaas* as a critical response to Schiller's novella further complicates the leading distinction that Schiller attributes to the literary case history in regard to its realist demand and the truth claim in the subtitle of the story. Both novellas provide an insight into the function of literary fiction for contemporary attempts to establish narrative forms for general psychological cognition. And both novellas examine the problem of discriminating between individual exceptions and general or generalizable norms. Insofar as they approach these questions through literary forms of storytelling, Schiller's *Criminal of Lost Honor* and Kleist's *Michael Kohlhaas* are literary case histories in a narrower sense. And insofar as both novellas critically examine the possibilities and impossibilities of discrimination between these forms of storytelling, they anticipate the institutional success of psychological case histories in forming and eventually reforming legal and forensic processes of decision making in the nineteenth century.

4

Conclusion

Literary Reference and Authorship

Chapters 1 through 3 implicitly presupposed that the novels and novellas discussed have literary status, and I have developed my argument under the assumption of their affiliation with an established literary system. Without any doubt, Goethe's and Moritz's novels as well as Schiller's and Kleist's novellas are part of today's German literary canon. But just as certainly, this literary canon did not yet exist around 1800. It cannot even be assumed that the writers of these texts considered themselves literary authors. The common practice of mentioning an editor where we expect to find the name of an author testifies to this. *Werther* and *Anton Reiser* conceal Goethe's and Moritz's authorship, and instead frame their novels by means of a fictitious editorship. In Schiller's and Kleist's novellas, the reference to the truthfulness of the story and the historically documented origin of the material have a similar function. If not as literature, how else should we be reading *Werther, Anton Reiser, The Criminal of Lost Honor,* and *Michael Kohlhaas*?

In other words, what might have been the premises of and motivations for writing about cases for Goethe, Moritz, Schiller, and Kleist when we assume that they did not write as literary authors? After all, Goethe and Kleist had studied law; Schiller was trained as a medical doctor; and Karl Philipp Moritz was inspired by the philosophical doctors of the Enlightenment period and held important pedagogical positions in Berlin. The reading of their cases as literary fiction obscures the fact that these novels and novellas might just as well be understood as vehicles for lawyers, medical doctors, pedagogues, and philanthropists to inform each other about the legal and mental status of the individual and, thus, to continue the medical and legal traditions of thinking, arguing, and writing in cases.

And yet the close reading of these texts shows that in them the representation of cases began to change, in two respects in particular. First, they could no longer be clearly attributed to a single disciplinary context. Although *Werther* seems to be a pertinent case from a moral and legal perspective, the novel takes a different direction when it develops the case primarily from the point of view of psychological development. Karl Philipp Moritz's *Erfahrungsseelenkunde* followed medical categories and also claimed to be suited for legal applications. The new focus on the inner history and the psychological motivation of the individual—which also frames Schiller's story of the criminal Christian Wolf—results in a blurring of the lines between legal, moral, and medical areas of expertise.

Second, a new narrative perspective develops in these cases, which further complicates the position of authorship. In the final part of *The Sufferings of Young Werther*, the editor takes over the narrative voice and significantly intervenes in the interpretation of the case. The same is true of the psychological novel *Anton Reiser*, which I read as an exercise in cold observation that Moritz had claimed to be the methodological foundation for practicing *Erfahrungsseelenkunde*. In Schiller's *The Criminal of Lost Honor*, the problem of narrative for the representation of cases becomes the central theme of the frames in which the case of the murderer Christian Wolf is narrated. And Kleist's *Michael Kohlhaas* further complicates the narrative distinctions that lead in Schiller's novella to the claim that historical storytelling is the only appropriate choice for the composition of cases.

These two changes regarding the disciplinary affiliation and narrative perspective of cases are interconnected: the change in narrative perspective answers to the problem of disciplinary uncertainty. Insofar as cases no longer refer to a specific system of reference guaranteed by their disciplinary context—whether that is law, medicine, or moral philosophy—they develop their own frame of reference for the representation of cases. They do so by establishing a narrative perspective that allows access to the inner motivation of the protagonist, and at the same time marks the position of an omniscient psychological narrator as a mediator between the outer circumstances and the inner history. Concurrently with the establishing of such a narrative perspective a different form of reference emerges that can be called *literary*, because it coincides with the emerging principles of literary authorship around 1800. The two versions of Goethe's *Werther* document this development in exemplary fashion when the second, revised version strengthens the position of the editor as omniscient narrator and, thus, reframes the case of Werther as a story of psychological development. Behind the fiction of editorship the contours become visible of an author who testifies not only to the authenticity and originality of the historical circumstances but is also the conduit to the inner history of the protagonist.[1] It is the negotiation of narrative reference and, as a result, the development of an omniscient psychological perspective, related to the emergence of literary authorship around 1800, by which these "new" cases set themselves apart from earlier forms of casuistic reasoning and contribute to the formation of an autonomous concept of literary fiction.

---

1. Uwe Wirth has discussed this transformation from editorship to authorship in Goethe's *Werther* in regard to the development of the narrator in chapter "6.5.1 Der Herausgeber-Erzähler des *Werther* als Geschichtsschreiber und Dichter" of his book, *Die Geburt des Autors aus dem Geist der Herausgeberfiktion: Editoriale Rahmung im Roman um 1800: Wieland, Goethe, Brentano, Jean Paul, E. T. A. Hoffmann* (Munich: Wilhelm Fink, 2008), 273–276.

Part II

The Case between Psychiatry, Law, and Literature

5

Schmolling, Hoffmann, Hitzig, and the Problem of Legal Responsibility

Law ~~and~~ Literature

In the course of the nineteenth century, case history was established as the preferred genre of newly developing scientific disciplines, from psychiatry at the beginning of the century to sexology and criminology toward the end. Emancipated from literary discourse and its aesthetic demands, the newly established disciplines were often driven by questions and problems of legal concern and meant to participate and intervene in the institutional framework of the law. This particular aspect—which, in the wake of Michel Foucault, has often been described as a dispute over competence between psychiatry and law[1]—is important here only when it is necessary

---

1. See Michel Foucault, *"Society Must Be Defended": Lectures at the Collège de France, 1975–1976*, trans. David Macey (Picador: New York, 1997); and Michel

to illuminate the literary perspective on cases. Literary authors throughout the nineteenth century followed the literary convention, established in the late eighteenth century, of referring to real occurrences and authentic cases and of focusing on an individual who could be identified as such only because he or she had breached a rule or deviated from societal norms. The literary reference to cases in the nineteenth century, however, developed a perspective that at least partially owed to the deployment of the case history as a genre of psychiatric intervention in legal decision making rather than to epistemic concerns. Thus, in Part II the focus will be no longer—as chapters 1 through 3—on literature's involvement in the development of case history as epistemic genre and the related formation of a literary discourse of the individual; it will instead be on the critical reaction of nineteenth-century literature to the institutional appropriation of narrative modes of casuistic representation. Rather than on literature's psychological contributions, the readings in chapters 5 through 7 will focus on literary forms of institutional critique that open new perspectives on the aesthetic foundation of casuistic reasoning.

Hitzig versus Hoffmann

Although the late eighteenth century witnessed the coevolution of modern literature and a scientific system of psychology, writers in the Romantic era broke the pact between literary production and anthropological cognition when they followed Novalis's and Friedrich Schlegel's appeal to turn the world into a poetic enterprise. When these authors dedicated themselves to the exploration of the spiritual abyss and the hidden layers of human subjectivity, they did so in the name of a speculative natural philosophy that was incompatible with the demands of scientific discourse. To put it briefly, the poetic products of Romanticism were of no use for contemporary

---

Foucault, *Abnormal: Lectures at the Collège de France, 1974–1975*, trans. Graham Burchell (Picador: New York, 1999).

psychology. Only Freud would later understand—albeit under different premises—reading Romantic poetry as case histories.[2]

In 1825 Julius Eduard Hitzig posthumously blamed his colleague and friend, the Romantic author and appellate court judge E. T. A. Hoffmann, for having been led by his poetic drive to overstep his legal competence in a criminal case that had been heard at the Berlin court a few years earlier. Only a footnote added by Hitzig to the publication of the proceedings from the murder case of Daniel Schmolling revealed Hoffmann's involvement in the case and his coauthorship of one of the deciding legal documents: "It might be interesting for the readers of this journal to learn that the following statements were written by the meanwhile deceased appellate court judge Hoffmann, the author of the Fantastic Tales in Callot's Manner, etc."[3] It is because of this footnote and its revelation of authorship that the Schmolling case has attracted the attention of literary scholars and led them to look for intersections between Hoffmann's legal writings and his literary works. A direct reference to the controversy over the question of accountability, however, to which the Schmolling case owes its particular legal-historical importance, does not exist in Hoffmann's literary oeuvre. Hitzig's footnote suggests that Hoffmann's involvement in the Schmolling case shows traces of the author's literary interest and could have compromised Hoffmann's legal ability to judge. By assigning authorship to a literary writer, Hitzig moves the reading of the legal document into close proximity with fantastical literature. Although this criticism can easily go unnoticed in the footnote quoted above, Hitzig is more explicit in his accusation in another footnote in the same issue of the *Zeitschrift für die Criminal-Rechts-Pflege*. The context

---

2. See, most prominently, Freud's reading of E. T. A. Hoffmann's novella *The Sandman* in his 1919 essay "The Uncanny," in *The Standard Edition of the Complete Psychological Works of Sigmund Freud, Vol. XVII (1917–1919): An Infantile Neurosis and Other Works*, ed. James Strachey (London: Vintage, 2001), 217–256.

3. E. T. A. Hoffmann, "Vertheidigungsschrift in zweiter Instanz für den Tabakspinnergesellen Daniel Schmolling welcher seine Geliebte ohne erkennbare Causa facinoris ermordete (Ein Beitrag zur Lehre der Zurechnungsfähigkeit)," in *Zeitschrift für die Criminal-Rechts-Pflege in den Preußischen Staaten mit Ausschluß der Rheinprovinzen*, ed. Julius Eduard Hitzig, vol. 1 (Berlin: Ferdinand Dümmler, 1825), 280.

of this second footnote is Hitzig's review of the psychiatric report prepared by the medical doctor Johann Christian August Clarus in the case of the murderer Woyzeck, on which Georg Büchner would base his drama of the same title, to be discussed in chapter 6. Hitzig praises Clarus's report as exemplary insofar as it limits itself to determining the degree to which the defendant's discernment had been compromised by mental illness without attempting to draw any legal conclusions. On the contrary, Hoffmann would have violated his authority in his statement in the Schmolling case. Due to "the peculiar direction of his mind," Hitzig claims, Hoffmann would have enjoyed seeing himself as a judge of questionable states of mind, a task that would only be appropriate for a forensic physician but not a judge.[4] Two years earlier, Hitzig had honored his recently deceased friend with the publication of a biography, in which he praised Hoffmann for his administrative talent and legal writing. In some cases, however, and specifically those that required the assessment of questionable states of mind, Hitzig claims Hoffmann let himself be tempted to draw conclusions based on his ingenuity and his fantastical creativity instead of rational and calm deliberation.[5] In other words, Hitzig criticizes Hoffmann directly for not having been able to appropriately distinguish in his statements between his legal and literary practices. But neither as judge

---

4. "In den hier gerügten Fehler ist der Concipient des Urtheils des Criminal-Senats des Kammergerichts in der Schmollingschen Sache, der verstorbene Kammergerichtsrath Hoffmann ... verfallen, der sich, in Folge der eigenthümlichen Richtung seines Geistes, besonders in Ausführungen über zweifelhafte Gemüthszustände gefiel" (Julius Eduard Hitzig, "Hofrath Doctor Clarus, Die Zurechnungsfähigkeit des Mörders Johann Christian Woyzeck," in Hitzig, *Zeitschrift für die Criminal-Rechts-Pflege*, 1:498).

5. "Nur in einzelnen Gattungen seiner criminalistischen Arbeiten, mag Hoffmann vielleicht der Vorwurf treffen, von seiner Individualität auf Irrwege geleitet worden zu sein, z. B. in Sachen, wo es auf einen Beweis durch künstlich ineinandergreifende Anzeigen von Verbrechen, oder auf Beurtheilung zweifelhafter Gemühtszustände, ankam. Dort gefiel er sich, hin und wieder, in Combinationen, die mehr von Scharfsinn, und zugleich von Fantasie, als von ruhiger Überlegung, zeigten;— hier, in Erörterungen, die nur in das Gebiet der psychischen Arzeneikunst, und nicht in das der Rechtswissenschaft, gehörten." (Julius Eduard Hitzig, *Aus Hoffmann's Leben und Nachlass*, Zweiter Teil [Berlin: Ferdinand Dümmler, 1823], 111.)

nor literary author would he have had the expertise and, thus, the authority to contradict psychiatric evaluations.

Before moving on to a more detailed discussion of the Schmolling case and Hoffmann's assessment of the psychiatric opinion, it is worth noticing a shift in reference to the status of literature. In the context of the legal-psychological discourse of the nineteenth century, there no longer seems to be a place for literature. Rather than being acknowledged as a testing ground for psychological observation, it can be concluded that literature is now excluded from the realm of psychiatric knowledge that aims at legal applicability and recognition as scientifically proven expertise, and this cannot risk being confused with the romantic concept of a philosophical speculation.

Against this background, Hoffmann's positioning in the Schmolling case is only superficially about the institutional rivalry between medicine and law. On a more profound level, the discussion reveals the irreconcilable discrepancy between the empirical requirements of the legal system and the speculative nature of the subjective experience of insanity. Thus, Hoffmann's claim to deny medical doctors any expertise in the assessment of legal responsibility is, on the other side, met by a poetic concept of experience and perception incompatible with legal reasoning.

The Schmolling Case

The Schmolling case attracted interest as one of the first cases in which the legal responsibility of the defendant was at stake due to the court's inability to determine the motivation for the murder. On September 25, 1817, the tobacco-rolling apprentice Daniel Schmolling stabbed his girlfriend, Henriette Lehne in Hasenheide, just outside of Berlin. The woman, who died from her severe injuries only one day later, had pointed to her lover as the perpetrator. Schmolling, who had a spotless reputation and had not been in conflict with the law until that day, confessed the deed without hesitation. In the following criminal investigation, he freely confessed to the crime and further declared that he had acted premeditatedly. He disclosed to the investigative judge that he had made the decision to murder his girlfriend about three weeks before committing the crime, and that for this purpose he had bought the knife with which he executed his plan. As a criminal case, the Schmolling case did not cause any difficulties: the circumstances of the deed were easy to determine; the victim herself had been recorded as a witness; the perpetrator was caught at the crime scene and did not even attempt to cover up his deed. However, the reasons for the deed remained unknown. What drove this thirty-eight-year-old man to commit such a dreadful crime? Asked about his motives, Schmolling explained that the thought of murdering his girlfriend had popped into his head suddenly and that he could not get rid of it until he had put it into practice. As no motive could be determined by criminal investigations, the judge decided to consult Dr. Merzdorff, a medical expert from the Berlin Charité, who diagnosed Schmolling with insanity and thus declared him not to be legally prosecutable. Although a second expert opinion by the medical officer of health, Dr. Horn, reinforced this diagnosis, the criminal court ruled that Schmolling was legally responsible and sentenced him to death by the wheel, but finally reduced his sentence to life in prison. After Schmolling killed a fellow inmate in 1827, he was once again sentenced to death and executed.

It was in this context of legal responsibility and the related discussion of the psychiatric intervention in matters of legal concern that Hitzig published the proceedings of the case in the 1825 issue of his *Zeitschrift für die Criminal-Rechts-Pflege*, a journal that he had founded in the interest of educational use for the criminalist and as a contribution to the most important contemporary debates on legislation. Programmatically, Hitzig had chosen a quote from the criminal superintendent H. B. Weber as a motto for the first edition of the *Zeitschrift*: "Regarding the necessary knowledge of the criminalist, it should not be limited to positive law.... The good criminalist must always be more than a mere judge; he must prove himself as a philosopher of law; he must be insightful particularly with regard to the inner and outer mechanism of human life; and he must ... study man not only theoretically but also practically."⁶

For the purpose of contributing to this educational goal, Hitzig's journal collected older cases consisting mainly of capital crimes such as infanticide, arson, and murder by poisoning, and discussed them anew against the background of current legal debates. It was an innovation of the journal that it included a distinct rubric for forensic medicine, under which medical and psychiatric reports as well as forensic papers were published. The proceedings of the Schmolling case appeared under the rubric "Pleadings" as a contribution to the study of legal responsibility, and comprised a short introduction by the editor and the legal reports of the case. The dossier of documents that Hitzig compiled exclusively follows the legal side of the debate and omits the reports of the medical experts who had been commissioned by the court and had triggered the debate on the mental state of the defendant. For the most part, the documents discuss the claim of Dr. Merzdorff, whose report concluded that Schmolling had committed the deed in a state of *amentia occulta*, and that in the decisive moment of the crime had lacked the freedom to determine his actions according to reason. *Amentia occulta* is the term with which the physician and anthropologist Ernst Platner had labeled a particular state of mind, called *manie sans délire* by the French psychiatrist Philippe Pinel a few years later: insanity without delusion.⁷

---

6. "Anlangend die für den Criminalisten nothwendigen Kenntnisse, so dürfen sich diese am wenigsten bloß auf positives Recht beschränken, denn gerade der Criminalist, er sei nun untersuchender oder erkennender Richter, bewegt sich in seiner durch das positive Recht immer nur lax umschriebenen Sphäre. Der gute Criminalist muß daher überall mehr, als nur Jurist (im gewöhnlichen Sinne des Wortes) seyn. Er muß sich als Rechts-Philosoph bewähren, er muß vorzüglich auch in das innere und äußere Triebwerk des Menschenlebens, in die allgemeinen und besonderen Verhältnisse des Staats und seiner Bewohner, gereifte Einsichten haben, er muß, um es kurz zu sagen, nicht nur den Menschen (theoretisch) sondern auch die Menschen (praktisch) kennen" (Hitzig, *Zeitschrift für die Criminal-Rechts-Pflege*, vol. 1).

7. In his discussion of the case, Hoffmann summarizes Merzdorff's medical evaluation, which refers directly to Ernst Platner and others: "Plattner [sic] nenne kranke Gemüthszustände dieser Art *amentia occulta*, Reil und Hoffbauer gäben

As the appellate court judge, E. T. A. Hoffmann was tasked with evaluating the legal consequences of Merzdorff's medical report, and he did not hesitate to conclude that the doctor's opinion would not be of higher value than any other opinion based on the given facts. Hoffmann criticizes the medical expert for not having given any medical evidence for his claims, and argues that the doctor overstepped his professional competence by drawing psychological conclusions. Merzdorff's diagnosis of *amentia occulta*, Hoffmann claims, is solely based on philosophical speculation and not on scientific experience. The deed itself was the only evidence that the doctor was able to give in support of the defendant's insanity, and a judge who followed this conclusion, Hoffmann sums up his argument, would blunder into "the vague realm of possibility."[8] But Hoffmann does not stop here. Although he generally acknowledges the importance of the medical profession for the detection of legally relevant physical conditions, he questions any medical competence for the psychological evaluation in legal matters. Alluding to Immanuel Kant, who in his *Anthropology from a Pragmatic Point of View* had assigned the examination of emotional states to philosophy,[9] Hoffmann shifts the conflict from that between medicine and law to that between medicine and philosophy. Against prominent medical authorities such as Johann Daniel Metzger, Johann Christian Reil, and the philosopher Johann Christoph Hoffbauer, Hoffmann argues that a philosopher without any medical training could come to a better understanding of psychological doctrines than a schooled medical expert. Hoffmann favors a philosophical psychology, such as Karl Philipp Moritz's *Erfahrungsseelenkunde*, which he references as evidence for his far-reaching critique.[10]

---

ihnen den unpassenden Namen von Wuth ohne Verstandesverwirrung. Hoffbauers Anreiz durch den gebundenen Vorsatz gehöre auch hierher, überhaupt sey die Existenz solcher wahrhaft kranken Gemüthszustände, den Ärzten und Psychologen längst bekannt" (Hoffmann, "Vertheidigungsschrift," 277).

8. Hoffmann, "Vertheidigungsschrift," 291.

9. "Aus diesem Grunde eignete Kant die Untersuchung des Gemüthszustandes ganz der philosophischen Fakultät zu" (Hoffmann, "Vertheidigungsschrift," 281).

10. "Und nur zu gewiß bleibt es, daß Männer von tief psychologischer Kenntniß, wie z. B. der verstorbene Moritz u.a., ohne Ärzte zu sein, irgendeinen zerrütteten Seelenzustand eines Menschen besser beurtheilen werden, als mancher Arzt,

It seems clear that a discussion of Hoffmann's legal opinion in the Schmolling case does not have to focus on the dispute over the murderer's motive nor does it have to delve into the details and circumstances of the individual murder case. What is at stake in Hoffmann's discussion of Daniel Schmolling's accountability is of general relevance, because it problematizes and attempts to determine the epistemological criteria under which legal decisions can be informed by a discourse on insanity. Indeed, Hoffmann's commentary is a vehement defense of the law against the speculative influence of a psychiatric discourse that did not have a sufficient epistemological basis on which legal decisions could be justified. The law must follow clearly defined rules to guarantee justice to the greatest possible extent, and thus cannot engage with any form of speculation. The law must be rigorously distinguished and protected from the influence of psychiatric as well as philosophical and literary discourses based on speculation. Therefore, on the one hand Hitzig is right in his critique of Hoffmann who indeed seems to favor a literary-philosophical approach to insanity over the claim of psychological competence by medical doctors. On the other hand, however, he overlooks the point that Hoffmann by no means attempts to claim legal competence for literary authors. Rather than blending the realms of law and literature, Hoffmann argues that law and literature follow from different premises that must not inform each other without undermining their respective claims of authority.

A passage in which Hoffmann's opinion takes on a rather unusual tone for this genre, sheds further light on this position:

> It is not granted to the human being involved in worldly life to fathom the depth of his own being. If the philosopher loses himself in speculations about this dark subject matter, the judge must hold on to that which has been established by unambiguous experiential data. Human freedom, considered from a metaphysical point of view, can never influence the practice of legislation and jurisdiction. When human freedom

---

dem jene Kenntniß, die sich nur auf die durchdringende Beobachtungsgabe und natürlichen Scharfsinn stützt, wenigstens im geringen Grade einwohnt" (Hoffmann, "Vertheidigungsschrift," 282).

is considered from a moral point of view, i.e., the faculty to determine one's will and its practical articulation according to a moral principle (arbitrium liberum), this kind of freedom is presupposed whenever penal sanctions are applied, and any doubt with regard to this has to be substantiated and convincingly presented to the judge if he is to take it into account.[11]

In her discussion of this passage from Hoffmann's statement, Dorothea von Mücke has argued that "Hoffmann radically departs from contemporary legal-philosophical and forensic psychiatric positions as he apodictically asserts the limits of human self-knowledge."[12] Recounting Hoffmann's discussion and ultimate rejection of the psychiatric concept of *amentia occulta*, Mücke concludes that Hoffmann fundamentally questions the assumption that the opaqueness of motive constitutes an anthropological condition that could be applied to the explanation of the individual case. Hoffmann claims "the mysterious unknown for the realm of philosophy and . . . for the realm of art."[13]

In Hoffmann's later writings literature develops its discursive form in confrontation with those legal and psychiatric institutions that he dealt with in his statement concerning the Schmolling case. It is my hypothesis that in regard to the institutional use of narrative cases of problematic forms of subjectivity, literary fiction begins to newly conceptualize and establish itself as a critical discourse that no longer contributes to a generally accepted knowledge of the self, but rather undermines institutional claims of certainty.

---

11. "Dem im irdischen Leben befangenen Menschen ist es nicht vergönnt, die Tiefe seiner eigenen Natur zu ergründen, und wenn der Philosoph sich über diese dunkle Materie in Spekulationen verliert, so darf der Richter sich nur daran halten, was die unzweideutigste Erfahrung festgestellt hat. Die Freiheit des Menschen, metaphysisch betrachtet, kann auf Gesetzgebung und Rechtspflege nie von Einfluß seyn, die moralische Freiheit des Menschen, d. h. das Vermögen, seinen Willen und dessen thätige Äußerung dem sittlichen Princip gemäß zu bestimmen (*arbitrium liberum*) wird als die Anwendung jeder Strafsanction bedingend vorausgesetzt, und jeder Zweifel dagegen muß dem Richter, soll er darauf achten, mit überzeugender Kraft dargethan werden" (Hoffmann, "Vertheidigungsschrift," 291).

12. Dorothea von Mücke, *The Seduction of the Occult and the Rise of the Fantastic Tale* (Stanford, CA: Stanford University Press, 2003), 113.

13. Mücke, *Seduction of the Occult*, 115.

The Case of Serapion

Around the same time that Hoffmann as a judge got involved in the Schmolling case, Hoffmann as a literary author worked on "The Story of Serapion," which he first published separately in a journal before it became the opening piece of the four volumes of collected stories, *The Serapion Brethren*. As an opening story that lends its name to the title of the publication and to the group of friends whose meetings and literary debates make up the framework of the story collection, it carries specific significance. Indeed, Hoffmann scholarship has devoted special attention to the story as the narrative framing of the poetological principle that informs Hoffmann's literary program.[14] Thus, "The Story of Serapion" is a case for a particular form of literary discourse and the founding document for a fictional artistic community that commits itself to the laws of the so-called Serapiontic principle. A constitutive part of this principle, however, is that its rules are not declared once and for all but are based on a story, and that these rules must be newly negotiated each time a story is told. The Serapiontic principle designates the object of literature to be the individual case and declares the intensity and communicability of the inner vision the only criterion for the evaluation of the poetic process. The literary institution suggested by the group of friends takes on the procedural form of storytelling that prefers visual over rational perspectives, fantastic imagination over the laws of reason.

---

14. To mention just a few publications on Hoffmann's Serapiontic principle: Hilda M. Brown, *E. T. A. Hoffmann and the Serapiontic Principle: Critique and Creativity* (Rochester, NY: Camden House, 2006); Lothar Pikulik, "*Die Serapions-Brüder*: Die Erzählung vom Einsiedler Serapion und das Serapion(t)ische Prinzip—E. T. A. Hoffmanns poetologische Reflexionen," in *Interpretationen: E. T. A. Hoffmann, Romane und Erzählungen*, ed. Günter Saße (Stuttgart: Reclam, 2006), 135–156; Uwe Japp, "Das serapiontische Prinzip," in *E. T. A. Hoffmann: Text + Kritik: Sonderband*, ed. Heinz Ludwig Arnold (Munich: Text + Kritik, 1992), 63–75; and Uwe Japp, "*Die Serapion-Brüder* (1819/21)," in *E. T. A. Hoffmann: Leben—Werk—Wirkung*, ed. Detlef Kremer (Berlin: Walter de Gruyter, 2012), 257–267.

"The Story of Serapion" revolves around the conflict between an outside world that supposedly reveals all its secrets to the rational mind and the fantastic inner world that finds its own truth in the production of authentic images. The old bearded hermit Serapion is first introduced by the narrator Cyprian who projects a strange and slightly uncanny appearance, whose gaze seems to lose itself in a remote distance, and who claims to be in the company of a group of wise men although he is clearly alone. Cyprian's strange encounter with the old man soon receives a rational explanation, supported by the medical status of the informant:

> Dr. S. told me all the story. This hermit had once been one of the most brilliant intellects, one of the most universally-accomplished men in M.; and belonging, as he did, to a very distinguished family, he was naturally appointed to an important diplomatic post as soon as he had completed his studies: the duties of this office he discharged with great ability and energy. Moreover, he had remarkable poetical gifts, and everything he wrote was inspired by a most brilliant fancy, a mind and imagination which sounded the profoundest depths of all subjects.... He had risen from step to step of his career, and was on the point of being dispatched on an important diplomatic mission, when he disappeared, in the most incomprehensible fashion, from M.[15]

After some time, a man in a brown robe appears in the Tyrolese mountains who claims to be the long-deceased martyr Serapion, and who is soon identified as the man who had disappeared from M. He is taken into custody and after violently resisting his arrest, taken care of by doctors and sent to the insane asylum, from which he manages to escape under mysterious circumstances. In the context of this history of the hermit Serapion, the direct institutional references are important, precisely because they overlap with Hoffmann's legal evaluation of the psychiatric opinion in the Schmolling case. The hermit's escape from the asylum is followed by a court decision informed by medical authorities to let the man live with his insanity as long as he does not pose a threat to society. Moreover, Cyprian himself, by applying the teachings of the recognized psy-

---

15. E. T. A. Hoffmann, *The Serapion Brethren*, trans. Major Alex Ewing, vol. 1 (London: George Bell, 1908), 11.

chiatric authorities Johann Christian Reil and Philippe Pinel decides to make it his task to cure the old man of his mental derangement, to help him return to the real world and reclaim his original identity. The scene in which the well-intended narrator approaches the hermit could hardly be more absurd and ends with the defeat of the psychiatric amateur. The hermit convincingly presents to the self-proclaimed psychiatrist the absurdity of his undertaking and beats him with his own weapons of reason:

> You maintain that it is a case of Fixed Idea that I believe myself to be Serapion the martyr—and I am quite aware that many persons hold the same opinion, or pretend that they do. Now, if I am really insane, none but a lunatic can think that he could argue me out of the Fixed Idea which insanity has engendered in me. . . . But if I am not mad, and if I am really Serapion the martyr, it is insane to set about arguing me out of that, and leading me to adopt the Fixed Idea that I am Count P. of M.[16]

Not only does the hermit's lecture shed light on his madness as a specific form of rationality, it makes reason itself a variation of insanity. With this inversion of madness and reason, Cyprian and Serapion also switch roles, and the latter now takes over as the storyteller whose novellas convey a poetic imagination unconfined by the limits of reason. With madness no longer being understood as the opposite of reason and instead being interpreted under aesthetic premises, the case of the madman Serapion turns into the case of romantic poetry. As the founding document for the group of friends who make the hermit their patron saint, and by transcending the limits of bourgeois subjectivity, "The Story of Serapion" contributes to the acceptance of a literary discourse that establishes a space for the imaginary beyond the confines of reason and rational demand. Literature here is not simply the opposite of reason; rather, this newly established literary discourse follows its own kind of reason and draws its critical potential from revealing the imaginary nature of absolute reason on the assumption of which legal bourgeois institutions rely. In this regard, Jutta Kolkenbrock-Netz emphasizes that the "modernism" of the author Hoffmann was based on the

---

16. Hoffmann, *Serapion Brethren*, 16.

critical debate with contemporary discourses of legal and medical-psychiatric institutions.[17] In "The Story of Serapion," a literary discourse is established that relates critically to the discourses of reason in a twofold sense. On the one hand, it undermines the position of the bourgeois individual by summoning those unconscious forces that radically question the possibility of transcendental self-creation and the autonomy of the subject. It is this literary-philosophical perspective that also informs Hoffmann's evaluation of the psychiatric opinion in the Schmolling case that caused Julius Eduard Hitzig to criticize Hoffmann for having overstepped his legal competence. On the other hand, this literary discourse establishes the author as a particularly gifted individual whose own psychological constitution makes him especially perceptive in understanding and depicting unconscious states of mind. It is this understanding of romantic authorship that will allow, toward the end of the nineteenth century, sexologists and criminologists to claim authority over the interpretation of literature from a medical-forensic perspective.

Chapters 6 and 7 each address these two critiques of reason and further discuss the development of literary discourses as new forms of institutional critique. Discussed in chapter 6, Georg Büchner's drama *Woyzeck* famously deals with the contemporary debates regarding the concept of legal responsibility that had already been at stake in the discussion of Hoffmann's contribution to the Schmolling case. Büchner, however, engages with the material of the Woyzeck case in the form of a drama that works on the disintegration of semantic and diegetic structures, and thus opens up a radically different perspective for the evaluation of casuistic reasoning. Discussed in chapter 7, Frank Wedekind's *Lulu* is part of a different historical constellation toward the end of the nineteenth century, in which the disciplinary formation of sexology and criminology essentially relies on casuistic forms of representation. Wedekind, too, chooses the dramatic genre to engage with these casuistic forms, to

---

17. Jutta Kolkenbrock-Netz, "Wahnsinn der Vernunft - juristische Institution - literarische Praxis: Das Gutachten zum Fall Schmolling und die Erzählung *Der Einsiedler Serapion* von E.T.A. Hoffmann," in *Wege der Literaturwissenschaft*, ed. Jutta Kolkenbrock-Netz, Gerhard Plumpe, and Hans Joachim Schrimpf (Bonn: Bouvier Verlag Herbert Grundmann, 1985), 144.

unfold their literary potential, and to undermine their claims of authority. Both texts represent a literary perspective that no longer attempts to compete with psychological explanations of questionable states of mind and instead establishes a form of literary critique by engaging with those casuistic forms by which a medical-forensic discourse attempts to take control over the interpretation and judgment of the human condition.

6

The Drama of the Case

Making the Case of Woyzeck

"All That Writing"

"What's the point of all that writing"—according to the psychiatric report by Dr. Johann Christian August Clarus, these are the words the murderer Johann Christian Woyzeck used to answer the question of why he had not been more cooperative before.[1] "What's the point of all that writing" can—retrospectively—also be read as an ironic commentary on the complex discourse network in which the wigmaker Woyzeck has become entangled since he murdered his girlfriend, the widow Johanna Christiane Woost,

---

1. "Wozu solle das viele Schreiben." (Georg Büchner, "Die Zurechnungsfähigkeit des Mörders Johann Christian Woyzeck, nach Grundsätzen der Staatsarzneikunde aktenmässig erwiesen von Dr. Johann Christian August Clarus," in *Sämtliche Werke und Briefe: Historisch-Kritische-Ausgabe*, ed. Werner R. Lehmann, vol. 1, *Dichtungen und Übersetzungen mit Dokumentationen zur Stoffgeschichte* [Hamburg: Christian Wegner Verlag, 1967], 506.)

on June 21, 1821. Yet the deed itself is a veritable trigger for the production of written documents: investigations begin, interrogations are conducted, results recorded, dossiers compiled. In the end, the verdict is rendered on the basis of these documents. Although highly recognized legal authorities such as Paul Johann Anselm von Feuerbach and Carl Joseph Anton Mittermaier vehemently argued against this practice and favored instituting oral and public trials, Johann Christian Woyzeck was still sentenced to death by a judge who only knew him from studying the files.[2] Among these documents was a medical evaluation of Woyzeck's emotional state provided by Hofrat Dr. Clarus, who, after five interviews with the defendant, came to the conclusion that he was responsible for his deed, and therefore legally prosecutable. The legal case of Woyzeck marks a historical transition: the old judicial procedures were still in effect, but the questions of the individual character of the perpetrator and the motives for the deed were considered of great importance to the verdict. In the case of Woyzeck, the verdict was still part of the old sovereign order of justice that Foucault has famously reduced to the formula "to make die and to let live."[3] The public execution was the theatrical spectacle in which power over life and death solemnly presented itself. But this power no longer went unquestioned; keen observers of human nature were already criticizing the idea of retaliation and deterrence as the purpose of punishment, and they were increasingly concerned about the public effects of the spectacularly dreadful show.[4] One such critical observer was the

---

2. See Paul Johann Anselm von Feuerbach, *Betrachtungen über die Öffentlichkeit und Mündlichkeit der Gerechtigkeitspflege*, 2 vols. (Giessen: Georg Friedrich Heyer, 1821); Carl Joseph Anton Mittermaier, "Bemerkungen über Geberdenprotokolle im Criminalprozesse," *Neues Archiv des Criminalrechts* 1, no. 3 (1816): 327–351; and for a scholarly discussion, see Peter Friedrich and Michael Niehaus, "Transparenz und Maskerade: Zur Diskussion über das öffentlich-mündliche Gerichtsverfahren um 1800 in Deutschland," in *Poetologien des Wissens um 1800*, ed. Joseph Vogl (Munich: Wilhelm Fink, 1998), 163–184.

3. Michel Foucault, "Lecture: 17 March 1976," in *"Society Must Be Defended": Lectures at the Collège de France, 1975–76*, trans. David Macey (New York: Picador, 2003), 239–264.

4. See Michel Foucault, *Discipline and Punish: The Birth of the Prison*, trans. Alan Sheridan (New York: Vintage, 1977).

scholar and translator of the work of the Italian criminologist Cesare Beccaria, *On Crime and Punishment*, Johann Adam Bergk. Bergk is credited with initiating the commissioning of medical experts for Woyzeck's criminal procedure.⁵ We know of Bergk's involvement in the case from a number of references in a second medical report that Dr. Clarus was asked to deliver after another successful intervention by Bergk. But the second comprehensive report on the legal responsibility of the murderer Woyzeck confirmed the earlier conclusions and resulted in the enforcement of the verdict: Johann Christian Woyzeck was executed on August 27, 1824. It was the last public execution in the city of Leipzig and, as it says in the report of a historical witness: "Of course, school was canceled that morning."⁶

The procedures leading up to the confirmation of the death sentence shape what was to be known as the Woyzeck case. By commissioning Dr. Clarus as a medical expert, the legal case, which was about the societal sanction of a criminal act, became a case of quite a different nature. The question that Dr. Clarus attempts to answer is not about the deed and its particular circumstances, but about the personality of the perpetrator and his motives. Moreover, he sought to understand the extent to which the personality of the wrongdoer is identical with his deed, and the extent the deed can be accounted to the doer. As mentioned earlier, the forensic attestation of accountability was a contested field throughout the nineteenth century, and the publication of Clarus's expertise triggered heated debates among legal scholars and doctors. But this debate on accountability and legal responsibility is not the sole focus of the following reading. Instead of merely discussing Woyzeck as a case of accountability, this chapter attempts

---

5. For more information about Bergk's involvement in the case, see Georg Büchner, "Der Korrespondent von und für Deutschland," no. 166, Sonnabend 9. Juni 1821, in *Sämtliche Werke und Schriften: Historisch-kritische Ausgabe mit Quellendokumentation und Kommentar*, vol. 7, *Woyzeck: Text Editionsbericht, Quellen, Erläuterungsteile*, ed. Burghard Dedner (Darmstadt: WBG, 2005), 361.

6. Nikolaus Dorsch and Jan-Christoph Hauschild, "Clarus und Woyzeck: Bilder des Hofrats und des Delinquenten," *Georg Büchner Jahrbuch* 4 (1984): 317–323.

to show that Georg Büchner's unfinished, yet canonical drama *Woyzeck*, based on the Woyzeck of the Clarus report, is essentially about the making of the case. Before discussing the literary adaptation, however, it is necessary to remain with the historical Woyzeck a bit longer and to recall some of the stakes of the medical-legal discussion.

The Drama of Recording

The document to which Büchner's *Woyzeck* refers verbatim is the second report that Dr. Clarus provided and that he published twice within only one year. The contexts of these publications vary significantly: the second publication of the report in the journal *Zeitschrift für Staatsarzneikunde* addresses a professional audience with an expert opinion on the question of forensic accountability, whereas the first publication seems to have a very different purpose. Clarus had his report printed as a brochure on the occasion of Woyzeck's public execution, and in his preface addresses the people who are expected to witness the convicted murderer's last moments. Clarus is not opposed to the death penalty; on the contrary, he understands its necessity in representing the inviolability of the law. His concern pertains to the theatrical effects of the execution that could trigger "banges Mitleid" in the audience, fear and pity for the fallen fellow human being.[7] In this regard, the publication of the report at the time of the execution can be understood as a security measure to prevent public rage by delivering a scientific justification for the death penalty. Rüdiger Campe has presented the more compelling and more far-reaching conclusion, however. He argues that the publication of Clarus's report is supposed to frame the spectacle of the execution in such a way as to break apart the traditional relation between the ceremony of punishment and tragic theatricality.[8] Framing the execution with the publishing of the expertise

---

7. Büchner, "Die Zurechnungsfähigkeit des Mörders," 488.
8. See Rüdiger Campe, "Johann Franz Woyzeck: Der Fall im Drama," in *Unzurechnungsfähigkeiten: Diskursivierungen unfreier Bewußtseinszustände seit*

confronts the tragic spectacle with a very different scene of observation, thereby weakening its theatrical effects. The forensic report presents a different gaze that is not merely concerned with actions and their effects, but with their causes; and it is based on a conception of drama that is very different from the theatricality of traditional tragedy.

This argument needs further elaboration and leads back to the expert report as a genre and to the form of its publication. An expert report is a document prepared by an authority invested with specialized knowledge that is considered necessary for making legal decisions, but exceeds the professional competence of the judicial authority. It makes observations and draws conclusions that must be presented in an objective, clear, and succinct manner. The first Woyzeck report that Clarus submitted to the court fulfilled all these requirements: Woyzeck's statements from his questioning are briefly summarized in indirect speech, followed by the results of the medical examination of his physical and mental state. One must assume that the second Clarus expert report on Woyzeck was not much more exhaustive. For its publication, however, Clarus revised and extended the actual document significantly and embedded it in a much more comprehensive and substantial presentation of the documents and legal proceedings. In this publication, the expert opinion becomes part of an elaborate statement of the case, of a case history that uses narrative organization to align Woyzeck's life story with the murder of his girlfriend. Every aspect of his life now appears in the light of his deed and is presented under the condition of his expertly proven accountability. Moreover, the causality with which the narration proceeds makes the murder appear an inescapable event and is therefore constitutive for the conclusion of accountability.

The document opens with the details of the murder followed by a circumstantial documentation of the legal proceedings. The presentation of the forensic investigation that follows not only provides insight into Woyzeck's biography and his mental constitution but

---

dem 18. Jahrhundert, ed. Michael Niehaus and Hans-Walter Schmidt-Hannissa (Frankurt am Main: Suhrkamp, 1998), 215.

also stages the examining gaze to which he is subjected. The investigative parts of the document are titled "While Reviewing the Files" and "While Examining the Delinquent,"[9] simulating a presence that imposes the perspective of the examining gaze onto the reader. The readers themselves are supposed to observe, to participate in Clarus's scene of investigation. To do this competently, they need to be familiarized with the rules and dramatic staging of the direct examination of the delinquent. Therefore, before Clarus presents the results of the examination, he explains the rules of the investigative procedure. First, he explains that he wants to persuade Woyzeck to speak freely and to say everything that is on his mind. Although the investigation is of utmost importance for his fate, he should neither regard the situation as a strict questioning nor consider Clarus his judge. Second, Clarus instructs Woyzeck to speak the truth and not to attempt to influence the outcome of the investigation by lying. Woyzeck would not be able to predict the conclusions the doctor will draw from his statements, and he should therefore speak honestly and fully unburden himself.

The dramatic situation informing first the forensic report and now the second version differs from other earlier forms of questioning in its lack of theatricality.[10] It is neither the theatrical presentation of affects that is at stake in this scene nor the staging of a discourse of truth and lying. Rather, it presents speech that does not know its own meaning, that can neither predict nor control the information it gives, a speech that needs to be analyzed by means of a special knowledge in order to fully reveal its truth. Woyzeck is presented to the reader as the subject of an investigation that, with the purpose of determining his accountability, effectively turns speech into action: what it says is less important than how it does so. Already on the level of this game of speaking and interpreting, Woyzeck proves to be accountable. He is a believable witness and reliable narrator of his own story, who patiently provides detailed information about his state of mind, particularly at the time of his

---

9. Büchner, "Die Zurechnungsfähigkeit des Mörders," 494, 503.

10. A comprehensive history of interrogation can be found in Michael Niehaus, *Das Verhör: Geschichte—Theorie—Fiktion* (Munich: Wilhelm Fink, 2003).

deed.[11] Hence, Woyzeck's accountability is produced on the level of speaking, and his ability to speak freely about his deed and its particular circumstances suggests that the deed itself can be accounted to him. One should not forget, however, that the deed itself is not what is under scrutiny in Clarus's expertise. The facts of the case have long been revealed by the legal investigation. Instead, Clarus attempts to demonstrate how the murder became inevitable, and to what degree the murderer Woyzeck is identical with his deed. To this end, the information from the files and the examination are arranged and brought into the form of a coherent narrative that is presented from the perspective of a scientifically rendered observation. One could, therefore, argue that narrative form and epistemological procedure converge in Clarus's publication and contribute to the formation of a text that makes Woyzeck a case of knowledge that derives from the examination of an individual.

Case and Drama

As argued earlier, a case has the special function of mediating between the particular and the general, the individual and the typical, the singular and the law. A case allows its result to be generalized based on an individual history and to be applied to an overall model of knowledge. Thus, case histories refer to knowledge that they themselves contribute to forming. This is also true for Clarus's pub-

---

11. Clarus reports about the mental state of the defendant: "Was den Verstand desselben anlangt, so fand ich an ihm weder Unstätigkeit und Zerstreuung, noch Ueberspannung, Abspannung, Vertiefung oder Verworrenheit der Gedanken und Vorstellungen sondern ungetheilte und anhaltend mehrere Stunden ausdauernde Aufmerksamkeit auf den Gegenstand der Unterredung, so daß er mit demselben, auch während ich von Zeit zu Zeit meine Bemerkungen niederschrieb, unterbrochen beschäftigt schien, und nachher öfters den Faden da wieder aufnahm, wo ich ihn hatte fallen lassen, in seinen Erzählungen meistens selbst erinnerte, wenn er sich von der Zeitfolge entfernte, oder bei Nebenumständen verweilte, auch nachher jedesmal von selbst in einer natürlichen und zusammenhängenden Gedankenfolge, zur Hauptsache zurückkehrte" (Büchner, "Die Zurechnungsfähigkeit des Mörders," 504–505).

lication of the Woyzeck case: although the forensic report was supposed to reach a conclusion on the accountability of the murderer, the published case history contributes to a general knowledge about the assessment of accountability. In both instances, the scene of investigation is transformed into a continuous narrative that reconstructs the psychological circumstances necessitating the occurrence of the unlawful event.

It is worth taking a closer look at this relation between drama and case in Georg Büchner's unfinished and fragmented drama *Woyzeck*. Clearly, *Woyzeck* is not simply the translation of a narrative plot back into dramatic action. But the dramatic form with which Büchner engages the case sets it apart from other literary adaptations of case histories, and constitutes its particular contribution to the understanding of the genre.

The connection that the drama refers to an actual case is a relatively recent discovery. When Georg Büchner died in 1837 at the age of twenty-three, he left a booklet of loose sheets with nearly illegible scribbles upon which every edition of the drama *Woyzeck* is based. In 1880 Karl Emil Franzos published the first edition of Georg Büchner's collected works, which also included the drama. But instead of Woyzeck, Franzos deciphered Wozzeck, and it was almost another forty years before the connection to the historical Woyzeck was discovered and the title of Büchner's drama changed.[12] Since then, the historical Woyzeck case has become an essential appendix to the drama and no critical edition of Büchner's work today goes without a reprint of at least Clarus's second report.[13] At times, Büchner's *Woyzeck* has been read as a counterdraft to Clarus's case history, and some interpreters have argued that the drama reestablishes Woyzeck's humanity by giving him back the voice that had been repressed and buried in the forensic representation of his case.[14] Behind this stands a notion of literature according to which literary discourse is a more appropriate, more humane

---

12. See Reinhard Pabst, "Zwei unbekannte Berichte über die Hinrichtung Johann Christian Woyzecks," *Georg Büchner Jahrbuch* 7 (1988/1989): 338–350.
13. See Campe, "Johann Franz Woyzeck," 211.
14. For example, Albert Meier, *Georg Büchner: Woyzeck* (Munich: Wilhelm Fink, 1980), 21–24.

form of representation than the objectifying representations of the sciences.

A more recent discussion of the drama and the case has been triggered by Rüdiger Campe, who argues that instead of merely citing from the content of the case, Büchner's drama refers to the modes of representation according to which case histories proceed.[15] In this reading, the drama *Woyzeck* primarily addresses problems of representation and framing. Following Campe's argument, most recent scholarship discusses Büchner's play in regard to the history of legal accountability and human experimentation. The dramatic form Büchner chose for his *Woyzeck* is seldom considered for the analysis of the play. Nicolas Pethes, in an article on the cultural history of human experimentation, simply reads Büchner's *Woyzeck* as a dramatic case study "drawing from as well as contributing to the discourse on human experiments and the anthropological concepts connected to them."[16] Here, the adjective *dramatic* makes a difference in regard to presence: "Instead of *reconstructing* the causes of the crime with the means of forensic psychiatry, the play *presents* Woyzeck's immediate reactions to situations that humiliate him, drive him crazy, and turn him into a murderer. . . . The play is able to show what psychiatry merely reconstructs."[17] Basically, Pethes argues that Büchner's *Woyzeck* offers an alternative version of the case, not as a dramatization of a psychiatric report but as an attempt to compete with psychiatry on the same level. I suggest a different reading: rather than being a dramatic case history, Büchner's *Woyzeck* should be read as the dramatic framing of a case history that in its mode of representation comments on the case and engages with the conditions of its formation. The drama neither redramatizes a case history nor competes with its form of representation; it is the staging of the case, its *making*.

I make two arguments to support this claim. The first concerns the drama's focus on scenes of observation that run through the

---

15. See Campe, "Johann Franz Woyzeck."
16. Nicolas Pethes, "'Viehdummes Individuum,' 'unsterbliche Experimente': Elements for a Cultural History of Human Experimentation in Georg Büchner's Dramatic Case Study *Woyzeck*," *Monatshefte* 98, no. 1 (2006): 70.
17. Pethes, "'Viehdummes Individuum,'" 76.

whole play as a guiding motif. The second argument leads back to Büchner's distinctive practice of citation and to the play's direct references to Clarus's case history.

Staging Observation

Without paying attention to the controversial question of the order of scenes in Büchner's play, one immediately notices the concentration of scenes with an emphasis on seeing and observing, scenes that either stage an invitation to observe or exhibit the observing gaze itself. Already the first of the four handwritten drafts of the play, in which Woyzeck is still called Louis, opens with an invitation to see. The scene is a fairground with booths, and a barker announces the upcoming show: "Look at this creature as God made it: he's nothing, nothing at all. Now see the effect of art: he walks upright, wears coat and pant, carries a sword! Ho! Take a bow! Good boy. Give me a kiss! . . . Ladies and gentlemen, here is to be seen the astronomical horse and the little cannery-birds—they're favorites of all crowned heads. The presentation will begin! The beginning of the beginning! The commencement of the commencement will start immediately."[18]

The scene, in which one can easily recognize a direct reference to theater itself, combines three of the elements that will be of utmost importance for the whole drama: observation, demonstration, and discipline. And by using a literal quote from the first fairground scene in a later scene of the same draft, Büchner connects this initial presentation of theater as a place combining observation, representation, and training with the scrutinizing and evaluating gaze of the sciences. In this scene that takes place in a tavern, a drunken barber shows off as the proud object of scientific investigation: "I am science. Every week I get half a florin for my scientific self. . . . I am a *spinosa pericyclyda*; I have a Latin backbone. I am a living skeleton, all mankind studies me."[19]

---

18. Georg Büchner, "Woyzeck," in *The Major Works*, ed. Matthew Wilson Smith, trans. Henry J. Schmidt (New York: W.W. Norton, 2012), 157.
19. Büchner, "Woyzeck," 160.

From the beginning of the play, from the commencement of the commencement, as Büchner says, scientific observation corresponds to spectacular demonstration and is subject to acts of representation. The barber, who announces himself to *be* science and identifies his individual self with fictitious conceptual abstractions, proudly presents himself as a case. The absurd and comical effect of this scene, however, is not so much due to what he says, but that it is he who says it. One does not turn oneself into a case simply by announcing it. The barber's speech refers to the absence of an authority and the lack of a perspective from which casuistic observation becomes possible. Regarding the question of accountability that is at stake in the historical Woyzeck case, one could say that his speech is not authorized and that it is, therefore, not accountable to him. On the other hand, it is the scientific object itself that speaks here, and it speaks directly to the reader and forces him or her into a perspective of a judging observer. Here is the scene at greater length:

> Sir, leave me alone! I am science. Every week I get half a florin for my scientific self—don't break me apart or I'll go hungry. I am a *spinoza pericyclyda*; I have a Latin backbone. I am a living skeleton, all mankind studies me.—What is man? Bones! Dust, sand, dirt. What is nature? Dust, sand, dirt. But those stupid people, those stupid people. Let's be friends. If I had no courage, there wouldn't be any science. Only nature, no amputation. What is an arm, flesh, bones, veins? What is dirt? Where will it be sticking in the dirt? So should I cut my arm off? No, man is egoistic, but he hits, shoots, stabs. There, now. We must. Friends, I am touched. Look, I wish our noses were two bottles and we could pour them down each other's throats. Oh, how beautiful the world is! Friend! My friend! The world! *(Moved.)* Look how the sun's coming out of the clouds, like a bedpan being emptied out. *(He cries.)*[20]

The speech of the barber hardly qualifies as scientific and could rather be called delusional as it fails to make sense on a discursive level. From being the object of scientific studies, however, the barber deduces the authority for reflecting on the nature of man. Con-

---

20. Büchner, "Woyzeck," 160. (Büchner discarded this scene, and it was not considered in later edits of the play.)

sidering himself a scientific case seems to connect him to mankind in general. In this regard his speech is indeed a speech act, one that fails as a speech but is successful as an act that accomplishes what it fails to articulate on the discursive level. Put differently, the barber turns into a case not by what he says, but by saying it. One can, therefore, understand the barber scene as an early reference to the dramatic game of speaking and interpreting on which Clarus's case history is essentially based.

Throughout the play, and throughout the different drafts, scenes addressing the relation between seeing and speaking frame the problem of the case.[21] *Woyzeck* does not stage the Woyzeck case itself; instead, the drama focuses on the framing conditions of the case and centers on the investigation as a game of seeing and speaking, of interpreting and representing. All this comes together and culminates in the famous doctor scene. In the transition from the first to the second draft, Louis and the barber are combined in the single character of the protagonist Woyzeck, who is haunted by mysterious voices, treated badly by his captain, cheated on by his girlfriend, and objectified by a career-oriented doctor who performs nutritional experiments on him in the interest of his new scientific theory. Not only is this scene the only one in which the problem of accountability, responsibility, and free will is explicitly addressed, it also comes closest to a depiction of the investigative situation from Clarus's case history. In the two early scenes from the first draft, we were given the perspective of direct and immediate observation. We were either prompted to observe, as in the fairground scene, or put into a position that challenged our own judgment and that forced the examining gaze upon us, as in the barber scene. In the doctor scene, we move into a more distanced perspective, from which we can observe observation itself. We are presented with the analyzing and diagnostic gaze of the medical-scientific expert, who is delighted and amazed by the apparently delusional state of his

---

21. In a recent article on the framing of case histories in Schiller, Büchner, and Musil, Johannes Lehmann has come to a similar conclusion in regard to Büchner's *Woyzeck*. See Johannes F. Lehmann, "Erfinden, was der Fall ist: Fallgeschichte und Rahmen bei Schiller, Büchner und Musil," *Zeitschrift für Germanistik* N.F. 19 (2009): 361–380.

human guinea pig: "You're an interesting case. Subject Woyzeck, you're getting a raise. Now behave yourself. Show me your pulse! Yes."[22]

But Woyzeck cannot be reduced to the role of a mere test case and object of a scientific experiment. He has his own will, be it free or not. He pissed against the wall, following nature's call and not the doctor's, who would have preferred to keep the urine for his experiment:

> DOCTOR: The call of nature, the call of nature! Nature! Haven't I proved that the *musculus constrictor versicae* is subject to the will? Nature! Woyzeck, man is free; in man alone is individuality exalted to freedom. Couldn't hold it in! *(Shakes his head, puts his hands behind his back, and paces back and forth.)*[23]

Neither nature's nor the doctor's call have anything to do with free will. Moreover, Woyzeck speaks and stands up for himself, and in his defense he not only acts freely and speaks consciously but also erases the conceptual distinctions upon which the scientific worldview of the doctor is based. When it comes to nature, language begins to fail Woyzeck. But in the doctor's world, speaking that fails to create meaning is called philosophy, and is only a step away from insanity, that is, speaking that fails to make sense:

> WOYZECK: You see, Doctor, sometimes you've got a certain character, a certain structure.—But with nature, that's something else, you see, with nature—*(He cracks his knuckles.)* that's like—how should I put it—for example . . .
> DOCTOR: Woyzeck, you're philosophizing again.
> WOYZECK: *(Confidingly.)* Doctor, have you ever seen anything of double nature? When the sun's standing high at noon and the world seems to be going up in flames, I've heard a terrible voice talking to me!
> DOCTOR: Woyzeck, you've got an *aberratio*!

---

22. Büchner, "Woyzeck," 145.
23. Büchner, "Woyzeck," 144.

WOYZECK: (*Puts his finger to his nose.*) The toadstools, Doctor. There—that's where it is. Have you seen how they grow in patterns? If only someone could read that.
DOCTOR: Woyzeck, you've got a marvelous *aberratio mentalis partialis*, second species, beautifully developed. Woyzeck, you're getting a raise. Second species: obsession with generally rational condition.[24]

Woyzeck and the doctor are clearly talking past one another, but this does not mean that one must accept the doctor's conclusion. The doctor is simply reacting to something he does not understand by making it available to his way of thinking in terms of scientific systems of classification. But what he classifies as second species of monomania is, of all things, Woyzeck's attempt to think outside the borders of taxonomy. The way Woyzeck observes nature mirrors and inverts the way the doctor observes him. And as Woyzeck is questioning the concepts of nature on which the scientific worldview relies, it could be concluded that he is in fact philosophizing.

Unaccountable Citation

So far, I have argued that Büchner's *Woyzeck* dramatically stages the investigation from Clarus's report by focusing on scenes of observation in which seeing and speaking are closely interconnected. In these scenes, Büchner's drama cites the investigative setting of the Woyzeck case without, however, adopting the perspective of casuistic representation. Without the frame of medical-legal knowledge and authority, the case appears to be nothing more than a dramatic arrangement of scenes in which the individual players keep talking past one another and seem to be aimlessly drifting without much orientation.[25]

---

24. Büchner, "Woyzeck," 144–145.
25. See Helmut Müller Sievers, *Desorientierung: Anatomie und Dichtung bei Georg Büchner* (Göttingen: Wallstein, 2003).

From the outset, the reliability of sense perception is at stake in Büchner's drama; and this, too, is a reference to the historical Woyzeck case. Indeed, the reason that the court commissions a psychiatric evaluation of the murderer was the defendant's statement that he had suffered from hallucinations and hearing strange voices in his head. The Woyzeck of the drama, too, is haunted by these voices. Büchner is well-known for his literary practice of citation, and in reference to *Woyzeck*, Campe and Helmut Müller-Sievers have emphasized the play's modified citation of the repeated *immer zu, immer zu* that drives Woyzeck throughout the play and eventually to commit the murder of his girlfriend.[26] *Immer zu, immer zu* refers to *immer drauf, immer drauf*,[27] with which Clarus cites the voices that keep haunting Woyzeck. And this is in fact the point: Büchner references what Clarus cites. The mysterious voices haunting Woyzeck, the same voices that tell him to murder his girlfriend, receive special treatment in Clarus's presentation of the case: only the voices appear in direct speech. Everything else that Woyzeck confesses is transformed into indirect speech and presented in a narrative structure. It seems that the voices escape the narrative mode of representation because of their lack of agency. Only once Clarus attempts to explain their origin. Woyzeck, Clarus writes, had the

---

26. See Rüdiger Campe, "Three Modes of Citation: Historical, Casuistic, and Literary Writing in Büchner," *Germanic Review: Literature, Culture, Theory* 89, no. 1 (2014): 44–59; Müller-Sievers, *Desorientierung*, 133–135.

27. Büchner cites the *immer drauf, immer drauf* from the Clarus report in the scene "Open field" [*Freies Feld*] that was part of the first draft of the play when Woyzeck was still called Louis: "WOYZECK On and on! On and on! [*Immer zu! immer zu!*] Shh—music. *(Stretches out on the ground.)* Ha—what, what are you saying? Louder, louder—stab, stab the bitch to death? Stab, stab the bitch to death. Should I? Must I? Do I hear it over there too, is the wind saying it too? Do I hear it on and on—stab her to death, to death" (Büchner, "Woyzeck," 148). In the same scene, Büchner not only cites the *immer drauf, immer drauf*, but references the entire passage from Clarus's report: "Als in Gohlis die Kirmse gewesen, habe er Abends im Bette gelegen und an die Woostin gedacht, daß diese wohl dort mit einem anderen zu Tanze seyn könne. Da sey es ihm ganz eigen gewesen, als ob er die Tanzmusik, Violinen und Bässe durcheinander, höre, und dazu im Takte die Worte: Immer drauf, immer drauf! Kurz vorher habe ihm von Musikanten geträumt, und das habe ihm immer was übles bedeutet. Am andern Tage habe er gehört, daß die Woostin wirklich mit einem andern in Gohlis gewesen sey und sich lustig gemacht habe!" (Büchner, "Die Zurechnungsfähigkeit des Mörders," 515).

habit to soliloquize, and thus, it was in the realm of possibility that he had mistaken his own words for the noise in his head and for an external voice addressing him. The voices, the medical expert concludes, could be attributed to a transposition of the subjective with the objective perspective.[28] But even the forensic report does not succeed in silencing the voices. On the contrary, in the end they are everything that is left of Woyzeck while the murderer's own speech is absorbed by the expert's narrative. In a text that deals with the problem of accountability, the voices remain that which cannot be accounted for; they have no speaker and thus escape the narrative order. Put differently, the voices are remnants of a dramatic order of the deed that the narrative order of the case must erase to successfully make its claim.

With the citation of the voices, Büchner references the case where the case itself uses citation. As there is no agent and no source that accounts for the voices, they only exist in a mode of citation. The repeated rhythmic doubling of *immer zu, immer zu* can be understood as the poetic expression of this logic.[29] The citation of the voices in the drama, thus, points to the center of the Woyzeck case, the problem of the defendant's accountability that would not have been questioned without the existence of the voices. Furthermore, the drama points to the fact that Woyzeck's accountability—his

---

28. "Bei Erklärung dieser Erscheinung [the voices] muß der Umstand in Erwägung gezogen werden, daß Woyzeck gewohnt gewesen ist, *mit sich selbst zu sprechen,* der es sehr denkbar macht, wie er, bei dem erhitzten Zustande seines Blutes und seiner Einbildungskraft, seine ebengedachten, oder laut ausgesprochenen Worte mit dem Lärme in seinem Kopfe verwechseln und selbigen bei seinem immer lebendigen Glauben an übernatürliche Einwirkungen für eine an ihn gerichtete fremde Stimme halten konnte. Diese Erklärung erhält dadurch noch größere Wahrscheinlichkeit, daß der Sinn dieser angeblich von einer *fremden* Stimme gehörten Worte sich fast immer auf das bezieht, was seine jedesmalige Gemüthsstimmung, oder eine natürliche Ideenassociation, ihm bei einem Selbstgespräche in den Mund legen konnte. So ist es höchst natürlich, daß er, als er mit einer Arbeit fertig gewesen, daran *gedacht* hat, was *er nun machen solle,* und zugleich bei den bereits vorausgegangenen Täuschungen seines Gehörs höchst wahrscheinlich, daß er, bei diesen gedachten, oder laut ausgesprochenen Worten, das *Subjektive* mit etwas *Objektivem* verwechselt habe" (Büchner, "Die Zurechnungsfähigkeit des Mörders," 522).

29. See Müller-Sievers, *Desorientierung,* 146; Campe, "Three Modes of Citation," 14.

status as a subject and legal person—depends on the ways in which his testimony and his statements are reported and cited in Clarus's case history. In this regard, Woyzeck's accountability is the effect of a citational practice and it underscores the importance of citation for casuistic reasoning, which in its claim to general validity vitally depends on the premise of being citable. Büchner's *Woyzeck* can hardly be understood as the redramatization of a case history; much more decisively, it does trace the Woyzeck case back to its dramatic terms and conditions. That is, Büchner references the case history precisely where it is itself dramatic. This is shown by the scene of observation upon which the case is based, and it applies to the voices that Clarus's narrative cannot control.

In Büchner's drama *Woyzeck* we encounter a change in perspective that dramatic literature offers on casuistic forms of representation. The historical background is the new status of the psychological case history in the nineteenth century as an integral part of legal decision making and medical-legal debates. Büchner's drama attempts to compete with neither the Woyzeck case institutionally nor with Clarus's psychological analysis. By choosing the dramatic form for his adaptation of the historical material, he takes a position that differs decisively from that of the forensic expert. Just as important is the drama's lack of any medical-legal frame that would allow it to be read within the contemporary debates; this was provided much later with the discovery of the relation to the historical Woyzeck case. Without this frame the world that the drama presents loses its stability, and this directly affects the dramatis personae. This is not only true for the protagonist Woyzeck, but for almost every character of the play, and not least the two characters who are supposed to display authority. The Captain pathetically clings to empty concepts of virtue and morality.[30] And the attempts of

---

30. In the famous barber scene, when Woyzeck shaves his Captain who keeps humiliating him, the latter significantly fails to explain the meaning of the word *morality* and thus demonstrates not only the meaninglessness of the concept but moreover that morality has become a mere convention of social norms: "Woyzeck, you're a good man, a good man—*(With dignity.)* but Woyzeck, you've got no morality. Morality—that's when you are moral, you understand. It's a good word. You have a child without the blessing of the church, as our Reverend Chaplain

the Doctor to defend his scientific worldview appear to be compulsive, desperate, and out of touch with everyday life.

Büchner's *Woyzeck* has often been declared the first modern drama to replace the closed form of the classic drama with an open order of scenes.[31] The drama pursues the disintegration of the narrative, and challenges those structures that are supposed to guarantee access to a meaningful order of the world. Only with the knowledge that the drama *Woyzeck* is based on a case Woyzeck can the disorientation of the drama be suspended and made accessible for a discursive and contextual reading. But even then, the drama does not contribute to the solution of the case or its open question of accountability, and it does not provide a final word on the nature of the deed or on Woyzeck's motivation and motives. By presenting an open order of scenes, the drama confronts its readers with a plurality of possible motives for the murder. Büchner leaves it to the readers to decide without enabling them to make such a decision. In doing so, his drama emphasizes the discrepancy that opens up between legal-psychiatric and literary discourse in the nineteenth century.

---

says, without the blessing of the church—*I didn't say it*" (Büchner, "Woyzeck," 142). It is significant for an interpretation of the play to notice that Woyzeck, in response to the Captain, points out the difference between conventional norms and moral behavior: "Cap'n, the good Lord isn't going to look at the poor little kid only because amen was said over it before it was created" (Büchner, "Woyzeck," 142).

31. See Volker Klotz, *Geschlossene und offene Form im Drama* (Munich: Hanser, 1960).

7

DRAMA, ANECDOTE, CASE

Wedekind's Lulu

Dangerous Individuals

Frank Wedekind's drama *Lulu* was written more than fifty years after *Woyzeck*, and unlike Büchner's drama and most literary texts discussed so far, it is not based on the adaptation of a singular historical case that would allow interpretive access to the documentary material. From a literary perspective, Wedekind has often been seen as a successor to Büchner, insofar as his dramatic work displays similar traits such as an open form and a lack of narrative closure.[1] Although not a single historical case can be identified as the model for the *Monstretragödie Lulu*, the modern form of the play can be

---

1. Ariane Martin summarizes and discusses the scholarly reception of this literary relationship in "Büchner und Wedekind," in *Büchner-Rezeptionen—interkulturell und intermedial*, ed. Marco Castellari and Alessandro Costazza (Bern: Peter Lang, 2015), 41–54.

understood as commentary and critique of contemporary discourses on sexuality and deviance that refer to forms of knowledge derived from cases.[2]

The historical constellation at the end of the nineteenth century in regard to medical-psychiatric interventions in social and legal practices differs significantly from that of the first half of the century. In particular, the question of accountability that defined earlier debates and the discussion in the cases of Schmolling and Woyzeck is replaced by new criminological theories of social defense that emphasize the importance for determining the dangerousness of individuals rather than the degree to which they can be held responsible for their actions.[3] Newly established disciplines of criminal anthropology, criminology, and sexology seek to provide scientific justifications for the effective prevention of crimes rather than accepting a legal system that only responds to offenses and, thus, fails to protect society from the malady of criminal aggression.[4] The emergence of these criminological disciplines is accompanied by the collection, representation, and publication of cases that do not simply stand in the service of legal decision making, but are meant to provide the basis for questioning the legal competence for crime

---

2. From here onward, I am referring to the original first version of the play in 1894, *Die Büchse der Pandora: Eine Monstretragödie*. Due to censorship concerns, Wedekind revised the play significantly. He split the five acts and turned them into the two plays *Erdgeist* and *Die Büchse der Pandora*. In this chapter, I will refer to the *Monstretragödie* with the title of the English translation *The First Lulu*.

3. In his lecture, *Die strafrechtliche Zurechnungsfähigkeit*, which he presented 1896 at the International Congress of Psychology, one of the leading figures in this debate, the jurist and legal scholar Franz von Liszt, vehemently argued in favor of giving up the concept of legal responsibility altogether and replacing it with that of dangerousness. Liszt illustrated the urgency of his claim by alluding to the case of Marie Schneider, a young schoolgirl who had murdered an infant in order to satisfy her craving for sweets. (Franz von Liszt, "Die strafrechtliche Zurechnungsfähigkeit: Vortrag, gehalten am 4. August 1896 auf dem III. Internationalen Psychologen-Kongreß," in *Strafrechtliche Aufsätze und Vorträge, Zweiter Band* [Berlin: J. Guttentag, 1905], 214–229.)

4. This line of argument led the famous psychiatrist Emil Kraepelin to demand the abolition of fixed sentences: Emil Kraepelin, "Die Abschaffung des Strafmaßes: Ein Vorschlag zur Reform der heutigen Strafrechtspflege (1880)," in Kraepelin, *Kriminologische und forensische Schriften*, ed. Wolfgang Burgmair, Eric J. Engstrom, and Paul Hoff (Munich: Belleville, 2001), 13–95.

altogether in favor of a psychiatrically informed intervention in the social body.[5] Famously, Michel Foucault has studied the history of the transformation that in the course of the nineteenth century leads from the discussion of the legal concept of accountability to that of dangerousness, and this results in an argument favoring the depenalization of crime with which criminal anthropologists challenge the established legal order.[6] In the wake of Foucault's historical studies, the influence of literature on the scientific formation of criminology and sexology has also been investigated.[7] In the most direct way, literature's influence on nineteenth-century criminology can be seen in its providing casuistic material that often substitutes for empirical studies as long as there is restricted access to penal and legal institutions.[8] It should also be mentioned that sexological and criminological uses of literature have resulted in some in-

---

5. I have discussed two of these cases in my book, *Epistemologie des Extremen: Lustmord in Kriminologie und Literatur um 1900* (Munich: Fink Verlag, 2012). Both the case of the schoolgirl Marie Schneider and the case of the private teacher Andreas Dippold were used repeatedly in various criminological and legal contributions to the debate about questions of accountability and the necessary measures for an effective system of social defense.

6. See Michel Foucault, "About the Concept of the 'Dangerous Individual' in 19th-Century Legal Psychiatry," *International Journal of Law and Psychiatry* 1 (1978): 1–18; Michel Foucault, *"Society Must Be Defended": Lectures at the Collège de France, 1975–1976*, trans. David Macey (Picador: New York, 1997). Following Foucault's lead, historians have researched this transformation. Here, I will list only the most notable examples: Pasquale Pasquino, "Criminology: The Birth of a Special Knowledge," in *The Foucault Effect: Studies in Governmentality*, ed. Graham Burchell, Colin Gordon, and Peter Miller (Chicago: University of Chicago Press, 1991), 235–250; Richard F. Wetzell, *Inventing the Criminal: A History of German Criminology 1880–1945* (Chapel Hill: University of North Carolina Press, 2000); and Peter Becker, *Verderbnis und Entartung: Eine Geschichte der Kriminologie des 19. Jahrhunderts als Diskurs und als Praxis* (Göttingen: Wallstein, 2002).

7. See Jörg Schönert, ed., *Erzählte Kriminalität: Zur Typologie und Funktion von narrativen Darstellungen in Strafrechtspflege, Publizistik und Literatur zwischen 1790 und 1920* (Tübingen: Niemeyer, 1991); Stefan Andriopoulos, *Unfall und Verbrechen: Konfigurationen zwischen juristischem und literarischem Diskurs um 1900* (Wiesbaden: Springer Verlag, 1996); and Höcker, *Epistemologie des Extremen*.

8. The jurist Jacques Stern, for example, discusses the value of literary fiction for criminology and legal scholarship in his 1906 essay, "Über den Wert der dichterischen Behandlung des Verbrechens für die Strafrechtswissenschaft," *Zeitschrift für die gesamte Strafrechtswissenschaft* 26 (1906), 145–171.

teresting readings that, from the perspective of literary studies, deserve to be taken seriously. One example is Albert Eulenburg's and Iwan Bloch's in-depth studies of the Marquis de Sade's works that follow an interest in the pathological condition of what had formerly been referred to as satyriasis and, since Richard von Krafft-Ebing's *Psychopathia sexualis*, became generally known under the label sadism. Eulenburg and Bloch not only studied the life and work of de Sade but also provided the basis for further studies with the German translation and publication of some of de Sade's almost forgotten and most infamous writings.[9] The sexological reception of de Sade around 1900 recognizes the literary oeuvre for its almost clinical and systematic depiction of pathological conditions and, at the same time, declares the author de Sade a case of the very perversion that his name has designated ever since. Iwan Bloch considered de Sade one of the founders of modern sexual pathology and his novels early predecessors of Krafft-Ebing's *Psychopathia sexualis*: "There is no doubt that, in anticipation of R. v. Krafft-Ebing, the Marquis de Sade deserves credit for having compiled in his novels an almost exhaustive collection of sexual-pathological types. And there is also no doubt that the great diversity of depicted sexual perversions and the precise individualization of the specific types in his work is based on real-life observations."[10] According to Bloch, the sexologist Albert Eulenburg deserves credit for having inaugurated the scholarly debate about the author de Sade.[11] Eulenburg's de Sade essay appeared in 1899 in Maximilian Harden's journal *Die Zukunft* with the declared goal of contributing

---

9. See Albert Eulenburg, "Der Marquis de Sade," *Die Zukunft* 26 (1899): 497–515; Iwan Bloch (as Eugen Dühren), *Der Marquis de Sade und seine Zeit: Ein Beitrag zur Kultur- und Sittengeschichte des 18. Jahrhunderts mit besonderer Beziehung auf die Lehre von der Psychopathia sexualis* (Berlin: H. Barsdorf, 1900); and Iwan Bloch (as Eugen Dühren), *Neue Forschungen über den Marquis de Sade und seine Zeit: Mit besonderer Berücksichtigung der Sexualphilosophie de Sade's auf Grund des neuentdeckten Original-Manuskriptes seines Hauptwerkes "Die 120 Tage von Sodom"* (Berlin: Max Harrwitz, 1904).

10. Bloch, *Der Marquis de Sade*, 429. "Was R. v. Krafft-Ebing in Form einer wissenschaftlichen Monographie getan hat, das hat schon hundert Jahre früher der Marquis de Sade in Form eines Romans geleistet" (Bloch, *Der Marquis de Sade*, 450).

11. Bloch, *Der Marquis de Sade*, 487.

to the sexological study of sexual perversions by shedding light on the life and character of the French author, whom Eulenburg considered not just another pornographic writer, but rather a "very unusual individual and literary appearance, and, I want to say, an antimoral force whose creativity originates from the center of evil itself."[12]

Bloch's and Eulenburg's treatment of de Sade and his work is characteristic of the way sexologists use literature as a source for casuistic material. The reference to the psychological disposition of the literary author justifies the recourse to literature as an archive of cases for the purpose of scientific studies of human pathologies. Literary authors and poets are seen to have an advantage in the depiction and representation of pathological conditions that must, however, be read scientifically to draw conclusions useful for sociohygienic purposes. In the preface to the first edition of his 1886 *Psychopathia sexualis*, which considerably influenced forensic psychiatry around 1900 and became famous as the first systematic collection of cases of sexual pathologies, Richard von Krafft-Ebing makes precisely this argument:

> The poets may be better psychologists than the psychologists and philosophers; but they are men of feeling rather than of understanding, and at least one-sided in their consideration of the subject. They cannot see the deep shadow behind the light and sunny warmth of that from which they draw their inspiration. The poetry of all times and nations would furnish inexhaustible material for a monograph on the psychology of love; but the great problem can be solved only with the help of Science, and especially with the aid of Medicine, which studies the psychological subject at its anatomical and physiological source, and views it from all sides.[13]

At the end of the nineteenth century, the transfer of literary texts into the psychopathological context essentially relies on a conception of authorship that is by no means an invention of Krafft-Ebing

---

12. Eulenburg, "Der Marquis de Sade," 499.
13. Richard von Krafft-Ebing, *Psychopathia sexualis: With Special Reference to Contrary Sexual Instinct: A Medico-Legal Study*, authorized translation of the 7th enlarged and revised German edition, trans. Charles Gilbert Chaddock (Philadelphia: F. A. Davis, 1892), iii–iv.

and his contemporaries, but rather, as Hoffmann's Serapiontic principle showed, can be traced back to literary Romanticism.[14] Literary representation of sexual deviance and criminal dispositions can serve as casuistic evidence for the medically trained expert. Literature, however, does not always comply with this role, as is the case with Frank Wedekind, whose work often engages with contemporary sexology. Rather than supplying sexological studies with more material, Wedekind's drama *Lulu* reverses the perspective and approaches contemporary sexology from a literary viewpoint.

Two particular aspects of Wedekind's *Lulu* interest me in the context of this study and guide my discussion of the play: First, the drama's connection to a contemporary sexological discourse that operates on the level of casuistic representation; and second, the specific literary procedure Wedekind develops in engaging with the sexological material aesthetically. Although no single case can be identified as the source for Wedekind's drama, the final scene featuring the infamous murderer Jack the Ripper provides ample evidence for placing the drama in the context of sexological and criminological discourses. What is more, the reference to Jack the Ripper carries special importance because this is the particular case criminologists used to argue for the urgency of their claims and to justify the severity of their suggested measures of control. The appearance of Jack the Ripper in Wedekind's *Lulu* does not reference just any case, but the one case that, unlike any other, stands for the connection of lust and cruelty for which Krafft-Ebing had suggested the name *sadism*. At the same time, Wedekind's reference to Jack the Ripper directly points to the imaginary center of a criminological discourse that took advantage of the series of dreadful and unsolved murders that gave rise to scary and uncanny fantasies and, in the years following the spectacular crimes, contributed to an atmosphere of uncertainty, fear, and the urgent demand for public safety.

The Ripper murders happened just two years after Krafft-Ebing had introduced the connection of lust and cruelty in his 1886

---

14. A demystification of the discourse of romantic authorship can be found in Heinrich Bosse, *Autorschaft ist Werkherrschaft: Über die Entstehung des Urheberrechts aus dem Geiste der Goethezeit* (Paderborn: Schöningh, 1981).

Psychopathia sexualis and the so-called *Lustmord* as the most radical aberration from a norm of masculinity that shows this combination to a much lesser degree. In the same year, Robert Louis Stevenson had published his gothic novella, *The Strange Case of Dr. Jekyll and Mr. Hyde*, which drew on the connection between the normal and the pathological by depicting the nineteenth-century Victorian facade behind which sexual lust and desire could reign almost uncontrollably. Deborah Cameron and Elisabeth Frazer, who have analyzed the blending of fact and fiction in the public reception of the Ripper murders in London's Whitechapel neighborhood in the 1888 "Autumn of Terror," have argued that Stevenson's gothic novella, produced as a stage play at the same time, "provided a neat and convenient framework for understanding contemporary events."[15] The historian Judith Walkowitz, in her book, *City of Dreadful Delight*, analyzes the cultural productivity of the Ripper case and demonstrates how modern norms of sex and gender emerged from narratives of sexual danger in late Victorian London.[16] The enormous influence of the Ripper murders in building public awareness of sexual deviance is displayed in the extent to which the phantom of Whitechapel haunts the literary and cultural production around 1900. Wedekind's *Lulu* is, by far, not the only literary text featuring the infamous murderer. Bram Stoker had Jack the Ripper in mind when he created the monster Dracula, whom he calls a criminal and "of criminal type" in reference to Cesare Lombroso and Max Nordau.[17] Alfred Döblin, who, according to Winfried G. Sebald, had been obsessed with the phenomenon of sexual murder, wrote a short story with the title *Das Leben Jacks, des Bauchaufschlitzers*.[18] And George Grosz, whose

---

15. Deborah Cameron and Elisabeth Frazer, *The Lust to Kill: A Feminist Investigation of Sexual Murder* (New York: Polity Press, 1987), 126.

16. See Judith Walkowitz, *City of Dreadful Delight: Narratives of Sexual Danger in Late-Victorian London* (Chicago: University of Chicago Press, 1992).

17. "The Count is a criminal and of criminal type. Nordau and Lombroso would so classify him, and qua criminal he is of imperfectly formed mind" (Bram Stoker, *Dracula* [New York: W. W. Norton, 1997], 427).

18. See Winfried G. Sebald, "Preußische Perversionen: Anmerkungen zum Thema Literatur und Gewalt, ausgehend vom Frühwerk Alfred Döblins," in *Inter-*

expressionist paintings often depict sexual murder, counts a pulp novel with the title *Jack, der geheimnisvolle Mädchenmörder* among his most important memories of his youth.[19]

Although Jack the Ripper was never caught, the murders were seen as evidence for the existence of the criminal type of *Lustmörder* that took on an important function for the formation and stabilization of the criminological discourse. The special atrocity and ferociousness of the crimes supported the criminologists' urgent call for new measures of social control. In addition, this new criminal type stood for a newly discovered connection between sexual desires and criminal behavior and thus became an important link between criminological, medical, and psychopathological forms of knowledge. And last, but not least, the figure of the *Lustmörder* connected criminological discourses with contemporary culture, which in turn provided it with a much wider audience and greater popularity. The criminal type of *Lustmörder* was created around 1900 at the intersection of sexological and criminological discourses with pop-cultural, journalistic, and literary forms of representation.

Thus, with the entry of Jack the Ripper in the final act of *The First Lulu*, Frank Wedekind calls onstage not only a nightmarish phantom that in 1894 was still present in public memory but also the discourse of sexual pathology and the bourgeois gender norms that this discourse reproduced under the cover of scientific and male-dominated expertise. There is no doubt that contemporary audiences knew how to interpret the murderer Jack's appearance, for example, as Karl Kraus's perceptive review of the play in *Die Fackel* strikingly shows.[20] Although the reception of Wedekind's *Lulu* has made these connections from the beginning, the play itself, as Ruth Florack has argued, eludes direct discursive links to contemporary scientific fields of knowledge.[21]

---

nationale Alfred-Döblin-Kolloquien, Basel 1980, New York 1981; Freiburg im Bresgau, 1993, ed. Werner Stauffacher (Bern: Peter Lang, 1986), 231–238.

19. See George Grosz, "Jugenderinnerungen," *Das Kunstblatt* 13 (1929): 166–174.

20. See Karl Kraus, "Die Büchse der Pandora," *Die Fackel* 182 (1905): 1–14.

21. "Denn einem unmittelbaren Anschluß an Wissenschaftsgeschichte verweigert sich Wedekinds Werk ganz offenbar." (Ruth Florack, "Aggression und Lust:

The First Lulu does not show any direct discursive engagement with contemporary sexology, but Wedekind's diaries contain evidence of his reading of sexological and criminological publications, in particular Krafft-Ebing's *Psychopathia sexualis*. It is here that one can find clues for the influence of sexological cases on Wedekind's literary-aesthetic production. Thus, before returning to the discussion of the drama *Lulu* and before engaging more closely with the appearance of Jack the Ripper in the context of the play, I will show how Wedekind develops a literary procedure from reading a case that he found in Krafft-Ebing's best seller. What interested him was not its sexological or psychological understanding but its grotesque and carnivalesque potential. It is the anecdotal potential of the case that allows Wedekind to engage with it on a dramatic and aesthetic level.

From Case to Anecdote

Under the heading "Unnatural Abuse, Sodomy," the following entry can be found in Richard von Krafft-Ebing's *Psychopathia sexualis*: "The intercourse of females with beasts is limited to dogs. A monstrous example of the moral depravity in large cities is related by Maschka ('Handb,' iii),—the case of a Parisian female who showed herself in the sexual act with a trained bull-dog, to a secret circle of *roues*, at 10 francs a head."[22] In a note from his diary, Frank Wedekind refers to this case.[23] On August 8, 1889, only three years after the first edition of the *Psychopathia sexualis* had been published, he writes: "Last night in bed I thought of the anecdote from Krafft-Ebing: the Parisian prostitute with the bull-dog. I visualize it all in detail, thinking how the girl enters, walk-

---

Anmerkungen zur Monstretragödie," in *Frank Wedekind*, ed. Ortrud Gutjahr [Würzburg: Königshausen & Neumann, 2001], 163.)

22. Krafft-Ebing, *Psychopathia sexualis*, 405.

23. Johannes G. Pankau discusses Wedekind's reference to this passage from the *Psychopathia sexualis*, and argues that Wedekind aesthetically processes the case. See Johannes G. Pankau, "Prostitution, Tochtererziehung und männlicher Blick in Wedekinds Tagebüchern," in Gutjahr, *Frank Wedekind*, 19–54.

ing on her hands, and collects money by holding her legs slightly apart. Then she gets monkeys to undress her, the whole point being her total passivity. Then at least three or four bulldogs are driven in and beaten. The girl lives and sleeps with a bitch for the sake of her spiritual aroma. I spend the entire afternoon trying to draw the girl."[24]

Wedekind's genre definition of the casuistic episode from the *Psychopathia sexualis* is both accurate and problematic. What he refers to as anecdote, in its original context claims the status of a case and empirical truth. In the *Psychopathia sexualis*, cases are labeled as observations—*Beobachtungen*—claiming authenticity, manifesting authority, and guiding the reader's reception of the book: observations are supposed to be read from a scientific, objective, and clinical perspective. The case of the Parisian prostitute does not belong to those cases labeled as observations; instead, it is authenticated by the reference to its original source, Josef Maschka's 1882 *Handbuch der gerichtlichen Medicin*. Following this reference, however, it does not seem completely inadequate to refer to the case as anecdote or even droll story as Maschka's own source is a rumor from the time he spent in Paris.[25]

Wedekind's genre designation "anecdote" says more about the way he—and probably the general public—read and received the *Psychopathia sexualis* than about Krafft-Ebing's sexological work itself. It is a well-known fact that the enormous success of the book was not owed to a sudden scientific interest and that Krafft-Ebing, to avoid misuse, translated some of the most scandalous and explicit passages into Latin. Clearly, this form of censorship was of limited success and certainly did not prevent anybody from using the book to find erotic stimulation.

---

24. Frank Wedekind, *Diary of an Erotic Life*, trans. W. E. Yuill (Oxford: Blackwell, 1990), 70–71.

25. "Zum Schlusse will ich noch erwähnen, dass sich vor Jahren während meines Aufenthaltes in Paris eine Frauensperson in heimlichen, geschlossenen Circeln gegen ein Entré von 10 Francs damit producirte, dass sie sich von einem eigens hierzu abgerichteten Bulldogg begatten liess." (Josef Maschka, "Zeichen der Jungfrauschaft und gesetzwidrige Befriedigung des Geschlechtstriebes," in *Handbuch der gerichtlichen Medicin* [Tübingen: A. Hirschwald, 1882], 3:191.)

For Wedekind, at least, reading *Psychopathia sexualis* had an inspiring effect, and the anecdotal potential he found in Krafft-Ebing's case histories remains a central aspect of his literary adaptation. A number of elements in this short diary entry are also constitutive of Wedekind's dramatic production. Johannes Pankau has listed them as circuslike, artistic, and prostitutive elements of trained femininity and the connection between commerce and sexuality.[26] Reading the case as an anecdote allows Wedekind to detach the story from its sexological context, actualize it as an event, and visualize it as dramatic action. Put differently, the anecdotal reading of the case makes it possible to reverse its reference to a general order of knowledge and to make it accessible on a level of representation that is in its core dramatic. This procedure does not appear to be arbitrary or accidental and, due to shared characteristics, the translation of a case into an anecdote does not seem to be too complicated.

As a story of a remarkable, noteworthy, and stimulating historical occurrence that focuses on a concise and significant characterization of a person or event, the anecdote shares many qualities with the cause célèbre from Pitaval and Schiller to Feuerbach's *Merkwürdige Criminal Rechtsfälle* (1808/1829) and Willibald Alexis's *Der Neue Pitaval* (1842–1890). Anecdote and case both report events that are considered remarkable and strange, and both refer to peculiar qualities that they claim to be the essential feature of their object of narration. They differ, however, in their referential orientation, as Hans Lipps mentioned in a 1931 attempt to give a definition of the case: "Something that one turns into a descriptive anecdote, relates as a curious story, or speaks of as a scandalous incident receives a quite different framing and method of treatment when it is presented as a *case*."[27] The anecdote stands for itself, while the case is supposed to contribute to a greater order of things that cannot be reduced to it. But while the case depends on truth and fac-

---

26. See Pankau, "Prostitution," 48.
27. Hans Lipps, "Instance, Example, Case, and the Relationship of the Legal Case to the Law," trans. Erica Weitzman, in *Exemplarity and Singularity: Thinking in Particulars in Philosophy, Literature, and Law*, ed. Michèle Lowrie and Susanne Lüdemann (London: Routledge, 2015), 21.

ticity, the anecdote, as Michael Niehaus explains, resides in a rather dubious sphere that cannot be completely apprehended by means of the categorical distinction between factual and fictitious narrative.[28] Literally, the anecdote is a text that has not been edited; an unaccounted text without origin and without an author.[29] While a case depends on its editor and that editor's scientific authority, the authenticity of the anecdote remains dubious. As the anecdote emphasizes the singularity of an event and is not bound to be conclusive, it does not have to comply with the laws of causality and finality, and often emphasizes what appears to be accidental and contingent. It thus obtains a different relation to history. The anecdote, as Joel Fineman puts it, "*lets history happen*.... [It] produces the effect of the real, the occurrence of contingency, by establishing an event as an event within and yet without the framing context of historical successivity."[30] It is the specific quality of the anecdote that distinguishes it from a case that Paul Fleming also emphasizes in his definition of the genre: "The anecdote is a narration that claims to present (whether true or not, verifiable or not) a historical event, usually a single event detached from other events. As a discrete isolated narrative, the anecdote doesn't have a chronological connection to any surrounding narration of events; even when collected—and anecdotes can only be collected, not 'sewn' together into a single story—an anecdote stands on its own."[31]

Taking into account this definition of the anecdote for a discussion of Wedekind's adaptation of Krafft-Ebing's case of the Parisian cocotte, one can draw conclusions regarding his artistic procedure. Obviously, Wedekind is not concerned with the authenticity of the

---

28. See Michael Niehaus, "Die sprechende und die stumme Anekdote," *Zeitschrift für deutsche Philologie* 133 (2013): 183–202.
29. "Anekdote, griech. an-ekdota (von ekdidonai = herausgeben, edieren), also 'nicht Herausgegebenes.'" (Elfriede Moser-Rath, "Anekdote," in *Enzyklopädie des Märchens: Handwörterbuch zur historischen und vergleichenden Erzählforschung*, vol. 1, ed. Kurt Ranke [Berlin: De Gruyter, 1999], 528.)
30. Joel Fineman, "The History of Anecdote: Fiction and Fiction," in *The New Historicism*, ed. Harold Aram Veeser (New York: Routledge, 1989), 61.
31. Paul Fleming, "The Perfect Story: Anecdote and Exemplarity in Linnaeus and Blumenberg," *Thesis Eleven* 104, no. 1 (2011): 74.

event, and his presentation shifts the historical focus from truth and comparability to singularity and peculiarity. His anecdotal retelling of the case emphasizes the event itself and reveals its artistic potential, which shows certain overlap with a circus and vaudeville act. The anecdotal reading of the case enables Wedekind to picture the scene and to manipulate it artistically.

A Bourgeois Tragedy

If what can be said about many of his literary contemporaries is true for Wedekind—that his diary is not only a data storage device but also the testing ground for literary arrangements—then one can understand Wedekind's reading of Krafft-Ebing's case as a model for a literary procedure that allows further assumptions about Wedekind's literary references to sexology. It is a well-established topos of Wedekind scholarship that he followed contemporary sexological debates and that he found inspiration here for his literary work.[32] Ruth Florack, for example, describes *Lulu* as a "montage of the grotesque" that refers to contemporary discourses of sexuality.[33] Yet with the exception of the diary entry, direct references to sexology are difficult to find in Wedekind's oeuvre. The appearance of Jack the Ripper in *The First Lulu* can, as shown earlier, justify a reading of the drama in this context, and recent interpretations have convincingly argued that sexological characteristics can also be found beneath the discursive level of the play. According to Hania Siebenpfeiffer, for instance, Jack the Ripper's sexual murder of Lulu is only the dreadful finale of the tragedy of femininity. The iconography, however, can be found throughout the entire

---

32. See Johannes Pankau, *Sexualität und Modernität: Studien zum deutschen Drama des Fin de Siècle* (Würzburg: Königshausen & Neumann, 2005); Elke Austermühl and Hartmut Vinçon, "Frank Wedekinds Dramen," in *Die literarische Moderne in Europa*, vol. 2, *Formationen der literarischen Avantgarde*, ed. Hans Joachim Piechotta, Ralph-Rainer Wuthenow, and Sabine Rothemann (Opladen: VS Verlag für Sozialwissenschaften, 1994), 304–321; and Elizabeth Boa, *The Sexual Circus: Wedekind's Theatre of Subversion* (Oxford: Blackwell, 1987).

33. See Florack, "Aggression und Lust."

play and is already present in the very beginning.[34] The first act takes place in an artist's studio, where the painter and Lulu's future husband, Eduard Schwarz, is supposed to paint Lulu's portrait commissioned by her current husband, the dean of the Medical School, Dr. Goll. The entire scene is sexually charged to the highest extent: While the painter is already "licking his paintbrushes,"[35] Goll asks him to throw her onto the canvas: "Hold the brush longer.—No impasto for her. She's not the super-colossal type" (Wedekind, 41). "A sight for sore eyes," he remarks of the female object who is "coming out of the bedroom as Pierrot" (Wedekind, 40). "Treat her as a still life" (Wedekind, 42), requests the journalist Dr. Franz Schöning who is also present. And once the others have left the studio and the painter is finally alone with his model, he savages his desired female object, chases her through the room, while she defends herself until he confesses his love, upon which she consents: "I am yours" (Wedekind, 57). In her studies of artistic depictions of sexual murder in the early twentieth century, the art historian Kathrin Hoffmann-Curtius has argued that modernist paintings by Rudolf Schlichter, George Grosz, and Otto Dix, among others demonstrate the structural violence that is at play in the transformation of the female body into a piece of art.[36] The first act of Wedekind's drama does precisely this: it stages the analogy between sexual violence and artistic practice that in the final act culminates in the sexual

---

34. See Hania Siebenpfeiffer, "Re-Writing Jack the Ripper: Zur Semiotik des Lustmords in Frank Wedekinds *Monstretragödie*," in *Lustmord: Medialisierungen eines kulturellen Phantasmas um 1900*, ed. Susanne Komfort-Heim and Susanne Scholz (Königstein: Ulrike Helmer, 2007), 55–72.

35. Frank Wedekind, *The First Lulu*, trans. Eric Bentley (New York: Applause Books, 1994), 39.

36. "Die Künstler setzen die Aktionen ins Bild, die der Entstehung des Bildes vorausgehen, das Ausschneiden von Anblicken, das Aussortieren von Körperteilen und ihr neues Zusammensetzen, aber sie thematisieren auch das Bearbeiten des Bildes von Weiblichkeit, die Verbindung des weiblichen Körpers mit dem Bildgrund, sein Stillstellen, sein Festlegen, die Transponierung des lebendigen Körpers in tote Materie, das Auskratzen, Ausschneiden, Ausstreichen, die Pinselschläge und vieles mehr." (Kathrin Hoffmann-Curtius, "Frauenmord als künstlerisches Thema der Moderne," in *Serienmord. Kriminologische und kulturwissenschaftliche Skizzierungen eines ungeheuerlichen Phänomens*, ed. Frank J. Robertz and Alexandra Thomas [Munich: Belleville, 2004], 282.)

murder of the female protagonist and connects it with the contemporary sexological context.

Although recent scholarship has paid attention to the drama's discursive and iconographic references to sexology, Johanna Bossinade alerts us to the fact that the form of the drama has rarely been considered in the discussion of Wedekind's often noticed references to contemporary critical writings on civilization and sexuality by Johann Jakob Bachofen, Friedrich Engels, Krafft-Ebing, Havelock Ellis, and Freud.[37] Yet it is important to follow Wedekind's references to sexology not only on the discursive level but also on the level of literary and, more specifically, dramatic form. How does this form relate to the material from a sexological context that essentially relies on casuistic forms of representation?

Wedekind's *Lulu* is not an easily accessible text and its modernism lies first and foremost in a rigorous rejection of the classic dramatic form. The play's dramatis personae are drafted neither as characters nor as types, and Wedekind renounces any kind of psychology altogether. The drama presents actions without psychological depth and the individual scenes are sequentially arranged as discrete acts without creating a consistent and successive narrative. The closeness of the classic dramatic form is willfully suspended and the individual scenes each exhibit their own semantic value. Seriality and repetition take the position of a causally arranged plot. And if someone attempted to retell the story, it would likely result in a series of grotesque events that could compete with Krafft-Ebing's *Psychopathia sexualis* if given the authority of clinical observation.

In short, Wedekind's drama works on the dissolution of the dramatic unities of action, place, and time, and his dramatis personae, accordingly, do not show any form of development. This directly affects the interactions and dialogues of the play that are for the most part limited to mere allusions to physical desires, whereas arbitrarily stated moral boundaries are challenged only to such a de-

---

37. See Johanna Bossinade, "Wedekinds *Monstretragödie* und die Frage der Separation (Lacan)," in Gutjahr, *Frank Wedekind*, 147.

gree that a return to socially accepted forms of conduct always remains possible. Rarely does someone finish a sentence—exclamations are followed by empty allusions going nowhere—the drama performs the avoidance of a discursive level of speech, and in those rare scenes in which speaking seems to cause real action and promises to result in the fulfillment of physical desires, the involved characters are quick to return to their trivial chitchat. Although the entire drama is sexually charged to the highest extent, the characters are denied sexual satisfaction. Only the protagonist Lulu gets what she wants. Already in the third act she confesses to the playwright Alwa: "To fall into the hands of a sex murderer could be interesting."[38]

Lulu is the clear center of the play. All other characters are defined only by their desire for her. And in turn, Lulu herself appears to be a woman without qualities who willingly agrees to become whatever her male admirers want her to be:

SCHWARZ: Be nice to me.
LULU: I am being nice to you.
SCHWARZ: Then get undressed.
LULU: What for?
SCHWARZ: That Pierrot costume . . .
LULU: But I am yours.
SCHWARZ: Nelly . . .
LULU: How'd you mean, my Pierrot . . . ?
SCHWARZ: Nelly . . . Nelly . . .
LULU: But I am not Nelly.
SCHWARZ: Your Pierrot costume . . .
LULU: My name is Lulu.
SCHWARZ: I would call you Eve.
LULU: As you wish.
SCHWARZ: Then be nice to me.
LULU: As you wish.
SCHWARZ: Eve.[39]

---

38. Wedekind, *First Lulu*, 108.
39. Wedekind, *First Lulu*, 57.

For her male admirers, Lulu is nothing more than the object of their desires onto which they can project their gender-specific fantasies.[40] She further defies any of the typical bourgeois role models. As Florack has argued, she neither fits the image of the wife whose sexuality stands in the service of procreation nor complies with the idea of the prostitute who sells her sexuality as a commodity.[41] As compliant wish fulfillment of men's own fantasies, Lulu does not fit any of the images of womanhood that bourgeois society has created and that sexological discourses have scientifically reaffirmed. As a mirror of male fantasies, she paradoxically defies all male attributions of femininity and gender-specific norms. And although she becomes whatever they want, her male admirers become exasperated with her:

SCHIGOLCH: I don't understand women.
ALWA: I never did understand them.
LULU: I understand them.[42]

In contrast to all the other men in the play, Jack appears to be a *Frauenversteher*, a connoisseur of women. As a moth is attracted to light, Karl Kraus wrote, the protagonist of Wedekind's play, Lulu, the most *unwomanly woman*, is driven toward the *manliest man*, the sex murderer Jack.[43] This ending of the play has often been understood as a critique of predominant bourgeois gender norms and the accompanying sexual ethics of the fin de siècle. That it is, of all people, the dreaded phantom of Whitechapel, Jack the Rip-

---

40. This is the standard interpretation of Wedekind's *Lulu* since Silvia Bovenschen's discussion of the play in her book, *Die imaginierte Weiblichkeit: Exemplarische Untersuchungen zu kulturgeschichtlichen und literarischen Präsentationsformen des Weiblichen* (Frankfurt am Main: Suhrkamp, 1979). That Bovenschen also sees in Lulu a "Substantialisierung des Weiblichen zu einem Natürlichen und Ursprünglichen" (44), is due to the version of Wedekind's play that her interpretation is still based on. Ruth Florack has argued that *The First Lulu*, other than the so-called *Doppeldrama*, consisting of the two plays *Der Erdgeist* and *Die Büchse der Pandora*, would not allow such an interpretation (Florack, "Aggression und Lust," 173).
41. See Florack, "Aggression und Lust," 173.
42. Wedekind, *First Lulu*, 174.
43. See Kraus, "Die Büchse der Pandora," 6.

per, whom the drama puts in charge of restoring civilized order by murdering the femme fatale Lulu, must be considered the real scandal of Wedekind's play. Although Jack the Ripper is a mythical figure composed of rumors, legends, and uncanny tales, his appearance in the final act is a reference to an extraliterary reality. According to Florack, Wedekind's drama calls attention to the limits of fictionalization: although there are no women like Lulu, there are men like Jack the Ripper. Thus, the realization is inescapable that the violence of the play is real.[44]

It is one of the difficulties of *The First Lulu* that on the level of the plot it neither develops a critical perspective nor presents a clearly identifiable critical program. Throughout the entire play, contemporary discourses on sexuality are affirmatively reproduced and dramatically staged. It is only with the final scene and its reference to the Jack the Ripper case that the drama takes a different turn. After Jack has finished his dreadful deed with the same indifference that one imagines a factory worker does his job, he shows excitement about his trophy: "I would have never thought of a thing like that.—That is a phenomenon, what would not happen every two hundred years.—I am a lucky dog, to find this curiosity. . . . When I am dead and my collection is put up to auction, the London Medical Club will pay a sum of three hundred pounds for that prodigy I have conquered this night. The professors and the students will say: That is astonishing!"[45]

With the sex murderer delivering his victims to the medical sciences and contributing to the greater good and progress of humanity, the violence of the discourse to which the drama uncompromisingly subscribed by taking it literally becomes evident. Not only does the sex murder function as a corrective in the name of dominant sexual morals and bourgeois conceptions of normalcy, which would be scandalous enough, but even more, the *Lustmord* appears

---

44. See Florack, "Aggression und Lust," 176.
45. Frank Wedekind, *Lulu: Die Büchse der Pandora: Eine Monstretragödie* (Frankfurt am Main: Suhrkamp, 1999), 200. (In the original German edition of the *play*, this passage is composed in English. I am quoting it here from the German edition of the text, as Eric Bentley's translation of *The First Lulu* that I otherwise used shows important omissions and misrepresentations of these particular passages.)

as scientific practice. When the sex murderer turns out to be a collector and anatomist and when his deed of dismembering a female body unambiguously refers to surgical and scientific practices, the violent criminal act suddenly appears in the light of the human sciences and their claim of contributing to humanity's progress. In Wedekind's drama, Jack the Ripper appears without the usual fascination and sensationalism to which he doubtless owes his fame. And when the drama presents his dreadful deed as rationally calculated business, the sex murderer no longer appears as the terrifying other, the criminal monster or beast in human form that threatens the natural civilized order. Instead, his deed turns into an event that seamlessly fits the order of the bourgeois society and contributes to its self-conception. If the dramatically staged act of *Lustmord*, therefore, can so smoothly and entirely be integrated in the rational discourse of the human sciences and even seems to unfold its proper significance in this context, the moral authority of this discourse can no longer be taken seriously.

Wedekind's drama refers to a pivotal aspect of the sexological definition of gender norms, in which female subjugation and the male conquest of women, whose love is supposed to be primarily directed toward motherhood, has to contribute to the stabilization of the civilized order. The introductory chapter of Krafft-Ebing's *Psychopathia sexualis* makes this perfectly clear:

> Undoubtedly man has a much more intense sexual appetite than woman. As a result of a powerful natural instinct, at a certain age, a man is drawn toward a woman. He loves sensually, and is influenced in his choice by physical beauty. In accordance with the nature of this powerful impulse, he is aggressive and violent in wooing. At the same time, this demand of nature does not constitute all of his mental existence. When his longing is satisfied, love temporarily retreats behind other vital and social interests.
>
> With a woman it is quite otherwise. If she is normally developed mentally, and well bred, her sexual desire is small. If this were not so the whole world would become a brothel and marriage and a family impossible. It is certain that the man that avoids women and the woman that seeks men are abnormal.[46]

---

46. Krafft-Ebing, *Psychopathia sexualis*, 13.

Krafft-Ebing's sexological gender model leaves no room for women such as Lulu. It does, however, still include the *Lustmörder* as the most extreme case of masculinity—or, to use Karl Kraus's pointed formulation, as the "manliest man."[47]

To sum up this argument and to shed further light on the critical perspective with which Wedekind challenges the sexologically approved order of sexes and bourgeois gender norms, I conclude with another anecdote. On May 29, 1905, Karl Kraus organized a performance of Wedekind's play for an exclusive group of invited guests in the Trianon theater in Vienna. Wedekind himself appeared onstage in the role of Jack the Ripper who murdered the protagonist Lulu, played by the stage actress Tilly Newes. It is more than just irony that Wedekind would marry the actress only one year later. It is certainly possible to interpret the casting for the play as a self-reflexive commentary on the gender-specific demeaning aspect of the artistic work, as Claudia Liebrand argues.[48] But as the continuation of a play that takes contemporary sexual norms and gender-specific role assignments literally, the wedding of the male perpetrator and his female victim fulfills sexological fantasies and provides a happy ending to *The First Lulu* as a bourgeois play.

---

47. See Kraus, "Die Büchse der Pandora," 6.
48. Claudia Liebrand, "Noch einmal: Das wilde, schöne Tier Lulu: Rezeptionsgeschichte und Text," in Gutjahr, *Frank Wedekind*, 187.

8

Conclusion

The Fiction of Authority

Part I of this book was concerned with the emergence of psychological description by means of narrative focalization and with the concomitant emergence of a new conception of literary authorship. The readings of Part II showed that while literary texts in the nineteenth century continued the convention of referencing historical cases, they did so in order to question institutional authority and to criticize the epistemological foundations and the legitimacy of legal judgments informed by psychological narrative. A scene from Hoffmann's "The Story of Serapion" in *The Serapion Brethren* may exemplify this new status of literary fiction in the nineteenth century. When the narrator Cyprian, who had confronted the hermit Serapion with the noble intention of curing him from his delusions, surrenders to the "methodological madness" of his opponent that appears to be the condition for his "extraordinary poetical genius,"[1] he acknowledges a new form of literary authorship that

---

1. E. T. A. Hoffmann, *The Serapion Brethren*, trans. Major Alex Ewing, vol. 1 (London: George Bell, 1908), 20.

displays the gift of exceptional fantastical creativity but forfeits the ability to distinguish between the inner vision of the fantastical mind and the rational authority of a critical observer. The psychological perspective that novels such as *Werther* and *Anton Reiser* had established for narrative literature is explicitly dismissed by Cyprian when he concedes to the hermit: "I took great care never again to essay my role of the psychological doctor."[2]

As seen earlier, this conflict over literary and narrative authority coincides with Hoffmann's positioning in the debate about legal responsibility surrounding the case of the murderer Daniel Schmolling. Hoffmann's rigorous rejection of medical authority in the analysis of states of mind for the purpose of legal decision making shows his deep concern about the predictability of the law and the dangers of compromising legal authority with knowledge based on philosophical speculation. Literary fiction, according to Hoffmann's rendering of romantic authorship, develops in opposition to psychological rationality and its claim to objectivity: poetical talent is based on *methodological madness*. This model of authorship, on the one hand, assigns to literary authors a special ability to depict questionable states of mind, and on the other hand locates this ability in authors' own special psychological intuition. It anticipates the tendency of sexological and criminological experts at the end of the nineteenth century who look for a psychopathological kinship between an author and his or her material and who elevate rational authority over the interpretation of literary fiction. Frank Wedekind's theater performance as Jack the Ripper in Karl Kraus's Viennese production of *Pandora's Box* is an ironic commentary on this development. *The First Lulu* presented artistic production fueled by violent fantasies of male dominance and, thus, perverted the authority of the bourgeois artist. Leaving the last word to Jack the Ripper and leaving to the dreaded murderer the task of reaffirming bourgeois norms of gender and sexuality, radically questions the authority of the dominating sexological discourses at the end of the nineteenth century that had made strategic use of cases to argue for replacing legal authority with medical and psychiatric expertise.

---

2. Hoffmann, *Serapion Brethren*, 21.

Both Wedekind's *Lulu* and Büchner's *Woyzeck* are critical attempts to undermine the casuistic display of authority by dissolving narrative coherence in dramatic action. Büchner's *Woyzeck* does not compete with Clarus's case history, which had confirmed the murderer's responsibility by lending coherence to his life story. Instead of establishing a perspective that could justify a decision in the Woyzeck case, Büchner lets the narrative disintegrate and thus, rather than displaying authority, stages its decomposition. The drama does not proceed by means of psychological narrative, nor does it simply stage the Woyzeck case. It does, however, present scenes and arrangements that reference the case and can be understood as critical commentary to the debate about legal responsibility to which Clarus's case history was meant to contribute. In particular, this is visible in the scenes in which the drama displays observation, and in doing so it also reflects on its own practice of dramatic staging. The protagonist Woyzeck appears to be under constant observation and his behavior is incessantly examined, interpreted, and judged: as the scientific guinea pig of an overly ambitious doctor; as a soldier who is unconditionally subjected to a military regime of discipline; as a betrayed lover who is exposed to everyone's mockery; and, not least, as the drama's main character who is ruthlessly exhibited on the dramatic stage. Woyzeck's restlessness and display of paranoid behavior must not be attributed to an individual pathological constitution but can simply be understood as the effect of being the object of uninterrupted surveillance. The dramatic form Büchner chose for his adaptation of the case intervenes in the logic of casuistic reasoning not only by breaking down its narrative order but also by displaying the observing gaze and its claim to authority.

Like the hermit Serapion in Hoffmann's story, these dramatic texts confront the audience with a difference in perception that, if taken seriously, will also affect the reader's own position. Undermining the authority of reason and intervening in the medical-legal debates over the question of accountability, Hoffmann, Büchner, and Wedekind—each in his particular way—inflict doubt on the casuistic display of certainty and in the process challenge the reader's forms of perception.

Part III

Novelistic Casuistry

9

Freud's Cases

Psychoanalysis and Literary Fiction

In the human sciences that dominate the public debate around 1900, literary fiction plays a rather dubious role. On the one hand, criminologists and sexologists often refer to literary material to substitute for the lack of empirical observations, and attribute special psychopathological value to the poetic depictions of the human struggle. On the other hand, the same discourses impute to literary authors a rather questionable relation to their poetic products, denying them psychological authority. In contrast to the psychologically and medically trained expert, literary authors, it is said, do not possess the ability to rationally and objectively oversee the entire consequences of their creations. The same mental disposition that qualifies poets to depict psychopathological conditions is responsible for disqualifying them as psychologists. In order to distinguish between scientists and poets, Richard von Krafft-Ebing characterized the latter as sentimentalists and located their special ability for depicting "the miseries of man and the dark sides of his existence" in their sensitive nature that would itself always run the risk of degenerating into a "horrid caricature."[1] As I have shown earlier in regard to the sexological reception of Marquis de Sade's work, attributing to authors a psychological kinship with their literary creations was meant to make their own biographies accessible to psychopathological interpretation and, thus, to produce additional casuistic material. The most radical consequence of this treatment of literature can be found in the two volumes of Max Nordau's 1892 book *Degeneration*, in which the social critic and physician presents a literary history of contemporary authors as a history of pathologies. Following in the footsteps of Cesare Lombroso's criminal anthropology, Nordau claims that "degenerates are not always criminals, prostitutes, anarchists, and pronounced lunatics; they are often authors and artists."[2] Nordau leaves no doubt about the pathological connection he sees between the author and his choice of material: "The artist who complacently represents what is reprehensible, vicious, criminal, approves of it, perhaps glorifies it, differs not in kind, but only in degree, from the criminal who actually commits it."[3]

Considering the 1906 publication of an essay titled "On the Value of the Literary Representation of Crime for Penology" in the *Zeitschrift für die gesamte Strafrechtswissenschaft*,[4] it must be assumed that this debate was still part of the general criminological agenda when Sigmund Freud approached a similar question in a short presentation one year later:[5] "We laymen have always

---

1. Richard von Krafft-Ebing, *Psychopathia sexualis: With Special Reference to Contrary Sexual Instinct: A Medico-Legal Study*, authorized translation of the 7th enlarged and revised German edition, trans. Charles Gilbert Chaddock (Philadelphia: F. A. Davis, 1892), vii.
2. Max Nordau, *Degeneration* (New York: D. Appleton, 1895), vii.
3. Nordau, *Degeneration*, 326.
4. See Jacques Stern, "Über den Wert der dichterischen Behandlung des Verbrechens für die Strafrechtswissenschaft," *Zeitschrift für die gesamte Strafrechtswissenschaft* 26 (1906): 145–171.
5. Debates about the psychopathological status of literature and the literary author in particular can also be found in Erich Wulffen's popular criminological

been intensely curious to know ... from what sources that strange being, the creative writer, draws his material, and how he manages to make such an impression on us with it and to arouse in us emotions of which, perhaps, we had not even thought ourselves capable."[6] Freud, however—and this can hardly be considered a surprise—arrives at conclusions very different from those of his medical colleagues Krafft-Ebing and Nordau. Indeed, his reevaluation of literary fiction not only contributes to enhancing its status by assigning to it new areas of psychological influence but also has a significant effect on literary production itself. Far from removing literature from the psychological context, Freud shifts the focus regarding the function of literary fiction for psychological cognition from authorship to form. As I discuss in this chapter, the question of literary form initially appears in Freud in connection with his case histories on hysteria and with the problem of casuistic representation. Freud, however, reverses the prevalent criminological perspective when he notes a certain proximity of his own scientific case histories to literature. This comparison concerns less the scientific value of Freud's case histories than it does literary fiction and its *reality value*, and, thus, his contribution to new conceptions of literary realism. Indeed, the definition of literary fiction in reference to reality is also at stake in Freud's 1907 presentation that was cited above, which I take as a point of departure for a discussion of Freud's treatment of literature before focusing more closely on the question of literary form in his case histories

In "Creative Writers and Day-Dreaming," Freud attributes to the poet the special ability to give aesthetic pleasure by helping the reader to solve mental tensions and to enjoy his or her own fantasies and dreams without feeling the need for self-criticism, censorship,

---

books such as *Ibsens Nora vor dem Strafrichter und Psychiater* (Halle: Marhold, 1907), and *Gerhard Hauptmann vor dem Forum der Kriminalpsychologie und Psychiatrie: Naturwissenschaftliche Studien* (Breslau: Langewort, 1908). Nordau's *Degeneration* and the publications following in his footsteps had a significant influence on later debates concerning the *degenerate art* in Nazi Germany.

6. Sigmund Freud, "Creative Writers and Day-Dreaming" (1907/198), in *The Standard Edition of the Complete Psychological Works of Sigmund Freud*, vol. 9 (1906–1908), trans. and ed. James Strachey (London: Hogarth Press, 2001), 143.

and shame. Poetry, for Freud, has a sociopsychological function; it is a medium of aesthetic entertainment with the benefit of psychological relief. To accept Freud's conclusion, however, one must first accept his comparison of the poet's creativity to that of the playing child and the distinction that goes along with it and further shapes his argument: "The opposite of play is not seriousness—it is reality."[7]

The understanding of literary fiction as play that consciously sets itself apart from reality is one of the main and most productive distinctions in the early period of psychoanalysis when it was not yet established as a discipline and still had to define its most basic concepts. Although it was not Freud's intention to contribute to literary interpretation or even to establish a new philological approach to literature, psychoanalytic approaches to literature have significantly added to its redefinition, with important effects on the development of modern forms of writing. Freud himself credited literature with being a major influence on psychoanalysis. He even attributed to literary authors the original discovery of the unconscious, though not without adding that it was he who discovered "the scientific method by which the unconscious can be studied."[8] The anthropological model of psychoanalysis, not unlike poetry, rests on the foundation of a linguistic system and thus, seems to run the risk of being itself taken for literature. This explains Freud's sometimes dismissive attitude toward literature and his emphasis of the scientific quality by which psychoanalysis distinguishes itself and defies the suspicion of being nothing more than a fragile system of literary interpretation.[9] Generously crediting poets with the discovery

---

7. Freud, "Creative Writers," 144.

8. Cited in Lionel Trilling, "Freud and Literature," in *The Liberal Imagination* (London: Doubleday Anchor, 1951), 34.

9. In this regard, Jean Starobinski has argued that Freud's seeming disregard for literature and art must be understood as a kind of defense mechanism to deflect from the "literary complex" belonging to psychoanalysis's own foundational background. While psychoanalysis intended to develop as the conscious discourse of reason over the irrational and the nondiscursive, Starobinski reminds us of the mythopoetic origin of many of its primary concepts. (See Jean Starobinski, "Psychoanalysis and Literary Understanding," in Starobinski, *The Living Eye*, trans. Arthur Goldhammer [Cambridge, MA: Harvard University Press, 1989], 129–148.)

of the unconscious while emphasizing the superiority of his own scientific perspective is a rhetorical trick we know from Krafft-Ebing, who in the introduction to his *Psychopathia sexualis* lauds poets and philosophers for their depiction of mental predispositions only to claim the importance of scientific expertise for psychological cognition. Unlike Krafft-Ebing, however, who explains the poet's ability to depict pathological states of mind on the basis of the author's psychological kinship, Freud's scientific system of psychoanalysis has a much deeper and more profound connection to poetic language as it takes into consideration the formal and aesthetic aspects of literature. In addition to the understanding of a literary text as a manifestation of its author's psychological state, Freud finds in literary fiction an exploration of the unconscious by means of poetic form that can be translated into scientific and rational language with the support of the psychoanalytic method. Indeed, the realization of the scientific claim in psychoanalysis is based on a technique of decoding by which a cryptic symbolic language is replaced with a conscious language of interpretation. The scientific rationality of psychoanalysis is essentially based on methods of interpretation, its material is that of language and linguistic expression in which the unconscious matter makes its way to the surface without being recognized. Accordingly, concepts such as fiction, play, and literature are not necessarily to be considered dismissive in psychoanalytic vocabulary, even when Freud strictly distinguishes them from the realm of reality. What *realizes* itself in the *play* of literary fiction is precisely what is not supposed to be part of reality. While this is a very limited understanding of literary fiction, it nevertheless shows the specific psychoanalytic access to literature and the advantage that Freud finds in literary expression for the study of the unconscious.

Below I address the question of the psychoanalytic potential of literary representation in Freud's case histories. As a point of departure, I focus on Freud's famous comparison of case and novella in which he complicates the relation between science and literature. With this comparison, Freud shifts the focus away from the casuistic material itself toward its linguistic and literary composition. The narrative model of the novella, however, with which Freud attaches his cases to forms of literary representation, does not prevail as the guiding model in Freud's later, more famous case histories. In the Dora case, published in 1905, Freud already questions the closed narrative form for casuistic representation and replaces the novelistic narrative of an omnipresent narrator with the rather fragmentary narrative of the patient herself. Although this places an even stronger emphasis on the question of representation, it requires a closer look at the literary conceptions of reality in their narrative composition. The discussion of some of Freud's most famous cases in the context of this study will contextualize the readings of two texts by Alfred Döblin and Robert Musil who again refer to historical cases in order to reevaluate the realist status of literature.

The Case as Novella

The problem of the distinction between literature and science accompanies the development of psychoanalysis and its methods from Freud's earliest studies. As evidence for the productive proximity of psychoanalysis to literature, literary critics have often pointed to the remark in the 1895 *Studies on Hysteria*, with which Freud introduces the epicrisis of the case of Elisabeth von R.:

> I have not always been a psychotherapist. Like other neuropathologists, I was trained to employ local diagnoses and electro-prognosis, and it still strikes me myself as strange that the case histories [*Krankengeschichten*] I write should read like short stories [*Novellen*] and that, as one might say, they lack the serious stamp of science. I must console myself with the reflection that the nature of the subject is evidently responsible for this, rather than any preference of my own. The fact is that local diagnosis and electrical reactions lead nowhere in the study of hysteria, whereas a detailed description of mental processes such as we are accustomed to find in the works of imaginative writers [*Dichter*] enables me, with the use of a few psychological formulas, to obtain at least some kind of insight into the course of that affection.[10]

---

10. Sigmund Freud and Josef Breuer, *Studies on Hysteria*, ed. and trans. James Strachey (New York: Basic Books, 1957), 160–161.

Freud's comparison of his case histories with novellas has triggered various reactions. Some interpreters have declared this passage the founding document of psychoanalysis.[11] Still others have referred to this statement to question the scientific value and to criticize the literary style of Freud's case histories.[12] Freud himself attributed the irritation caused by the literary proximity of his case histories to his scientific upbringing. Beginning in 1883, he had learned how to compose case histories in Theodor Meynert's psychiatric clinic. In comparison with his famous psychoanalytic case histories, however, these early written recordings are highly formalized and do not show any specific individual engagement of their author.[13]

But Freud's genre comparison is not sufficiently understood by reducing it to a perspective that challenges the scientific quality of

---

11. See Steven Marcus, "Freud und Dora: Roman, Geschichte, Krankengeschichte," *Psyche* 28, no. 1 (1974): 32–79; Jutta Prasse, "Was ist wirklich geschehen?" in *Sprache und Fremdsprache. Psychoanalytische Aufsätze*, ed. Claus-Dieter Rath (Bielefeld: transcript, 2004), 183–193; and Marianne Schuller, "Erzählen Machen: Narrative Wendungen in der Psychoanalyse nach Freud," in *Wissen: Erzählen: Narrative der Humanwissenschaften*, ed. Arne Höcker, Jeannie Moser, and Philippe Weber (Bielefeld: transcript, 2006), 207–220.

12. See Adolf-Ernst Meyer, "Nieder mit der Novelle als Psychoanalysedarstellung: Hoch lebe die Interaktionsgeschichte," in *Die Fallgeschichte: Beiträge zu ihrer Bedeutung als Forschungsinstrument*, ed. Ulrich Stuhr and Friedrich-Wilhelm Deneke (Heidelberg: Asanger Roland Verlag, 1993), 61–84.

13. See Albrecht Hirschmüller, *Freuds Begegnung mit der Psychiatrie* (Tübingen: Diskord, 1991), 208. Although his psychoanalytic case histories differ significantly from these earlier more clinical recordings in their use of less standardized forms and a more refined narrative structure, Freud emphatically claimed his psychoanalytic practice to follow in the footsteps of the medical tradition. Freud's continuous use of the term *Krankengeschichte* (medical history) instead of *Fallgeschichte* (case history) could be interpreted as such an enforcement of this claim, as Mai Wegener argues. (See Mai Wegener, "Fälle, Ausfälle, Sündenfälle: Zu den Krankengeschichten Freuds," in *Fall—Fallgeschichte—Fallstudie: Theorie und Geschichte einer Wissensform*, ed. Susanne Düwell and Nicolas Pethes [Frankfurt am Main: Campus, 2014], 170.) However, Stefan Goldmann has shown that the term *Fallgeschichte* was only established in Germany after World War II, and that Freud did not make a decision against it when using the generally accepted term *Krankengeschichte*. (See Stefan Goldmann, "Kasus—Krankengeschichte—Novelle," in *"Fakta, und kein moralisches Geschwätz": Zu den Fallgeschichten im "Magazin zur Erfahrungsseelenkunde" [1783–1793]*, ed. Sheila Dickson, Stefan Goldmann, and Christof Wingertszahn [Göttingen: Wallstein, 2011], 44.)

his studies. Freud himself thought of it as comforting that the literary form resulted from the object of his scientific interest and did not come from his well-known personal preference for literary fiction. That his case histories read like novellas can first and foremost be attributed to the important psychoanalytic insight that his patients' symptoms did not correspond to what he called "Realitätszeichen," signs of reality, in a letter to his friend Wilhelm Fließ,[14] and that they must rather be decoded according to the fictitious value that was hidden somewhere within the patients' narratives. This again leads to the far-reaching conclusion essential for the clinical picture of hysteria that fictions have important effects on the formation of reality. Thus, it is what Jutta Prasse calls "the veracity of fiction"[15] that is at stake in the passage from the *Studies on Hysteria* quoted above, if not—as one could claim with some confidence—in psychoanalysis in general.

But Freud's comparison of case histories with novellas has even more dimensions than the one that Freud himself emphasized when lamenting the challenge for the medical-scientific value of his studies. Indeed, Freud just reverses what has already been successfully practiced by the end of the nineteenth century, that novellas can be read as case histories.[16] Considering the scientific value that was attributed to literary novellas by some of his sexological contem-

---

14. Sigmund Freud, *Briefe an Wilhelm Fließ: 1887–1904*, ed. Jeffrey Moussaieff Masson (Frankfurt am Main: S. Fischer, 1986), 283.

15. Prasse, "Was ist wirklich geschehen," 190.

16. In addition to the examples discussed so far in this book, Georg Büchner's 1836 novella *Lenz* is based on the case of the *Storm and Stress* author Michael Reinhold Lenz. In his 1888 novella *Lineman Thiel*, Gerhard Hauptmann presents the protagonist's sudden and intense discharge of mental energies with catastrophic results. And one must also mention E. T. A. Hoffmann's 1816 novella, *The Sandman*, which Freud himself famously read as a case history. (See Freud, "The Uncanny," in *The Standard Edition of the Complete Psychological Works of Sigmund Freud, Vol. XVII (1917–1919): An Infantile Neurosis and Other Works*, ed. James Strachey [London: Vintage, 2001], 217–256.) The close proximity between novella and case history can be traced back to Cervantes, whose novellas, as Stefan Goldmann argues, influenced and inspired Freud's own literary style. (See Stefan Goldmann, "Sigmund Freud und Hermann Sudermann oder die wiedergefundene wie eine Krankengeschichte zu lesende Novelle," in *Literatur, Mythos und Freud*, ed. Helmut Peitsch and Eva Lezzi [Potsdam: Universität Potsdam, 2009], 55.)

poraries, Freud's concern regarding the scientific appearance of his case histories might come as a surprise. On the one hand, it could be argued that Freud only pretended to be concerned about his finding and that his true intention was to emphasize the importance of literary forms of representation for the psychoanalytic method. On the other hand, one must recognize that Freud's work, in comparison with contemporary sexological discourses, takes the reference to literature to a new level. Although the strict distinction between literature and science remained an important element for the self-conception of sexology, Freud's confession scandalizes by radically undermining the distinction between poet and scientist and claiming an intrinsic connection between the two forms that are generally considered to be mutually exclusive. For Freud, literature is not valued simply as a supplier of material for psychological research that claims for itself the ability to read and interpret poetry rationally from the perspective of the human sciences. Rather, case histories that can be read as novellas adumbrate a direct connection between literary form and scientific cognition.

Another indicator of Freud's intention to attribute to literary fiction an important function for the formation of psychoanalytic knowledge is that his comparison makes reference to the genre of the novella instead of simply alluding to narrative qualities. As a genre, the novella shares many characteristics with the case history. In one of the first genre-specific studies of the case from 1930, the literary critic André Jolles recognized the case as an early form of the novella. According to Jolles, a case only needed a few additions to be turned from a simple form to the artistically and aesthetically more accomplished form of the novella.[17] But his definition of the case as a simple form that challenges the law and the norm shows even more similarities with the definition of the novella since Goethe. In his conversations with Johann Peter Eckermann, Goethe famously characterizes the novella as a "peculiar and as yet unheard-of event."[18] Furthermore, he refers to his 1809 novel, *Elective Affini-*

---

17. See André Jolles, *Simple Forms: Legend, Saga, Myth, Riddle, Saying, Case, Memorabile, Fairytale, Joke*, trans. Peter J. Schwartz (New York: Verso, 2017), 146.
18. Johann Wolfgang von Goethe, *Conversations of Goethe with Eckermann and Soret*, trans. John Oxenford (London: George Bell, 1874), 209.

ties, in which he not only highlights the primacy of novelty and noteworthiness of the novella but also emphasizes that it centers in form and content around a "conflict between law and violence, commonsense and reason, passion and prejudice."[19] Friedrich Theodor Vischer summarized these characteristics in his 1857 *Aesthetics*, where he writes that the novella "does not present the complete development of a character, but an excerpt from the life of a human being that is marked by friction and is in crisis, and that exhibits to us with clarity and by means of a reversal of fate and emotional complication what human life is in general."[20] One could take Vischer's definition of the novella and apply it directly to Freud's case histories from the *Studies on Hysteria*. Against this background, it will not be surprising to find that Freud's famous comparison is placed at the epicrisis and thus at just the part of a case history that is supposed to develop and accentuate the central conflict of the case. And when Vischer emphasizes the special usefulness of the novella for the depiction and understanding of human life, the genre's close proximity to the case history becomes strikingly evident. Novellas presenting individual lives in crisis in such a way that they take on an exemplary character for the understanding of human life in general can indeed be read like case histories with their epistemological tendency to draw general conclusions from the representation of individual histories.

Freud surely would have liked to claim authorship for his comparison of case with novella. Its originality, however, cannot solely be attributed to the innovative potential of the psychoanalytic method. Freud was an attentive reader of novellas, and Stefan Goldmann has argued that nineteenth-century novelistic fiction formed an almost inexhaustible archive of casuistry for Freud, who took great advantage of it for his own work.[21] In Hermann Sudermann's 1894 novella *Der Wunsch*, Goldmann was even able to

---

19. Johann Wolfgang Goethe, *Elective Affinities*, trans. R. J. Hollingdale (London: Penguin, 1971), 235.
20. Friedrich Theodor Vischer, *Ästhetik oder Wissenschaft des Schönen: Zum Gebrauche der Vorlesungen: Dritter Theil, Zweiter Abschnitt* (Stuttgart: Mäcken, 1857), 1318.
21. See Goldmann, "Sigmund Freud und Hermann Sudermann," 61.

identify a model for the very case in the *Studies on Hysteria* from which Freud's famous comparison originates. The relation between Freud's case histories and literature, however, cannot be reduced to the literary archive that Freud might have accessed. Freud's case histories are based on a literary structure that, although posing a challenge to the scientific claim of psychoanalysis, remains responsible for its epistemic dynamic and indispensable for psychoanalytic cognition. It is worth repeating Freud's own assessment that the literariness of his case histories is not based on his own decision or even preference, but that it comes with the object of his investigation. The object of Freud's study is the unconscious, the structure of which Jacques Lacan once compared to that of language, itself a medium that disguises and obscures rather than offering transparency. It is against this backdrop that Mai Wegener concludes that it is the status and condition of language by which psychoanalysis detaches itself from the scientific model of the case,[22] and thus, one is tempted to add, opens itself for a poetic experience.

Recording the Case of Dora

In the preface to his most famous case history, published in 1905 as "Fragment of an Analysis of Hysteria" and better known as the Dora case, Freud addresses some problems regarding the composition and publication of his cases. Although he expresses concern about the violation of his patients' privacy that a publication of the most intimate details of their lives would certainly entail, those difficulties he refers to as being "of a technical kind"[23] and that concern the narrative composition of the case history, are of great importance in this context and will be given close attention below.

Freud leaves no doubt that he considers the publication of his cases his scientific duty as long as he can avoid the direct injury of

---

22. See Wegener, "Fälle, Ausfälle, Sündenfälle," 176.
23. Sigmund Freud, *Dora: An Analysis of a Case of Hysteria*, ed. Philip Rieff (New York: Touchstone, 1997), 2.

the individual. The delicacy of the intimate matters discussed during the therapeutic sessions, however, has a more direct influence on its scientific recording. It excludes the possibility of note taking during the psychotherapeutic treatment "for fear of shaking the patient's confidence and of disturbing his own view of the material under observation."[24] Thus, in particular, the recording of treatments of longer duration poses a problem for which Freud claims not to have found a solution yet. On the one hand, the Dora case offers itself for publication because the treatment spans only a relatively short period of time and its solution centers around only two dreams. On the other hand, Freud's interest in the publication of this case is not simply owed to its particular exemplarity and peculiar features, but concerns the composition of case histories in general. It would not have been very difficult, Freud writes, to record the case of Dora from the perspective of its solution and to give a "full and concise medical report." This, however, would have meant "plac[ing] the reader in a very different situation from that of the medical observer."[25] One cannot sufficiently stress the relevance of this remark for an adequate evaluation of Freud's cases. He is not content with presenting a clinical picture and instead tasks himself with demonstrating the psychoanalytic technique. Thus, Freud deliberately decides against influencing the form of the narrative even when it affects the consistency of the report. Steven Marcus thus attributes formal similarities of the Dora case to a modern experimental novel: "Its narrative and expository course, for example, is neither linear nor rectilinear; instead its organization is plastic, involuted, and heterogeneous, and follows spontaneously an inner logic that seems frequently to be at odds with itself; it often loops back around itself and is multidimensional in its representation of both its material and itself."[26] From Freud's own perspective, the literary form Marcus describes is precisely what guarantees the scientific value of his procedure. This is due to two factors. First, it is

---

24. Freud, *Dora*, 4.
25. Freud, *Dora*, 9.
26. Steven Marcus, "Freud and Dora: Story, History, Case History," in *Freud: A Collection of Critical Essays*, ed. Perry Meisel (Englewood Cliffs, NJ: Prentice Hall, 1981), 189.

the status of language on which Freud's psychotherapeutic method relies, through which he attempts to find access to the concealed source of his patient's symptoms and by means of which he delivers his scientific results. In other words, language is simultaneously both the channel through which the unconscious sends coded messages and the medium of scientific rationality. In Freud's practice, then, language has two opposing functions, to conceal and to detect, to distort and to clarify. And this leads to the second factor concerning the narrative structure of Freud's cases. A case is based on a history that can be told differently from the perspective of the patient and that of a rational observer who is able to oversee the presented material in its entirety. A footnote that Freud added to the Dora case reveals a relevant and interesting detail concerning the importance of narrative for the psychotherapeutic method. Freud here refers to another patient who was sent to him with hysteric symptoms. However, after the patient told her history, which "came out perfectly clearly and connectedly in spite of the remarkable events it dealt with," Freud concludes "that the case could not be one of hysteria," a diagnosis that was later confirmed by "a careful physical examination."[27] In sum, those who can tell their own history coherently, with clarity in expression and without contradictions, cannot be considered neurotic. On the flip side, it must be assumed that hysterics are poor storytellers.

It is Dora's own narrative that confronts Freud with the problem of representation that surfaces in almost all his case histories, which also are always histories of observation and histories of psychotherapeutic treatments. In the case of the "Wolfman" from 1918, Freud states: "I can neither write a purely historical nor a purely pragmatic history of my patient, I can neither provide a treatment history nor a case history, but shall find myself obliged to combine the two approaches."[28] In the case histories from the *Studies on Hysteria*, Freud still followed the model of the clinical case where

---

27. Freud, *Dora*, 10n3.
28. Sigmund Freud, "From the History of an Infantile Neurosis [The 'Wolfman']," in *The 'Wolfman' and Other Cases*, trans. Louise Adey Huish (New York: Penguin, 2003), 211.

he started with the symptoms and, as he writes in the preface to the Dora case, "aimed at clearing them up one after the other."[29] Since then, however, he found this method to be inadequate in facing the structure of the neurosis and he abandoned it in favor of a more refined technique: "I now let the patient himself choose the subject of the day's work, and in that way I start out from whatever surface his unconscious happens to be presenting to his notice at the moment. But on this plan everything that has to do with the clearing-up of a particular symptom emerges piecemeal, woven into various contexts, and distributed over widely separated periods of time. In spite of this apparent disadvantage, the new technique is far superior to the old, and indeed there can be no doubt that it is the only possible one."[30]

As a result of this new technique, Freud's cases appear to be incomplete, piecemeal, and fragmentary. Instead of creating coherence, they are disruptive, they break apart connections and align themselves with the generation of inconsistencies and gaps, in which shall become manifest what Freud refers to as the "necessary correlate of the symptoms . . . which is theoretically requisite."[31] Thus, when Freud publishes the Dora case as "Fragment of an Analysis of Hysteria," he not only alludes to the incompleteness of this specific analysis because of Dora's decision not to continue with the treatment. In fact, the title designates the essential technique of psychoanalysis for the composition of case histories. A preliminary conclusion could therefore be that the literary genre that Freud's cases are fundamentally based on is not so much the novella as the fragment.

Literary Modernism and Psychoanalysis

On the occasion of Freud's seventieth birthday, the literary author and medical doctor Alfred Döblin, congratulated him with a speech

---

29. Freud, *Dora*, 6.
30. Freud, *Dora*, 6–7.
31. Freud, *Dora*, 11.

in which he also addressed the connection between psychoanalysis and literary fiction. Döblin refers to Freud's novella/case analogy to demonstrate how psychoanalysis profited from adapting literary forms and by drawing knowledge from the realm of literature. Döblin, however, rejects the popular opinion that Freud had influenced literary fiction: "One has suggested that Freud's depth psychology would be followed by a depth poetry. Complete nonsense! Dostojewski still lived before Freud, Ibsen and Strindberg wrote before Freud. And we certainly know that Freud himself learned from them and used them as evidence."[32] In other contexts, Döblin is more generous when it comes to evaluating the psychoanalytic impact on modern literature. For instance, he refers to psychoanalytic technique as an important influence for rejecting criticism that he had adapted the literary style of *Berlin Alexanderplatz* from James Joyce. In fact, psychoanalysis undoubtedly had a great impact on modernist prose, and Thomas Anz convincingly claims in a 1997 research report on psychoanalysis and literary modernism that twentieth-century literary history could not be appropriately understood without the history of the reception of psychoanalysis.[33] But Anz also emphasizes the differences and quotes Robert Musil: "Literature differs from psychology, as literature differs from science.... The difference itself is simple: literature does not communicate knowledge and cognition. But: literature makes use of knowledge and cognition."[34] Even where psychoanalytic insights inform the production of literary fiction, the literary text does not intend a medical diagnosis or psychological case history.

Considering his influence on modernist literature, it seems remarkable that Freud himself remained committed to a rather

---

32. Alfred Döblin, "Sigmund Freud zum 70. Geburtstage," in *Die Zeitlupe: Kleine Prosa*, ed. Walter Muschg (Olten: Walter Verlag, 1962), 87.

33. See Thomas Anz, "Psychoanalyse in der literarischen Moderne: Ein Forschungsbericht und Projektentwurf," in *Die Literatur und die Wissenschaften 1770–1930*, ed. Karl Richter, Jörg Schönert, and Michael Titzmann (Stuttgart: Metzler, 1997), 377–413.

34. Robert Musil, "Fallengelassenes Vorwort zu: Nachlass zu Lebzeiten–Selbstkritik u–Biogr. [1935]," in *Gesammelte Werke: Prosa und Stücke, Kleine Prosa, Aphorismen, Autobiographisches*, ed. Adolf Frisé (Reinbek bei Hamburg: Rowohlt, 1978), 967.

classical literary concept. The transition from the novella to the fragment for the composition of psychoanalytic cases could be interpreted as paving the way for the transition from realist to modernist prose forms at the turn of the twentieth century. Although this holds true from the perspective of many modernist authors who refer to psychoanalysis as one of their major influences, it means giving too much credit to Freud to attribute to him the role of godfather of literary modernism. For Freud, the fragment is not an independent and self-contained literary form. Instead, it signals the incompleteness of the narrative and is supposed to support psychological cognition. The fragment is characterized by a deficiency, and in Freud's psychotherapeutic setup the neurosis is mastered when the analyst succeeds in making the patient familiar with her own history. In the parlance of literary history one feels reminded of Goethe's famous saying that Classicism is an expression of health whereas Romanticism is one of disease.[35] The completeness and closure of the narrative remains the ultimate goal of psychoanalysis, and this is where it differs from both the Romantic notion of literature and that of the early twentieth century.

In conclusion, literary authors adapted from psychoanalysis the fragmentary forms of writing without, however, subscribing to its dedication to completion and the notion of a *healthy* narrative. Modernist forms of writing exhibit the futility of such an endeavor and have indeed quite successfully shown that every story rests on a foundation that is in itself contingent and by no means provides a stable and readily available ground of meaning. When modernist authors at the beginning of the twentieth century keep producing literary case histories by following the literary tradition of referencing historically authentic cases, they no longer aim at displaying coherency and stability. Instead they exhibit the fragmentary, contingent, and indissoluble character of an individual history that escapes the rational attempts to contain it by means of scientific precision. In the literary context of the early twentieth century, a case

---

35. "Das Klassische nenne ich das Gesunde und das Romantische das Kranke." (Johann Peter Eckermann, *Gespräche mit Goethe*, ed. Ernst Beutler [München: dtv, 1976], 332.)

no longer appears as a case of a general order of things, but it is precisely this connection that modernist forms of writing intend to dissolve and expose in its arbitrariness.

Freud's psychoanalytic technique is still based on the promise of the cultural institution of literature since Goethe; he remains indebted to the *dispositif* of *Bildung*, according to which one reaches the status of a responsible subject when one masters one's own history by means of narrative. Even in his most fragmented case histories, Freud still follows the model of the *Bildungsroman*, which tells the story of how one became what one always was already. At the same time, however, Freud's cases demonstrate the work and discipline that are necessary to successfully gain control over one's own history and life, and thus offer insight into the formal conditions of this complicated endeavor.

10

FANTASY OF FACTS

Döblin's Poetics of Uncertainty

Outsiders of Society

"This is how it happened; even the protagonists believe it. But it also did not happen this way."[1] This paradoxical comment concludes Alfred Döblin's literary case history, *The Two Girlfriends and Their Murder by Poisoning*; it is also a literary agenda. For it demonstrates, on the one hand, the limits of narrative representation, and claims, on the other, new responsibilities for literary authors. Döblin's adaptation of the case of Elli Klein, who was accused together with her girlfriend, Grete Nebbe, of having poisoned her husband, appeared only a few months after the sensational trial of the women had been concluded. The literary case history was pub-

---

1. Alfred Döblin, *Die beiden Freundinnen und ihr Giftmord* (Düsseldorf: Artemis & Winkler, 2001), 79.

lished in 1924 as the first volume of a series that the communist and poet Rudolf Leonhard initiated under the title *Outsiders of Society: The Crimes of Today* in collaboration with the Berlin publishing house *Die Schmiede*. Leonhard managed to solicit a number of well-known authors to observe and document some of the most spectacular criminal trials. Overall, fourteen volumes were published between 1924 and 1925 before the series was discontinued for financial reasons. The fourteen books, however, covered a wide range of different trials. Ernst Weiß's *Der Fall Vukobrankovic* presented another case of murder by poison; Theodor Lessing documented the trial of the serial killer Fritz Haarmann; and Egon Erwin Kisch contributed a short book about Generalstabchef Redl, a homosexual Austrian colonel who spied for the Russian secret service. Although the *Outsider* series aimed at critically rethinking the possibilities of the genre of the criminal case history, its authors basically did nothing other than what criminologists and other professionals in penal matters do: they attentively listened to the stories of the defendants and meticulously read letters, diaries, newspapers, and expert opinions, in order to write a story that contributed to an understanding of the case. For this, the Berlin lawyer Heinrich Lindenau reviewed and praised the book series as "an unprecedented attempt to put the artistic intuition into service of criminal-psychological research."[2]

Scholarship has mostly seen the *Outsider* series in the tradition of the *Pitaval*, but has also emphasized its critical stance toward criminology and medical-forensic approaches to crime. Joachim Linder, for example, highlights the subversive potential of the book series and argues that it decisively breaks with Pitaval's realism and claim of authenticity.[3] Stefan Andriopoulos, on the other hand,

---

2. Heinrich Lindenau, "Außenseiter der Gesellschaft," *Deutsche Juristen-Zeitung* 31 (1926): 1656.
3. See Joachim Linder, "'Sie müssen das entschuldigen, Herr Staatsanwalt, aber es ist so: wir trauen euch nicht...' Strafjustiz, Strafrechtsreform und Justizkritik im *März*, 1907–1911," in *Erzählte Kriminalität: Zur Typologie und Funktion von narrativen Darstellungen in Strafrechtspflege, Publizistik und Literatur zwischen 1790 und 1920*, ed. Jörg Schönert (Tübingen: Niemeyer, 1991), 533–570.

sees a rhetorical complicity of the literary cases with their legal models.[4] As the opening case of the *Outsider* series, Döblin's short book can be seen as a precedent, doing justice to both positions that either emphasize the series' critical or rather reactionary character. With his double identity as a trained, practicing medical doctor with a pronounced interest in psychiatry and psychoanalysis and as a literary author, Döblin embodies the connection at stake in the series and seems an ideal representative of its program. This fact did not go unnoticed at the time of publication of Döblin's contribution. One of the first critics wrote: "Here, we are dealing not with three people, but five. The three involved in the trial, and then the writer Döblin and the doctor Döblin."[5] And another review, published in the psychoanalytic journal *Imago*, reads: "It is a fortunate fact that Döblin unites the doctor and the poet in one person."[6]

The Case of Elli Klein and Grete Nebbe

Between March 12 and 16, 1923, the case of two women was presented to the court in Berlin. Twenty-three-year-old Elli Klein and her friend Grete Nebbe were accused of murdering Elli's husband. Investigations for the trial reconstructed the following story. In 1919 Elli met the carpenter Willi Klein in Berlin and married him one year later. Together they shared an apartment with Willi's mother, and the marriage appeared doomed from the beginning. During the in-

---

4. See Stefan Andriopoulos, *Unfall und Verbrechen: Konfigurationen zwischen juristischem und literarischem Diskurs um 1900* (Wiesbaden: Springer Verlag, 1996), 93–95.

5. Hans Siemsen, *Die Weltbühne* 21, no. 1 (1925): 360–361, in Döblin, *Alfred Döblin im Spiegel der zeitgenössischen Kritik*, ed. Ingrid Schuster and Ingrid Bode (Bern: Franke Verlag, 1973), 158.

6. "Ein glücklicher Umstand, daß in Döblin der Arzt und Dichter in einer Person vereinigt sind. Er sieht mit dem Auge des Arztes, mit sicherem Blick erfaßt er die Dynamik der Triebe, die entscheidenden Konflikte, die kritischen Situationen. Und er hat die Einstellung des Arztes für das Herausfinden des Verschobenen, Veränderten im Seelischen. Was der Arzt gesehen hat, das erzählt hier der Dichter mit der blitzartig beleuchtenden Präzision seiner großen, sicheren Sprachkraft" (Gerö, *Imago* 14 [1928]: 524–525, in Döblin, *Alfred Döblin im Spiegel der zeitgenössischen Kritik*, 159).

terrogations related to the trial, Elli reported on being hated by her mother-in-law and about the disgusting impertinences committed by her husband. After six months she tried to escape and asked for protection from her parents, who did nothing and sent her back. Nothing changed after this incident. In her testimony during the trial, Elli recounted daily sexual assaults and physical abuses, and her mother, who insisted that Elli stay with her husband, admitted that she had been aware of this.

In 1921 Elli met Grete Nebbe, who was also stuck in an unhappy marriage, but unlike Elli had found support from her mother, who began treating Elli as if she were her own daughter. A close friendship developed between the three women, and soon Elli and Grete fell in love with each other. Secretly, they sent numerous letters to each other every day. These letters, more than six hundred in less than a year, were of great importance during the trial, where they were treated as evidence not only of the murder itself but also of the homosexual relationship between the two women.

In January 1922 Elli left her husband again and moved to her own apartment in Berlin. But her parents were able to convince her to return to her husband, who had promised to reform. Elli wanted to believe him and she returned, but soon found herself in the same unfortunate situation. After considering suicide she began thinking about an alternative solution. She bought arsenic, which was sold in pharmacies for the purpose of poisoning rats, and mixed small doses in her husband's food. In her letters she told Grete about her plan, and during the following weeks, the deed became a means of proving her love to her friend. On April 1 the poison produced its desired effect. Willi Klein was brought to the hospital where he died on the same day. His mother, however, suspected her daughter-in-law of being involved in the death of her son and sent the police to pursue her. In May 1922 Elli Klein and Grete Nebbe were arrested and charged with conspiracy to murder Willi Klein.

After the arrest, extensive investigations began. Medical experts were instructed to give their opinion on the lethality of arsenic, its effects on the human body, and the symptoms of poisoning. Three psychiatrists, one of them the famous sexologist Magnus Hirschfeld, were asked to examine the psychological state of the defendants.

The three expert reports read as if they had not been based on the same case. One expert emphasized the inhuman perfidiousness of the two women, whereas his colleagues pictured them as inculpable victims of male brutality.[7]

In March 1923 the case was finally brought to court. The trial generated intense public interest.[8] The press covered the trial in detail. On the second day, the letters were read in the courtroom and attracted a great deal of attention. Their content was widely considered evidence for the premeditated nature of the crime and led to the conclusion that Elli was not merely the victim of her husband's brutality, but a coldblooded killer. The letters show the "total amorality of her nature," the *Deutsche Allgemeine Zeitung* wrote and concluded: "All these letters express a limitless cruelty, a crudity of the heart, and an attitude that one could never have considered possible."[9] The letters were also considered evidence of Elli's homosexual relationship with Grete and provided grounds for identifying sexual motives for the murder. "The last word in this case," the *Vorwärts* concluded, "should be given to sexology rather than to psychiatry."[10]

The case of the two women seemed to confirm what sexologists and criminologists had determined to be the typical female crime. The perfidiousness, the disingenuousness, the cunning, and the hypocrisy they had applied to the crime of poisoning were seen as typical female attributes deriving from a specific female sexuality. In his 1917 *Psychology of Murder by Poisoning*, the criminologist, legal scholar, and author of crime novels Erich Wulffen presented the female murder by poisoning as the equivalent of the male crime of *Lustmord* (sex murder),[11] an assessment supported by the 1930 *Bilder-Lexikon der Sexualwissenschaft*, where one can read: "In

---

7. A detailed discussion of the expert opinions in this case can be found in Hania Siebenpfeiffer, *Böse Lust: Gewaltverbrechen in Diskursen der Weimarer Republik* (Cologne: Böhlau, 2005), 111–117.

8. Hania Siebenpfeiffer has reconstructed the coverage of the trial in her book *Böse Lust*, 104–111.

9. "Die Giftmischerinnen," *Deutsche Allgemeine Zeitung*, March 14, 1923.

10. "Der Prozeß der Giftmischerinnen," *Vorwärz*, March 15, 1923.

11. See Erich Wulffen, *Psychologie des Giftmordes* (Vienna: Urania, 1917).

most cases, female poisoners suffer from a sexually pathological disposition. The murder by poisoning represents the *Lustmord* of a woman, who uses this method due to a lack of physical strength."[12]

When the court finally rendered its judgment and sentenced Elli Klein to four years in prison, and her friend Grete Nebbe to one and a half years in the penitentiary, public outrage was the result. The reason was not that the penalty did not seem appropriate for the crime, but that it did not account sufficiently for the pathological constitution of the murderesses. If the murder had been pathologically determined and if it could be attributed to a sexually degenerate instinct, a few years in prison would neither change the women nor sufficiently protect society from further crimes they would be ready to commit once released. And yet one can also find the opposite reaction. Only a few days after the judgment was rendered, Robert Musil commented on the case in a short essay, in which he concludes: "Against the background of cases like this, one should ask more than ever how far society is guilty by not preventing it before it is too late. Indeed, an energetic criminal contains more bad than a good person, but also more seeds of the good, says J[ohn]. St[uart]. Mill."[13]

In contrast to Musil, Alfred Döblin does not take a clear position in his literary adaptation of the case. But he also does not content himself with merely reconstructing the case and providing insight into the psychological history of the protagonists. Instead, he questions the representational means by which psychologists and novelists offer their contribution to an understanding of criminality in particular, and the human condition in general. In a review of the best books of 1924, Robert Musil praises Döblin's literary treatment of the case: "Indeed, one can analyze psychologically, but it is impossible to reconstruct from these elements; something remains, the unsystematic, the actual, the specific composition, the fate, the

---

12. *Bilder-Lexikon der Sexualwissenschaft* (Hamburg: Institut für Sexualforschung, 1961), 344.
13. Robert Musil, "Das verbrecherische Liebespaar: Die Geschichte zweier unglücklicher Ehen [20. März 1923]," in *Gesammelte Werke: Prosa und Stücke, Kleine Prosa, Aphorismen, Autobiographisches*, ed. Adolf Frisé (Reinbek bei Hamburg: Rowohlt, 1978), 671.

contingent, and hence the individual: it is this for which Döblin in a totally objective and unsentimental way has found emotionally touching possibilities of expression in this small piece of work."[14] Following Musil's assessment of Döblin's approach to the case, my reading focuses on the poetological debate to which Döblin's case history contributes, which results in nothing short of the request for a reevaluation of the cognitive and critical potential of narrative literature.

Döblin's Casuistry

In *The Two Girlfriends and Their Murder by Poisoning*, Alfred Döblin does not content himself with merely telling the unfortunate story of the crime and its investigation. The short book consists of four parts, the first and most comprehensive being the case history itself, written in the documentary style of a report. It is followed by an outline of the case referring to seventeen tables that Döblin describes as "a topographic presentation of the development of the soul," which can be found as an attachment to the first edition. This is followed by a brief epilogue in which Döblin sums up the case and questions the ability of casuistic representation to provide a comprehensive understanding of human behavior. Yet even this critical epilogue is not the end of the book, not its final word. Instead, Döblin closes with two samples of Elli's and Grete's handwriting that he undertakes to analyze by means of graphology.

The initial case history presents the historical development from Elli's unhappy marriage to the trial, and thereby follows the psychological standards that Döblin, a former student of the psychiatrist Alfred Hoche and a practicing neurologist, was certainly familiar with. Döblin does not focus on the crime itself, but pays exclusive attention to the psychological development of the protag-

---

14. Robert Musil, "[Bemerkenswerte Bücher] Almanach auf das Jahr 1925 mit den dreihundertfünfundsechzig Geschenkbüchern überreicht von der Hellerischen Buchhandlung (Wien I)," in *Gesammelte Werke: Essays und Reden: Kritik* (Reinbek bei Hamburg: Rowohlt, 1978), 1715.

onists, and he does not shy away from generalizing interpretations. Elli is pictured as a boy-like girl,[15] naive and sexually immature, whereas her husband is characterized by a heightened sexual drive that hopelessly seeks satisfaction. Familial heredity and degenerative dispositions are offered as explanations for his brutal behavior against his wife.[16] Elli, however, develops from a tomboy into the active partner in her relationship with Grete, and she becomes the driving force in the conspiracy against her husband. In accordance with contemporary studies on female homosexuality, Döblin attributes to Elli specifically masculine features to explain her active role. He writes: "Elli's activity, her male decisiveness fell on sexual ground and took a dangerous direction."[17] In fact, although Döblin also presents the detailed circumstances of the murder, his explanations are exclusively based on the level of sexual drives and natural dispositions. On account of this, the tragic progression of the story appears to be unavoidably determined, and the question of guilt is systematically eliminated. Döblin's case history thereby anticipates the question that dominated the trial of the two women. As he later

---

15. The opening paragraph of Döblin's case history alludes to her boyishness: "Es passierte ihr ein kleiner Bubenstreich" (Döblin, *Die beiden Freundinnen*, 5).

16. "Immer deutlicher drängte sich um diese Zeit in das Leben und durch das Leben dieses Mannes das Schicksal seines Vaters, der mit Erhängen geendet hatte. Je mehr er verfiel, umso mehr wurde er Beute, Darstellungsmittel dieses alten Schicksals. Er war um diese Zeit auch ohne Zutun der Frau auf dem Weg des Todes. Seine Zerrüttung war enorm. Die Zeichen epileptischer Entartung traten hervor.

"Sein geschlechtlicher Drang war gesteigert. Er suchte häufiger und intensiver sich und die Frau zu erniedrigen. Er lockte sie wieder und trieb sie in die finstere Haßsphäre. Erregte in ihr diese Triebe, die sich dann furchtbar gegen ihn selbst richten sollten. Es war im Grunde sein eigener Haßtrieb, der ihn später umbrachte. Er mußte in ihrem Leib wühlen, Sinnlichkeit aus jeder Hautfalte herausfühlen. Er hatte den Drang, sie unbildlich, fast körperlich zu verschlingen. Es war kein bloßes Wort, wenn er ihr in der wilden Verschlingung sagte: er müsse ihren Kot haben, er müsse ihn essen, verschlucken. Das kam in der Trunkenheit vor, aber auch ohne den Alkohol. Es war einmal Selbstpeitschung, Unterwerfung, Kasteiung, Buße für die eigene Minderwertigkeit und Schlechtigkeit. Es war auch ein Heilungsversuch dieses Minderwertigkeitsgefühls: durch Beseitigung des Mehrwertigen, Unabhängig davon die wilde Lust, Mordwut, in bestialische Zärtlichkeit gehüllt" (Döblin, *Die beiden Freundinnen*, 35).

17. Döblin, *Die beiden Freundinnen*, 29.

summarizes: "In every case, it was not the deed that stood in the center, the poisoning itself, but rather the opposite of a deed: namely how this course of events came to be, how it was possible. Indeed, one set out to demonstrate how this event was unavoidable. One was not even playing on the field of guilt and innocence any longer, but on a very different one, the awfully precarious field of coherences, cognition, and understanding" (Döblin 99–100).

In his reconstruction of the case, Döblin realizes what the psychological method demands: the complete recording of psychological circumstances from which one can retroactively deduce the predictability of the crime. In this regard, the literary case history of the two girlfriends is no less astounding than statistical calculation, as Döblin claims later in the epilogue:

> Overlooking the whole, it is just like in the story "a wind came and knocked down the tree." I don't know what kind of wind it was and where it came from. The whole thing is tapestry, made up of many individual scraps, cloth, silk, even pieces of metal and clumps of clay. It is stuffed with straw, wire, and yarn and in many places the pieces are not bound together. Nevertheless, everything is consistent and bears the stamp of truth. It has become part of our customary processes of thinking and feeling. This is how it happened; even the protagonists believe it. But it also did not happen this way. (Döblin 112)

Döblin sums up his case history by vehemently questioning the principles of causality with which such narratives aim to provide explanations. This is how it happened, and at the same time it is not. Döblin leaves it at that and does not approach the question that the legal court was tasked with: Could it have been different? Up for discussion here are neither the question of accountability nor the astounding laws of probability, but the representational means of comprehension:

> At first, there are the awfully ambiguous words one has to use for the description of such processes and correlations. Faded and washed-out things everywhere, often palpably childish. The sweepingly stupid words for the description of emotional reactions: affinity, aversion, repulsion, love, feeling of vengeance. A mishmash and disorder, made for daily

communicational use.... The danger of these words is always that one believes in their ability to contribute to our understanding; but, thereby, they obstruct access to the facts. No chemist would work with such unpurified substances. By presenting us with such biographies many times, newspaper reports and novels have significantly contributed to us being satisfied with these empty words. Most psychological analyses are nothing but novelistic fictions. (Döblin 113)

The facts threaten to vanish behind the discursivity of the event. Words only obscure what they are supposed to explain. And even Döblin's own reconstruction of the case remains on a level of representation that is based on already established forms from which the truth of the event shall be deduced. But instead of trusting these words and attributing to them a value of truth, one needs to "take for granted the facts of the case, the letters, [and] actions, and must systematically refuse any objective explanation" (Döblin 112).

An Epistolary Case

From the perspective of the epilogue, the case of the two girlfriends appears to be a discursive construct, a coherent text made from heterogeneous material. Against this background, Döblin's case history can be read as criticism of criminological forms of representation. It is, however, not the self-reflexive epilogue with which the first volume of the *Outsider* series ends, but yet another attachment: two samples of the women's handwriting that Döblin attempts to analyze graphologically. This analysis confirms and supports the results of the case narrative: "Elli's handwriting more disturbing, more dangerous despite her neat and bourgeois attitude. Margarete sociable and weak despite her brusque and impulsive appearance" (Döblin app.). Even after the publication of his book, the interpretation of the handwriting samples still occupied Döblin's mind. He asked Ludwig Klages, whose study *Handschrift und Charakter* had been published a few years earlier in 1917, for his expert opinion: "I had to analyze and present a criminal case.... I have attached two handwriting samples, one from each of the two offenders, and added a few comments myself. The case itself is somehow obscure. (There are two homosexual women; they poisoned the husband of one of them; they attempted to poison the husband of the other; who was the active one?) I would like to ask you: would you take a look at the small book, consider the facts, and then tell me what you think about the handwriting . . . in terms of graphology."[18] Döblin's insistence on clarifying the question as to which of the two women had been the more active one, confirms his intention to find an explanation for the case. He does not critically question the medical-legal explanatory models according to which Elli's active dominance indicates *sexual inversion*. It is the means to arrive at these explanations, the purity of the material, that is up for discussion.

Döblin's criticism is based on a critique of language and a fundamental skepticism regarding the signifying function of words and concepts as not suited to penetrate the things themselves and to depict what really happened. That is why the graphological analysis of the women's handwriting uses the materiality of writing as another mode of scientific examination. In a somewhat twisted way, Döblin seems to hit the mark in the case when he considers writing not simply a carrier of meaning that needs to be extracted in interpretation, but rather a fact per se, a *Tat-Sache*, literally a matter of deed. In the case of Elli Klein and Grete Nebbe, the written text precedes the chain of events. The two women only put into action what they had drafted before in their letters. Against this background, it seems obvious to treat the letters as deeds themselves. However, if words are in fact deeds, then the narrative logic of events in cases becomes radically unstable. One leaves behind the sphere of realist storytelling that creates rational plots within a space defined by sovereign individuals and their actions.[19] In contrast, the murder of Elli's husband occurs in a space that is defined by the act of writing:

---

18. Alfred Döblin, "An Ludwig Klages 23.12.1924," in Döblin, *Briefe* (Olten: Walter Verlag, 1970), 126.

19. See Wolfgang Schäffner, "Psychiatrische Erfahrung und Literatur: Antihermeneutik bei Alfred Döblin," in *Alfred Döblin-Kolloquien Münster 1989*, ed. Werner Stauffacher (Marbach: Peter Lang, 1993), 44–56.

> The writing of letters, this peculiar writing of letters, began between the two women, who lived on the same street, saw each other on a daily basis, and during the short periods of absence still had to continue their conversation, their efforts and defense. The lover and the beloved, the chaser and the chased were taking hold of each other. First, they did not write much. Then they found pleasure in writing. They noticed that in the absence of the other there was something special in pursuing the game that is called friendship, chase, love. It was something strangely exciting, a sweet secrecy. Partly conscious, partly unconscious, they continued on this path in writing. . . . The letters seemed to be a means for mutual support, the conspiracy against the husbands, and at the same time, specifically an instrument of self-intoxication. They spurred each other on, calmed each other down, and deceived the other. The letters were a big step on the path toward new secrecy.[20]

According to Döblin's description, the letter writing sets in motion a dynamic in which writing and acting produce one another and in which the murder is dramatically inscribed. The husband's poisoning no longer appears to be the result of a conspiracy that was rationally and coldbloodedly planned. Rather, in Döblin's presentation, the women's letters create a poetic order of the deed that cannot be attributed to individual agents in control of the narrative or even of language itself. Far from authoring their own lives by means of writing, the two women seem to be carried away by the power of the words they address to each other. The truth of these words is not revealed by their meaning but by their effects; the women act on the basis of a language that lacks referential validity, and its effects cannot be reduced to the intention of an individual agent.

Thus, every attempt to contribute to an understanding of the crime by means of hermeneutic practices leads to arbitrary results. "Not even by going deeper into the case," Döblin writes in the epilogue, "would anything have happened" (Döblin 112). Instead of depth psychology, he suggests a topographical model that bypasses personal entities and instead maps a field of connections, effects and intensities. The "Topographic Presentation of the Development of the Soul" presents what Döblin claims to have learned when he "contemplated over the three, four people involved in this affair":

---

20. Döblin, *Die beiden Freundinnen*, 28–29.

> The life or the phase of an individual human being cannot be understood by itself. Humans symbiotically relate with others and other beings. Touch each other, approach each other, and grow on each other. This already is a reality: the symbiosis with others and also with apartments, houses, streets, places. I consider this a certain, although obscure truth. Picking a single individual, it is as if I look at a leaf or a joint of a finger when attempting to describe its nature and development. But they cannot be captured like this; the branch, the tree, or the hand and the animal must also be described. (Döblin 114)

This is a clear rejection of the logic of the case that derives an event's cause from an individual agent and sacrifices complexity for narrative causality. Although the topographic presentation that Döblin attaches does not itself claim scientific plausibility, it nevertheless shows the attempt to implement the critique from the epilogue and to suggest models alternative to that of narrative causality with its vanishing point of the responsible and sovereign individual. Similarly, the graphological approach to the women's handwriting neither focuses on the letters' content nor attempts to judge their authors' intention. Döblin's interest is directed toward what is unintentional about the act of writing and suited to undermining the hermeneutical practices of psychological understanding.

Away from the Human!

Döblin openly criticizes the narrative model of psychological casuistry for the naiveté and credulity with which it proceeds and influences institutional decisions, but he presents an alternative model in the epilogue to his book that he considers more appropriate and that, I argue, defines new standards for literary fiction: "Chemistry has very concrete ideas about the ways and degrees to which substances react to each other. There are laws of mass actions, a doctrine of affinity, specific affinity coefficients. Reactions occur with different speeds that can be precisely determined; substances become active under specific circumstances; accurately studied balances are established. Here, substances and their behavior toward each other are studied properly; all influences are controlled and detected. This method is good" (Döblin 116).

But what could this possibly mean for literature? It is useful to return to a short text that is clearly connected to the 1924 case study, the so-called *Berlin Program*, which Döblin published in 1913 under the title *To Novelists and Their Critics*. Here, Döblin already intends to show a way out of psychological prose. "One must learn from psychiatry," he writes, "the only science that captures the psychic human life in its entirety. It has long recognized the naiveté of psychology and confines itself to noting affective reactions and movements, and shrugs its shoulders at anything further, the 'whys' and 'hows.'"[21] In a study on Döblin's "poetology of knowledge," Wolfgang Schäffner has shown that Döblin is indeed aware of the newest contemporary developments of psychiatry, which, around 1910, had discovered metabolism to be the pivotal influence on human behavior.[22] Against the background of the case of the two women, it is interesting to note that contemporary research on homosexuality experimented with hormones and their influence on human glands. In his *Berlin Program*, Döblin gives an impression of how he imagines a literature that follows this biochemical psychiatric model. First and foremost, this new kind of literature must not arrange a plot and must not narrate. According to the psychiatric method of merely noting observed reactions and movements, Döblin's ideal novel must limit its use of words, arrange for a rapid course of action, and subvert its own organization with catchwords. He calls this literary method a "Kinostil," a *kinematic style*, in which the phenomena must flash by in a highly compact and precise way, and in which "the whole must not appear as spoken but as present." The consequence of this depsychologization of the novel is "the relinquishing of the author, depersonalization." Döblin thus rejects

---

21. Alfred Döblin, "An Romanautoren und ihre Kritiker: Berliner Programm" (1913), in *Schriften zu Ästhetik, Poetik und Literatur* (Olten: Walter Verlag, 1989), 121.
22. See Wolfgang Schäffner, *Die Ordnung des Wahns. Zur Poetologie psychiatrischen Wissens bei Alfred Döblin* (München: Fink, 1995), 214.

what had been constitutive for the genre of the modern novel from the beginning of its historical appearance: the inner history of man and the constitution of the sovereign individual. Certainly, Döblin is aware of this provocation when he calls on the addressees of his programmatic essay, the novelists and their critics, to get rid of the human: "Away from the human! Have courage for kinetic fantasy, and for recognizing the amazingly real contours! Fantasy of facts!"[23]

It would be an exaggeration to claim that Döblin's 1924 case history implemented this literary program. Yet the book exhibits the connection between novelistic storytelling and psychological cognition and demonstrates their effects on institutional processes of decision making. Döblin writes that he wanted "to show the difficulties of the case ... and to question the impression that one understood everything or at least most things about such a massive chunk of life." Indeed, "we understand it," he adds, "on a certain level."[24]

What is important here, however, is that Döblin discusses the representation of an authentic criminal case on the level of a poetological program that is supposed to contribute to a modern reevaluation of literature and, more precisely, to the transformation of literary fiction from a model of novelistic and psychological narrative to a psychiatric and media-technological system of recording.[25] In *The Two Girlfriends and Their Murder by Poisoning*, Döblin attempts to break with the literary tradition of psychological storytelling and to transform it into a poetics of contingency in which what does not comply with the laws of reason and escapes the order of self-determining subjectivity can find expression. By juxtaposing the different forms of interpretation in his small book, Döblin undermines their exclusive claims to authority. There is the case narrative itself; the self-reflexive and critical epilogue; the letters that not only can be read but also graphologically studied; and finally, seventeen tables depicting the mental development of the

---

23. Döblin, "An Romanautoren und ihre Kritiker," 121–123.
24. Döblin, *Die beiden Freundinnen*, 117.
25. In reference to Friedrich Kittler's famous book it would be appropriate to use the term *Aufschreibesystem* for Döblin's new literary system. See Friedrich Kittler, *Aufschreibesysteme. 1800. 1900* (Munich: Wilhelm Fink, 1985).

protagonists. Each of these representations claims to be true or at least to contribute to the understanding of the case, but their juxtaposition results in a representation of uncertainty that exceeds the concern about the two women's legal sentences, which caused such public outrage. Instead, it applies more generally to the means and operations through which both public and institutional judgments are formed.

Although it is true that Döblin's little book criticizes the characterological means of criminal psychology, his literary project is still indebted to the search for motives. Döblin does not abandon the truth claim of literature altogether. He simply locates it on a different level, that of chemical reactions and energetic processes. In a short autobiographical essay of 1927 titled "Doctor and Poet," Döblin makes a claim that must be taken seriously not only for the doctor but also for the poet Döblin: "I felt that psychological analysis was not sufficient. One must examine the body, but not the brains, rather the endocrine glands, the metabolism."[26] We also find this biochemical model in the 1924 case history, where it supports Döblin's request that literature give up depicting individual characters and personality profiles in favor of impersonal and material descriptions of affective reactions. It seems plausible to recognize in Döblin's poetological program of a *fantasy of facts* the same pathos of coldness and distance that we found at the outset in Karl Philipp Moritz's call for *Fakta*, and in Schiller's request for *cold* storytelling. Döblin's literary program, however, does not result in a naive form of realism. It is better understood as a poetics of contingency that produces uncertainty in regard to the precarious question of judgment, and thus directly affects our belief in our means of cognition and understanding.

---

26. Alfred Döblin, "Arzt und Dichter: Merkwürdiger Lebenslauf eines Autors," in *Autobiographische Schriften und Aufzeichnungen*, ed. Edgar Pässler (Olten: Walter Verlag, 1980), 25.

11

THE MAN OF POSSIBILITIES

Musil's Moosbrugger

Qualitativelessness

In the 1920s and 1930s, Robert Musil's literary production also follows the formula of contingency, which the protagonist of his novel *The Man without Qualities* connects with the "principle of insufficient cause." One of the central objectives of this sprawling text is to take this principle seriously and to make it the basis for a literary program that would surpass the representation of the real world with the realization of the possible one. The protagonist Ulrich specifies the principle of insufficient cause in a conversation with the banker Leo Fischel: "I give you my solemn word that neither I nor anyone else knows what 'the true' is; but I can assure you it is on the point of realisation."[1]

---

1. Robert Musil, *The Man without Qualities*, vol. 1, trans. Sophie Wilkins (New York: Vintage, 1995), 141.

It is one of the major differences between Döblin and Musil's poetologies that Döblin's literary program is centered around facts and based on a material foundation, but Musil's novel is interested in that which is possible. To Döblin's call for a fantasy of facts Musil responds with the concept of fantastic precision (*phantastische Genauigkeit*). And whereas Döblin demands from literature to get closer to reality,[2] Musil claims in an interview of 1926 that he is not interested "in the real explanation of real events."[3] In fact, Döblin's and Musil's realism can be distinguished by the opposite direction of their reference to reality. Whereas Döblin attempts to depict its specific composition, Musil's writing practices the decomposition of mere reality by attempting to capture the eventfulness of the event, its singularity. And yet, much more than Döblin, Musil remains indebted to the literary tradition. Döblin bids farewell to the human, but Musil announces the invention of the inner man.[4] When it comes to the implementation of their literary programs, however, it is Musil who seems to be more accomplished in regard to modern forms of writing.

To this effect, at the beginning of *The Man without Qualities* a decision is announced that has serious consequences for the genre of the novel: the protagonist Ulrich takes time off from life. Ever since Blanckenburg's first theory of the novel, Goethe's *Wilhelm Meister's Apprenticeship*, and Schlegel's *Letter about the Novel*, the

---

2. "Der wirklich Produktive ... muß zwei Schritte tun: er muß ganz nah an die Realität heran, an ihre Sachlichkeit, ihr Blut, ihren Geruch, und dann hat er die Sache zu durchstoßen, einige Oberflächen der Realität.... Denn wie denkt man die Realität zu durchstoßen, wenn man keine Anstalten trifft und auch oft kein Vermögen hat, die Realität anzupacken." (Alfred Döblin, "Der Bau des epischen Werkes," in *Aufsätze zur Literatur* [Olten: Walter Verlag, 1963], 107.) For a discussion of Döblin's realism, see Walter Delabar, "Experimente mit dem modernen Erzählen: Skizze zu den Rahmenbedingungen von Alfred Döblins Romanwerk bis 1933," in *Realistisches Schreiben in der Weimarer Republik*, ed. Sabine Kyora and Stefan Neuhaus (Würzburg: Königshausen & Neumann, 2006), 123–138.

3. Robert Musil, "Was arbeiten Sie? Gespräch mit Robert Musil [30. April 1926]," in *Gesammelte Werke: Prosa und Stücke, Kleine Prosa, Aphorismen, Autobiographisches*, ed. Adolf Frisé (Reinbek bei Hamburg: Rowohlt, 1978), 939.

4. See Robert Musil, "Skizze der Erkenntnis des Dichters [1918]," in *Gesammelte Werke: Essays und Reden: Kritik*, ed. Adolf Frisé (Reinbek bei Hamburg: Rowohlt, 1978), 1028.

genre's form was considered to align itself with that of life, and by doing so it offered evidence for the assumption that life could be thought of in terms of form.[5] "Vacation from life" must be understood as a fundamental step in the conception of Musil's novel that takes leave of the tradition of storytelling and replaces the principle of pragmatic narrative and its focus on causality with that of insufficient cause and its modus of contingency.

In regard to the novelistic parameters of subjectivity and individuality, Musil introduces the concept of *qualitativelessness*, which reacts to the characterological, psychological, and, more generally, disciplinary appropriation of personal identities.[6] In a conversation with his cousin Diotima, Ulrich gives the corresponding assessment of the present status quo: "The self is losing its status as a sovereign making its own laws. We are learning to know the rules by which it develops, the influence of its environment, its structural types, its disappearance in moments of the most intense activity: in short, the laws regulating its formation and its conduct. Think of it, cousin, the laws of personality! . . . What with laws being the most impersonal thing in the world, the personality becomes no more than the imaginary meeting point of all that's impersonal."[7] *Qualitativelessness* can thus be understood as reaction to a form of life that with increasing formalization has become increasingly formless and is only committed to the pragmatism of functionality, efficiency, and calculability. Subtracting individual responsibility from this system, one ends up in a world in which events have no agents and individual lives become uneventful. In other words, the individual's sovereignty to make decisions will be contained in the private sphere. And consequently, the

---

5. On the relation between form and life in the theory of the novel, see Rüdiger Campe, "Form und Leben in der Theorie des Romans," in *Vita Aesthetica: Szenarien ästhetischer Lebendigkeit*, ed. Armen Avanessian, Winfried Menninghaus, and Jan Völker (Berlin: Diaphanes, 2009), 193–211.

6. An interesting scholarly discussion of the program of qualitativelessness informed by psychoanalytic and sociological perspectives can be found in Klaus Laermann, *Eigenschaftslosigkeit: Reflexionen zu Musils Roman "Der Mann ohne Eigenschaften,"* (Stuttgart: Metzler Verlag, 1970).

7. Musil, *Man without Qualities*, 516.

novel as the inner history of the sovereign individual is reduced to the status of a case.

From this perspective, it makes sense that Musil makes use of a criminal case that undermines these distinctions to illustrate his novel's poetological program. The case of the sex murderer Moosbrugger demonstrates the medical-legal attempts to separate the criminal deed from the doer by reducing the event to the motivation of an individual agent. Yet when Moosbrugger's "insubordinate state of being" withstands these efforts to resolve his deed in individual responsibility, his case becomes the venue for competing forms of representation that desperately attempt to protect the human world from the intrusion of the unforeseeable, or, one might say: *the real*. In fact, Musil did not have to invent anything when drafting the Moosbrugger case. As Karl Corino has shown, he modeled the sex murderer after the historical case of Christian Voigt, and could take advantage of the detailed coverage provided by journalistic and criminological reports.[8]

Moosbrugger and Voigt

The case of Christian Voigt can be reconstructed from the historical documents: On the morning of August 14, 1910, the twenty-year-old prostitute Josephine Peer was found dead in the Vienna Prater. Her body was dreadfully disfigured. The autopsy revealed forty-four stabs and cuts with a knife; one of the cuts extended from the right to the left shoulder and had nearly cut off one of her breasts. Another cut began at the belly and made its way through to her back. One week after this horrific discovery, the thirty-two-year-old carpenter Christian Voigt was arrested under strong suspicion of being the wanted murderer. After a few helpless attempts at denial he finally confessed to the deed and did so, as he later specified in court, in order to do the police commissioner a favor.

---

8. See Karl Corino, "Zerstückelt und Durchdunkelt: Der Sexualmörder Moosbrugger im 'Mann ohne Eigenschaften' und sein Modell," *Musil-Forum* 10 (1984): 105–119.

It turned out that eight years earlier, on September 3, 1902, Voigt had committed a similar crime in Lauscha in Thüringen, killing seventeen-year-old Ella Protowsky by repeatedly stabbing her in the throat. The district court in Meiningen had ordered that Voigt be taken into custody, and a medical-forensic evaluation of the murderer was commissioned. This report was provided by the famous psychiatrist Otto Binswanger, who diagnosed Voigt with "clear signs of an epileptic transformation of the character" and "an increase of brute instincts."[9] Accordingly, Binswanger expressed his doubt in the legal responsibility of the subject, and the court dismissed the charge against Voigt, who instead was detained in the insane asylum in Bayreuth, from which he was released as cured in 1909.

In the case of 1910, the situation was much more complicated. Two of the court's medical experts expressed their inability to give a decisive diagnosis. And Voigt himself now claimed that he had only simulated the earlier diagnosed epilepsy, and now insisted on the acknowledgement of his responsibility. But he argued that he had not acted premeditatedly and that the court could only charge him with manslaughter instead of murder. The court ordered another psychiatric evaluation of the defendant, which, on the one hand, concluded that Voigt was "an innately degenerate and predominantly ethically defective individual with a specific affinity toward acts of violence," but stated, on the other hand, that there was no evidence of "an illness or defective consciousness exceeding the limits of degeneration."[10] On August 17, 1911, Christian Voigt was charged with the murder of Josephine Peer. He was sentenced to death by hanging, but was amnestied to a life sentence in prison one year later. He was released in 1930 and died eight years later without having committed another crime.

The case of Voigt is extraordinarily well-documented. The Viennese press provided daily coverage of the case and its investigation. From the results of the autopsy to Voigt's appearance in court, every

---

9. Cited in Siegfried Türkel, "Der Lustmörder Christian Voigt: Ein kriminalistisch-psychiatrischer Beitrag zur Lehre vom Lustmord," *Archiv für Kriminalanthropologie und Kriminalistik* 55 (1913): 56.

10. Türkel, "Der Lustmörder Christian Voigt," 96–97.

detail seemed to be worth publishing. Criminologists also had an interest in the crime, the murderer, his motives and mental constitution. In an issue of the 1913 *Archiv für Kriminalanthropologie und Kriminalistik*, one of criminology's most prominent journals since the late nineteenth century, the sexologist Siegfried Türkel published a scholarly article investigating the case of Voigt as a criminological and psychiatric contribution to the crime of *Lustmord*. Finally, Voigt became a part of literary fiction when Robert Musil modeled one of the main characters in his *Man without Qualities*, the sex murderer Christian Moosbrugger, after this case.

At first glance, Musil's novel is one of many examples of a productive exchange between criminology and literature between 1890 and 1930, an exchange to which the *Lustmörder* owed his immense popularity at the time, and that furthermore contributed considerably to the psychological understanding of the connection between criminality and sexuality.[11] And yet Musil's novel should not simply be read as just another attempt to psychologically investigate the criminal mind by means of literary empathy. Musil's depiction of the murderer Moosbrugger is an attempt to make the sex murderer an embodiment of a poetological problem in which the epistemological conditions of literature are themselves brought up for discussion. Below I argue that the novel uses the case of Moosbrugger to present its analytical discourse and its formal demands for a poetics of contingency.

A Borderline Case

Without much modification, Musil modeled the murderer Moosbrugger after the original sources in the historical Voigt case. In the context of the novel, however, the case takes on a different complexity. "The contemporary truth," the protagonist Ulrich comments

---

11. A comprehensive discussion of this exchange can be found in Martin Lindner, "Der Mythos 'Lustmord': Serienmörder in der deutschen Literatur, dem Film und der bildenden Kunst zwischen 1892 und 1932," in *Verbrechen–Justiz–Medien: Konstellationen in Deutschland von 1900 bis zur Gegenwart*, ed. Joachim Linder and Claus-Michael Ort (Tübingen: Niemeyer, 1999), 273–305.

on the case, is "that he had merely read all about it in the newspaper."[12] In the novel, the character Moosbrugger appears to be a patchwork of rumors, reports, public and expert opinions, an object of attention that is as mysterious and fascinating as it is threatening and frightening. From a legal perspective, however, everything "could be summed up in one sentence: He was one of those borderline cases in law and forensic medicine known even to the layman as a case of diminished responsibility" (Musil 261).

As a "borderline case," Moosbrugger is one of those cases that is used by criminologists and penologists to criticize the legal concept of responsibility. Most prominently, in his 1896 lecture *Die strafrechtliche Zurechnungsfähigkeit*, it was the jurist Franz von Liszt who called for dismissing the legal term of responsibility altogether and replacing it with that of social dangerousness. Liszt's critique targeted the concept of diminished responsibility in particular, a concept that marks a precarious place in the system of the criminal law where the principles of penal distinctions become blurred. The concept of diminished responsibility is a compromise between health and illness, sanity and insanity, culpability and inculpability, criminality and madness, and thus between justice and psychiatry. It is a compromise that commits neither to the one side nor the other, and instead embraces both. "To the legal mind," however, "insanity is an all-or-nothing-proposition," as Musil laconically sums up the debate in the title of the chapter in which Ulrich's father in his capacity as a legal scholar takes the paradox to its extremes: "The social view holds that the criminally degenerate individual must be judged not morally but only insofar as he is likely to harm society as a whole. Hence the more dangerous he is, the more responsible he is for his actions, with the inescapable logical consequence that those criminals who seem to be the most innocent, the mentally sick, who are by nature least susceptible to correction by punishment, must be threatened with the harshest penalties, harsher than those for sane persons, so that the deterrent factor of the punishment be equal for all" (Musil 587).

---

12. Musil, *Man without Qualities*, 68.

With this inescapable logic, according to which the insane criminal must be treated more sanely than the sane criminal, even Moosbrugger's strange behavior during his trial will no longer appear mysterious. In fact, Moosbrugger precisely points to the paradoxical quintessence of this logic by vehemently insisting on his responsibility while at the same time applauding the prosecutor when emphasizing his social dangerousness, and by finally affirmatively agreeing to his death penalty, though not without adding that "you have condemned a madman" (Musil 76). What seems to be clear madness, as Ulrich concludes, is indeed an accurate characterization of the inner logic of the debate against the background of which even the *Lustmörder* Moosbrugger can appear to be a figure of eminent rationality. As a borderline case and a case of *diminished responsibility*, Moosbrugger exemplifies the logic by which the judicial distinctions are confronted with their own limits. Thus, one can still tell Moosbrugger's story, and a case history can even ascribe to it a certain rationale, but—as can be read later in the novel—"when Moosbrugger's case was shorn of all its individual romantic elements, ... not much more was left of it than what could be gathered from the list of references to works cited that Ulrich's father had enclosed in a recent letter to his son":

> Such a list looks like this: AH. AMP. AAC. AKA. AP. ASZ. BKL. BGK. BUD. CN. DTJ. DJZ. FBvM. GA. GS. JKV. KBSA. MMW. NG. PNW. R. VSvM. WNM. ZGS. ZMB. ZP. ZSS. Addickes ibid. Beling ibid., and so on. Written out, these would read: Annales d'Hygiene Publique et de Medicine legale, ed. Brouardel, Paris; Annales Medico-Psychologiques, ed. Ritti . . . etc., etc., making a list a page long even when reduced to the briefest of abbreviations. . . . So there [Moosbrugger] sat, the wild, captive threat of a dreaded act (*wilde, eingesperrte Möglichkeit einer gefürchteten Handlung*), like an uninhabited coral island in a boundless sea of scientific papers that surrounded him invisibly on all sides. (Musil 581–582)

In the novel, Moosbrugger appears to be both a particular individuality whose inner history reveals itself through narrative and a generic type who can be objectified by means of scientific forms of representation resulting in a seemingly endless list of abbreviations, citations, treatises, and expert opinions. "Compared with the strenuous brainwork he imposes on the pundits of the law," Musil polemicizes, "a criminal's life can often be a picnic" (Musil 583).

Musil's novel is not interested in reconstructing the individual history of the murderer Moosbrugger from the facts given by the historical material and it does not attempt to draw a psychological profile. In difference to contemporary literary texts dealing with the phenomenon of *Lustmord*, Musil's novel does not take on the social function of making the dreadful crime accessible to a cultural-semiotic understanding. Quite the contrary, as "dangerous individual" and "mere possibility of a dreaded act," Moosbrugger appears to be a "desiccated case," his "name was forgotten, the details were forgotten," and what solely remained were the abbreviations of criminological and psychological publications that surrounded the murderer "invisibly" (Musil 580). Against this backdrop, it is impossible to make the criminal and his deed available to psychological comprehension by means of literature. The mere attempt to understand the criminal act from the personality of the criminal person results in the dissolution of corresponding or opposing discursive segments in an ongoing game of competing systems of recording. For this reason, Musil claims in a 1926 fragment "Charakterologie und Dichtung" that "the few words asthenic, schizothyme type have more meaning than a long individual characterization."[13]

With the confrontation of the individual and the typical in the case of Moosbrugger, two systems of recording are confronted with each other. One can be called scientific, the other, literary, in the broadest sense. In any case, Moosbrugger cannot be thought of as being on only one side of this distinction. In fact, for Musil he assumes his aesthetic quality primarily from occupying a sphere of uncertainty. As a borderline case between scientific and literary forms of representation, Moosbrugger is best understood as an embodiment of the novel's controversy between a logical and an aesthetic notion of truth, between a scientifically exact concept of reality and Musil's literary-aesthetic notion of possibility. Although the former is spelled out in legal terms of responsibility, Moosbrugger's

---

13. Robert Musil, "Charakterologie und Dichtung," in *Gesammelte Werke: Essays und Reden: Kritik*, 1403.

constant struggle to appropriately express himself, his lingual titubation, and his helpless attempts to take possession of language are directly linked with the realm of a poetic immediacy. Thus, Moosbrugger's "inordinate state of existence," as Roger Willemsen once put it, can be read as an allegory for literature that eludes the conceptual determinedness of rational discourse.[14] In the 1914 fragment, "Possibilities of an Aesthetic," Musil demands poetry "to imply cognition, but to carry it forward to the borderland of premonition, ambiguity, and singularities, which is not accessible by the mere means of reason."[15] In this regard, the sex murderer Moosbrugger can be seen as the model for Musil's aesthetic agenda, although "cracked and obscured," but at the same time that which would be the result "if mankind could dream as a whole."[16]

Imaginary Precision and the Utopia of Essayism

In the context of the novel, the case of Moosbrugger cannot be reduced to an exemplary case of medical-legal responsibility. Presenting the case as a borderline case between conceptual-discursive and intuitive forms of cognition, it takes on a more important and programmatic function for the general conception of Musil's literary project. Therefore, it is not enough to trace back the case of the murderer Moosbrugger to its historical origin, and it would not be sufficient to make it the occasion for an analysis of criminological and medical-legal discourse. More than that, the case stands for Musil's literary-aesthetic agenda, called in a famous chapter of the novel "The Utopia of Essayism" (Musil 267), a particular form of writing with which the novel aims to make the realm of possibility accessible.

The literary agenda of the *utopia of essayism* is supposed to be accomplished by means of what the novel emphatically introduces

---

14. See Roger Willemsen, *Robert Musil: Vom intellektuellen Eros* (Munich: Piper, 1985), 116.
15. Robert Musil, "[Von der Möglichkeit einer Ästhetik] [Ohne Titel - vermutlich von 1914]," in *Gesammelte Werke: Essays und Reden: Kritik*, 1327.
16. Musil, *Man without Qualities*, 76–77.

as "imaginary precision" (Musil 267), a methodological tool that withstands the tendency to solidify independent meaning, to generalize, and to erase distinctions. Instead, "imaginary precision" will create an open network of connections from which, as Musil predicts, "man as the quintessence of his possibilities, potential man" will emerge (Musil 270). And yet "imaginary precision" must also be understood as a critique of strictly scientific methods of cognition, a "pedantic precision," as the novel refers to it, akin to that "with which Moosbrugger's peculiar mentality was fitted into a two-thousand-year-old system of legal concepts, [similar to] a madman's pedantic insistence on trying to spear a free-flying bird with a pin" (Musil 267).

While pedantic precision creates cases and relates them to general causalities and principles, the imaginary precision of Musil's essayism leads into a sphere of exceptions, particularities, curiosities, and circumstances, and makes accessible "a field of energy," in which actions and events will be arranged in ways of "certain chemical combinations" (Musil 270).

Already in a 1914 fragment "On the Essay," Musil depicts the essay as such a field of energy and defines its particular position as one between science and art. From science, it would take its "form and method," from art its "matter": "The essay seeks to establish an order. It presents not characters but a connection of thoughts, that is, a logical connection, and it proceeds from facts, like the natural sciences, to which the essay imparts an order. Except that these facts are not generally observable, and also their connections are in many cases only a singularity. There is no total solution, but only a series of particular ones. But the essay does present evidence, and investigates."[17]

As a literary form, the essay belongs to those areas, as Musil continues, "in which it is not truth that dominates, and in which probability is something more than an approach to truth."[18] This essayistic

---

17. Robert Musil, "[On the Essay]," in *Precision and Soul: Essays and Addresses*, trans. and ed. Burton Pike and David S. Luft (Chicago: University of Chicago Press, 1990), 49.

18. Robert Musil, "[On the Essay]," in *Precision and Soul: Essays and Addresses*, 49.

probability withstands the attempts of predictability and calculability with which psychological and criminological profiling impose the principles of scientific rationality. For Musil, what the writers know is to be found in a depiction of the singular rather than the law, "the dominance of the exception over the rule": "This is the territory of the writer, the realm in which his reason reigns. While his counterpart seeks the solid and fixed, and is content when he can establish for his computations as many equations as he finds unknowns, there is in the writer's territory from the start no end of unknowns, of equations, and of possible solutions. The task is to discover ever new solutions, connections, constellations, variables, to set up prototypes of an order of events, appealing models of how one can be human, to *invent* the inner person."[19]

In his 1911 essay, "The Obscene and Pathological in Art," Musil further sheds light on the artistic presentation corresponding to the poet's cognition. Art, he claims, does not proceed conceptually, but intuitively; its objects are not general but individual cases. And again, Musil's definition of art derives from a confrontation with scientific rationality:

> Given the same case, a doctor is interested in the generally valid causal connections, the artist in an individual web of feelings, the scientist in a summary schema of the empirical data. The artist is further concerned with expanding the range of what is inwardly still possible, and therefore art's sagacity is not the sagacity of the law, but—a different one. It sets forth the people, impulses, events it creates not in a many-sided way, but one-sidedly. To love something as an artist, therefore, means to be shaken not by its ultimate value or lack of value, but by a side of it that suddenly opens up. Where art has value it shows things that few have seen. It is conquering, not pacifying.[20]

Essayistic art carries with it the distinction between art and science, it does not claim to replace scientific cognition with poetic cognition, but confronts the rational sphere of concepts and discourse with a sphere that is characterized by intuition, sentiment, and

---

19. Robert Musil, "The Knowledge of the Writer," in *Precision and Soul*, 64.
20. Robert Musil, "The Obscene and the Pathological in Art," in *Precision and Soul*, 7.

poetic expression. After all, according to Musil, both art and science seek knowledge. However, art seeks knowledge by focusing on the individual and not the general, by depicting exceptions and not rules, aberrations instead of norms. And yet art contributes to general cognition by representing "the obscene and the pathological by means of their relation to the decent and healthy, which is to say: art expands its knowledge of the decent and healthy."[21]

Seven years earlier, the young author Alfred Döblin had advertised his first novel *Der schwarze Vorhang* to the publisher Axel Juncker with a similar thought: "Sexual pathology is projected onto normal psychological behavior, and by means of intensification is made comprehensible and artistically representable."[22] "Any perversity can be depicted," Musil writes a few years later, "the way it is constructed out of normal elements can be depicted, since otherwise the depiction would not be understood."[23] From the perspective of artistic representation, the depiction of the pathological contributes to a reevaluation of normatively drawn boundaries and distinctions. "To give an example: one must admit that a Lustmörder can be sick, that he can be healthy and immoral, or that he can be healthy and moral; in the case of murderers these distinctions are indeed made."[24]

Various reasons can be given for the appearance of the *Lustmörder* at this crucial point in Musil's 1911 pamphlet. From a historical perspective, it can be speculated that here Musil refers for the first time to the case of Christian Voigt, which fascinated the Viennese public around the same time. And it allows connections to be drawn between Musil's earlier aesthetic writing and the figure that under the name of Moosbrugger plays a central role in *The Man without Qualities* and embodies the novel's literary agenda. It is indeed the same artistic program that the *Lustmörder* exemplifies in Musil's 1911 essay "The Obscene and Pathological in Art." Rather than focusing on a systematic approach to the individual case that allows its subsumption under a general rule, Musil is interested in that

---

21. Musil, "Obscene and the Pathological in Art," 6.
22. Alfred Döblin, "Brief an Axel Juncker, 9. April 1904," in *Briefe*, 23.
23. Musil, "Obscene and the Pathological in Art," 8.
24. Musil, "Obscene and the Pathological in Art," 8.

which escapes the order of casuistic representation. "The typical of an event," Musil notes fifteen years later in the already cited fragment "Charakterologie und Dichtung," "does not prevent the individual; it features both. In other words, psychology, characterology, typology, sociology lead to an idea of human existence in a very unknown universe. Statements regarding the existence of man; an intensely acting being against a vast background that only slowly elucidates. This is the initial feeling of the challenging mission of the new literature."[25]

Hence, for Musil it is not literature's goal to confront the individual with the typical. Instead, the new literature must depict individual affects against the background of the typical, must depict these affects in "their specific composition," in regard to their specific "functions and relations,"[26] to which everything comes down as soon as one begins to analyze it. The Moosbrugger case in *The Man without Qualities* carries out the artistic program that the *Lustmörder* exemplifies in Musil's critical essay of 1911. Against the background of Musil's early writing, Moosbrugger can now be understood as a paradigmatic case for the epistemological function that Musil attributes to literature. Aside from the dreadful circumstances of his deed, Moosbrugger eludes the typological screening of his personality and withstands the systematic attempts to categorize his existence. As a media sensation—a dangerous monster—he only serves the filthy fantasies of the bourgeois citizen who is bored in his marital bedroom. In the context of the novel, however, the extreme case of the pathological begins to fall apart and dissolves into separate and unrelated pieces. And at the same time, the concepts and the representational means, which ought to domesticate what threatened to escape the normative symbolic order, become questionable. With the case of Moosbrugger, the novel reflects on both the symbolic construction of reality and its decomposition into segments of mere possibilities that depict Moosbrugger's inaccessible world of experience as a state of momentary and transitory potentialities. Moosbrugger's mere existence withstands

---

25. Musil, "Charakterologie und Dichtung," 1404.
26. Musil, "Charakterologie und Dichtung," 1404.

the discursive attempts that were meant to define him and opens up a space in which events become possible. The case of Moosbrugger combines the two different systems on which Musil's epistemological and aesthetic distinction is essentially based: the order of discourse that aims to define and constitute the case as *Lustmord* without leaving any room for ambiguity, and the emblematic and unreasonable world of suddenly occurring events, which have their place in literature. Between these two opposing systems Moosbrugger's dreadful deed seems an isolated event, and every attempt to rationally conceptualize it, to make it part of our world of experience, will and must fail.

12

Conclusion

The Function of Fiction

"The world is everything that is the case," the famous opening statement from Ludwig Wittgenstein's 1921 *Tractatus Logico-Philosophicus* reads.[1] It declares that in the twentieth century the unity of the world has splintered to such a degree that it can only be comprehended and imagined as a totality of cases. Above all, writers who were sensitive to the lapsarian overtones in the concept of case bemoaned this new situation. Georg Lukács's *Theory of the Novel* (1914) is an extended lament over the loss of narrative and existential coherence, and over the fact that the modern novel cannot but represent cases of failed reconciliation with the world.[2] In his essay, "The Position of the Narrator in the Con-

---

1. Ludwig Wittgenstein, *Tractatus Logico-Philosophicus*, trans. C. K. Ogden (New York: Dover, 1998), 29.
2. See Georg Lukács, *Die Theorie des Romans: Ein geschichtsphilosophischer Versuch über die Form der großen Epik* (Bielefeld: Aisthesis 2009), 30.

temporary Novel," Theodor W. Adorno laments the erosion of critical perspectives and the standardization of cultural forms.[3] The experience and cultivation of individual subjectivity that since the end of the eighteenth century was inextricably tied to literary discourse and narrative forms of storytelling seems to have been absorbed completely into a thinking and writing in cases.

I read Robert Musil's and Alfred Döblin's novels as poetological responses to this development. In *The Man without Qualities*, Musil suggests an essayistic style of writing with which the literary text distances itself from scientific and rational discourse without, however, lapsing into mere fiction. Moreover, the essay sets out to fictionalize rational discourse and pushes it to the very point where it coincides with the fiction that precedes it. Döblin, in contrast, confines his critique to that of narrative while affirming the validity of scientific methods. As a consequence, he rejects any psychological truth claim of literary discourse and attempts to turn the novel into a modern epos that approaches life in its unfiltered totality.

In this study, Musil and Döblin mark the end point of a literary tradition that began in the final decades of the eighteenth century with novels such as Goethe's *Werther* and Moritz's *Anton Reiser* and that made use of authentic cases to capture the psychological depth of human subjectivity. The three main parts of this book followed this literary tradition throughout the long nineteenth century in three phases of the discourse of literature. Each of these phases reflects a transformation in the function of fiction that defines the particular historical status of narrative literature.

In the first phase at the end of the eighteenth century, a modern discourse of literature developed that was directed toward the individual and was increasingly focused on the narrative depiction of the inner history of its protagonists. New modes of writing emerged that fulfilled a twofold function, neatly embodied in the two versions of Goethe's *Werther*: they established a new psychological discourse and, at the same time, contributed to a new type of literary

---

3. See Theodor W. Adorno, "The Position of the Narrator in the Contemporary Novel," in *Notes to Literature*, vol. 1, trans. Sherry Weber Nicholsen, ed. Rolf Tiedemann (New York: Columbia University Press, 1991), 31.

fiction that could no longer be reduced to poetological standards, but positioned itself as the presentation of an individual biography. A thinking in cases, which was situated primarily in medicine and jurisprudence, influenced this development of new narrative forms at the end of the eighteenth century. As Karl Philipp Moritz's genre designation "psychological novel" shows, literary and epistemic genres began to merge, and informed psychological projects such as Moritz's *Erfahrungsseelenkunde*. Schiller's *The Criminal of Lost Honor* can still be read as part of this project. But the poetological discussion of *cold* and *hot* storytelling in the beginning of the novella, reveals a self-reflexive quality of literary discourse that set out to change its focus from poetics to psychology, from the emotional effect of poetic language and form to cold, *objective* observation. Schiller's novella—and in reference to it, Kleist's *Michael Kohlhaas*—counterbalances the *coldness* of psychological storytelling with a narrative that, by evoking empathy for the unfortunate protagonists, does not surrender to the scientific demands of objectivity. Literary case histories around 1800 cannot simply be reduced to the question of their subject matter; they also reflect on the modes of casuistic storytelling—a *writing in cases*—and thus, on the functions of literary narrative.

References to authentic cases remained a common literary practice throughout the nineteenth century and contributed to the success of what is referred to as poetic or bourgeois realism. My interest in this second phase was focused on literary fiction that critically questioned the narrative logic used to provide the basis for psychological assessments and legal decision making. Especially poignant are cases that attempt to crisscross the border between madness and reason at a time when a fungible concept of legal responsibility was a high priority for juridical and psychiatric thought and practice. In this phase, the most advanced writers of literary fiction positioned themselves in subversive opposition to the legal establishment. E. T. A. Hoffmann's *Serapiontic principle* claimed a new place for narrative fiction in confrontation with the prevalent psychological discourse but without sacrificing its own claims to reason. Büchner and Wedekind let narrative form and dramatic closure disintegrate and thus challenge contemporary attempts to capture narrative exposition for psychological cognition and psychiatric intervention in legal decision making. Whereas Büchner's *Woyzeck* complicates the relation to the documented case by offering an irreducible plurality of perspectives, Wedekind multiplies the number and status of cases when he refers to sexological and criminological discourses that scandalize bourgeois norms of gender and sexuality. The dramatic engagement with cases and the dissolution of narrative elements challenge the function of narrative to guarantee psychological certainty and to provide stability and justification for societal norms and values.

Around 1900—this is the third phase—Freud's insights into the importance of fiction for the formation of psychic reality, and into the epistemological relevance of narrative, directed attention to the structure and composition of cases and gave new impulses to literary fiction. Psychoanalysis offered an alternative to the sexological and criminological appropriation of narrative literature to provide evidence for their demands of social control. Even though Freud remained committed to a classical concept of narrative that can be traced back to the ideal of the *Bildungsroman*, the insights from his case histories inspired authors at the beginning of the twentieth century to newly explore the reality effects of narrative forms of representation. Döblin's call for a "Tatsachenphantasie" (fantasy of facts), and Musil's *utopia of essayism*, which counters the "Wirklichkeitssinn" (sense of reality) of scientific precision with the "Möglichkeitssinn" (sense of possibility) of imaginary precision, must be understood as attempts to establish new forms of literary realism. Both Döblin and Musil continue the tradition of literary references to cases in order to complicate and challenge conventions of understanding and cognition. Where a case seems to provide a certainty of judgment, the *fantasy of facts* and the *imaginary precision* instead dissect the case into its individual elements and circumstances. Döblin's and Musil's references to cases complicate the problem of judgment and question the role of narrative conditions for locating the possibilities of decision making in the individual. That they do so while also challenging the form of the novel shows the intimate connection between case and novel that the preceding pages have attempted to elucidate.

Postscript: The Case of Josef K.

I end this book by taking a brief look at a novel that most effectively speaks to the crisis of modern subjectivity and has often been used as evidence for the dilemma of modern conceptions of life between individual freedom, socially sanctioned rituals, and institutionalized forms of responsibility. In *The Trial*, written in 1914–1915 and published posthumously in 1925, Franz Kafka has taken seriously the genre's promise to grant unrestricted freedom of individual self-fulfillment, only to demonstrate how every attempt of the protagonist Josef K. to claim authority over his own life collides with the constraints and pressure of social responsibility. Kafka's novel evolves from the conflict of case and individual that shaped the modern discourse of literature after Goethe's *Werther*. The entire novel is framed as a criminal case: in the beginning Josef K. wakes up to being arrested in the name of a mysterious but omnipresent institution, and the novel ends with the protagonist's execution. In between, we witness Josef K.'s continued attempts to stand up against the institution of the legal court by desperately looking for acknowledgment of his individual autonomy. A passage from the chapter "Lawyer, Manufacturer, Painter," in which Josef K. makes plans to take action in his own case, contains the novel's conflict in a nutshell:

> The thought of his trial never left him now. He had often considered whether it might not be advisable to prepare a written defense and submit it to the court. In it he would offer a brief overview of his life, and for each event of any particular importance, explain why he had acted as he did, whether in his present judgment this course of action deserved approval or censure, and what reasons he could advance for the one or the other. The advantages of such a written defense over simply leaving things in the hands of his lawyer, who was far from perfect anyway, were obvious.[4]

Josef K. never executes this plan of composing what would appear to be his autobiography, the *novel* of his life. The failure of

---

4. Franz Kafka, *The Trial*, trans. Breon Mitchell (New York: Schocken, 1999), 112.

proceeding with the plan can be attributed, on the one hand, to the impossibility of its completion, as K. later laments, and, on the other hand, to the fact that he considered it a defense from the beginning and thus would have to compose it under the terms and conditions of the legal institution against which he attempts to stand his ground as a sovereign individual. Under these conditions, the individual history will only become an addition to the files, a case history that is irrelevant in regard to the displayed individual biography, and only matters to the extent to which it contributes to the subject's classification and his further integration into the administrative processes that govern the norms of social communication. "Perhaps," Josef K. contemplates, "someday after retirement, it might provide a suitable occupation for a mind turned childish, and help to while away the lengthening days. But now, . . . when he wished to enjoy the brief evenings and nights as a young man, now he was supposed to start writing his petition."[5]

It has often been noted that Josef K.'s scene of writing mirrors Franz Kafka's own situation.[6] This is interesting insofar as it can be understood in regard to a particular approach to literary fiction and its composition that sets out to examine life from the perspective of art and its promise of free individual development. Under the conditions of modernity, however, this premise leads directly to the double bind that Josef K. faces when planning his petition: the writing of the autobiography seems unavoidable, even necessary to claim his sovereignty as a free individual, and at the same time, he only gets more entangled in the networks of a regime of bureaucratic administration to which an individual life only matters insofar as it contributes to establishing societal norms. In this regard, Kafka's novel *The Trial* must be considered more than the story of the

---

5. Kafka, *Trial*, 127.
6. See Wolf Kittler, "Heimlichkeit und Schriftlichkeit: Das österreichische Strafprozessrecht in Franz Kafkas Roman *Der Proceß*," *Germanic Review* 78 (2003), 194–222; Rüdiger Campe, "Kafkas Institutionenroman: *Der Proceß, Das Schloss*," in *Gesetz: Ironie: Festschrift für Manfred Schneider*, ed. Rüdiger Campe and Michael Niehaus (Heidelberg: Synchron, 2004), 197–208; and Arne Höcker, "Literatur durch Verfahren: Beschreibung eines Kampfes," in *Kafkas Institutionen*, ed. Arne Höcker and Oliver Simons (Bielefeld: transcript, 2007), 235–253.

enigmatic prosecution of its protagonist. More than just dealing with the case of Josef K., the novel is about the case of literature.

David Wellbery once claimed that with Kafka's short text, "The Silence of the Sirens," the two-thousand-year-old literary tradition of unfolding the possibilities of fictionalization comes to an end.[7] With *The Trial*, Kafka terminates another literary tradition, one that since Goethe had made reference to historical cases in order to create the powerful illusion of self-determined biographical fulfillment. For Kafka's hero Josef K., as for Kafka himself, there is neither a choice nor an alternative to writing and to literature. The novel, however, demonstrates that literature does not offer a solution or escape; at best, it allows for a suspension of the obligation to judge.

---

7. See David E. Wellbery, "Scheinvorgang: Kafkas *Das Schweigen der Sirenen*," in *Seiltänzer des Paradoxalen: Aufsätze zur ästhetischen Wissenschaft* (Munich: Hanser, 2006), 177–195.

Bibliography

Adorno, Theodor W. "The Position of the Narrator in the Contemporary Novel." In *Notes to Literature*, vol. 1, edited by Rolf Tiedemann, translated by Sherry Weber Nicholsen, 30–36. New York: Columbia University Press, 1991.
Alewyn, Richard. "Klopstock!" *Euphorion* 73 (1979): 357–364.
Andree, Martin. *Wenn Texte töten: Über Werther, Medienwirkung und Mediengewalt.* Munich: Fink Verlag, 2006.
Andriopoulos, Stefan. *Unfall und Verbrechen: Konfigurationen zwischen juristischem und literarischem Diskurs um 1900.* Wiesbaden: Springer Verlag, 1996.
Anz, Thomas. "Psychoanalyse in der literarischen Moderne: Ein Forschungsbericht und Projektentwurf." In *Die Literatur und die Wissenschaften 1770–1930*, edited by Karl Richter, Jörg Schönert, and Michael Titzmann, 377–413. Stuttgart: Metzler, 1997.
Arndt, Christiane. *Abschied von der Wirklichkeit: Probleme bei der Darstellung von Realität im deutschsprachigen literarischen Realismus.* Freiburg im Breisgau: Rombach, 2009.
Austermühl, Elke, and Hartmut Vinçon. "Frank Wedekinds Dramen." In *Die literarische Moderne in Europa*, vol. 2, *Formationen der literarischen*

Avantgarde, edited by Hans Joachim Piechotta, Ralph-Rainer Wuthenow, and Sabine Rothemann, 304–321. Opladen: VS Verlag für Sozialwissenschaften, 1994.

Balke, Friedrich. "Kohlhaas und K.: Zur Prozessführung bei Kleist und Kafka." *Zeitschrift für Deutsche Philologie* 130, no. 4 (2011): 503–530.

Becker, Peter. *Verderbnis und Entartung: Eine Geschichte der Kriminologie des 19. Jahrhunderts als Diskurs und als Praxis*. Göttingen: Wallstein, 2002.

Bezold, Raimund. *Popularphilosophie und Erfahrungsseelenkunde im Werk von Karl Philipp Moritz*. Würzburg: Königshausen & Neumann, 1984.

Blamberger, Günter et al., ed. *Kleist-Jahrbuch*. Stuttgart: J. B. Metzler, 2003.

Blanckenburg, Friedrich von. "Die Leiden des jungen Werthers." In *Texte zur Romantheorie II (1732–1780), mit Anmerkungen, Nachwort und Bibliographie von Ernst Weber*, 392–441. Munich: Fink Verlag, 1981.

Blanckenburg, Friedrich von. *Versuch über den Roman: Faksimiledruck der Originalausgabe von 1774. Mit einem Nachwort von Eberhard Lämmert*. Stuttgart: J. B. Metzler, 1965.

Bloch, Ernst. *Naturrecht und menschliche Würde*. Frankfurt am Main: Suhrkamp, 1961.

Bloch, Iwan (as Eugen Dühren). *Der Marquis de Sade und seine Zeit: Ein Beitrag zur Kultur- und Sittengeschichte des 18. Jahrhunderts mit besonderer Beziehung auf die Lehre von der Psychopathia sexualis*. Berlin: H. Barsdorf, 1900.

Bloch, Iwan (as Eugen Dühren). *Neue Forschungen über den Marquis de Sade und seine Zeit: Mit besonderer Berücksichtigung der Sexualphilosophie de Sade's auf Grund des neuentdeckten Original-Manuskriptes seines Hauptwerkes "Die 120 Tage von Sodom."* Berlin: Max Harrwitz, 1904.

Boa, Elizabeth. *The Sexual Circus: Wedekind's Theatre of Subversion*. Oxford: Blackwell, 1987.

Bosse, Heinrich. *Autorschaft ist Werkherrschaft: Über die Entstehung des Urheberrechts aus dem Geiste der Goethezeit*. Paderborn: Schöningh, 1981.

Bossinade, Johanna. "Wedekinds *Monstretragödie* und die Frage der Separation (Lacan)." In Gutjahr, *Frank Wedekind*, 143–162.

Bovenschen, Silvia. *Die imaginierte Weiblichkeit: Exemplarische Untersuchungen zu kulturgeschichtlichen und literarischen Präsentationsformen des Weiblichen*. Frankfurt am Main: Suhrkamp, 1979.

Brown, Hilda M. *E. T. A. Hoffmann and the Serapiontic Principle: Critique and Creativity*. Rochester, NY: Camden House, 2006.

Büchner, Georg. "Der Korrespondent von und für Deutschland," no. 166, Sonnabend 9. Juni 1821. In *Sämtliche Werke und Schriften*, 7. Darmstadt: WBG, 2005.

Büchner, Georg. *Sämtliche Werke und Schriften: Historisch-kritische Ausgabe mit Quellendokumentation und Kommentar*, vol. 7, *Woyzeck: Text Editionsbericht, Quellen, Erläuterungsteile*. Edited by Burghard Dedner. Darmstadt: WBG, 2005.

Büchner, Georg. "Woyzeck." In *The Major Works*, edited by Matthew Wilson Smith, translated by Henry J. Schmidt, 133–169. New York: W.W. Norton, 2012.
Cameron, Deborah, and Elisabeth Frazer. *The Lust to Kill: A Feminist Investigation of Sexual Murder*. New York: Polity Press, 1987.
Campe, Rüdiger. "Form and Life in the Theory of the Novel." *Constellations* 18, no. 1 (2011): 53–66.
Campe, Rüdiger. "Form und Leben in der Theorie des Romans." In *Vita Aesthetica: Szenarien ästhetischer Lebendigkeit*, edited by Armen Avanessian, Winfried Menninghaus, and Jan Völker, 193–211. Berlin: Diaphanes, 2009.
Campe, Rüdiger. *The Game of Probability: Literature and Calculation from Pascal to Kleist*. Translated by Ellwood H. Wiggins Jr. Stanford, CA: Stanford University Press, 2013.
Campe, Rüdiger. "Johann Franz Woyzeck: Der Fall im Drama." In *Unzurechnungsfähigkeiten. Diskursivierungen unfreier Bewußtseinszustände seit dem 18. Jahrhundert*, edited by Michael Niehaus and Hans-Walter Schmidt-Hannissa, 206–236. Frankfurt am Main: Suhrkamp, 1998.
Campe, Rüdiger. "Kafkas Institutionenroman: *Der Proceß, Das Schloss*." In *Gesetz: Ironie: Festschrift für Manfred Schneider*, edited by Rüdiger Campe and Michael Niehaus, 197–208. Heidelberg: Synchron, 2004.
Campe, Rüdiger. "Three Modes of Citation: Historical, Casuistic, and Literary Writing in Büchner." *Germanic Review: Literature, Culture, Theory* 88, no. 1 (2014): 44–59.
Campe, Rüdiger. "Von Fall zu Fall: Goethes *Werther*, Büchners 'Lenz.'" In *Was der Fall ist: Casus und Lapsus*, edited by Inka Mülder-Bach and Michaela Ott, 33–55. Paderborn: Wilhelm Fink, 2014.
Campe, Rüdiger, and Arne Höcker. "Introduction: The Case of Citation: On Literary and Pragmatic Reference." *Germanic Review: Literature, Culture, Theory* 88, no. 1 (2014): 40–43.
Clarus, Johann Christian August. "Die Zurechnungsfähigkeit des Mörders Johann Christian Woyzeck, nach Grundsätzen der Staatsarzneikunde aktenmässig erwiesen von Dr. Johann Christian August Clarus." In Georg Büchner, *Sämtliche Werke und Briefe: Historisch-Kritische-Ausgabe*, edited by Werner R. Lehmann, vol. 1, *Dichtungen und Übersetzungen mit Dokumentationen zur Stoffgeschichte*, 487–549. Hamburg: Christian Wegner Verlag, 1967.
Class, Monika. "K. P. Moritz's Case Poetics: Aesthetic Autonomy Reconsidered." *Literature and Medicine* 32 (2014): 46–73.
Corino, Karl. "Zerstückelt und Durchdunkelt: Der Sexualmörder Moosbrugger im 'Mann ohne Eigenschaften' und sein Modell." *Musil-Forum* 10 (1984): 105–119.
Delabar, Walter. "Experimente mit dem modernen Erzählen: Skizze zu den Rahmenbedingungen von Alfred Döblins Romanwerk bis 1933." In *Realistisches Schreiben in der Weimarer Republik*, edited by Sabine Kyora and Stefan Neuhaus, 123–138. Würzburg: Königshausen & Neumann, 2006.

Döblin, Alfred. *Alfred Döblin im Spiegel der zeitgenössischen Kritik*. Edited by Ingrid Schuster and Ingrid Bode. Bern: Franke Verlag, 1973.
Döblin, Alfred. "Arzt und Dichter: Merkwürdiger Lebenslauf eines Autors." In *Autobiographische Schriften und Aufzeichnungen*, edited by Edgar Pässler, 23–29. Olten: Walter Verlag, 1980.
Döblin, Alfred. *Briefe*. Olten: Walter Verlag, 1970.
Döblin, Alfred. "Der Bau des epischen Werkes." In *Aufsätze zur Literatur*, edited by Walter Muschg, 103–133. Olten: Walter Verlag, 1963.
Döblin, Alfred. *Die beiden Freundinnen und ihr Giftmord*. Düsseldorf: Artemis & Winkler, 2001.
Döblin, Alfred. "An Romanautoren und ihre Kritiker. Berliner Programm" (1913). In *Schriften zu Ästhetik, Poetik und Literatur*, 119–123. Olten: Walter Verlag, 1989.
Döblin, Alfred. "Sigmund Freud zum 70. Geburtstage." In *Die Zeitlupe: Kleine Prosa*, edited by Walter Muschg, 80–88. Olten: Walter Verlag, 1962.
Dörr, Volker C. *Reminiscenzien: Goethe und Karl Philipp Moritz in intertextuellen Lektüren*. Würzburg: Königshausen & Neumann, 1999.
Dorsch, Nikolaus, and Jan-Christoph Hauschild. "Clarus und Woyzeck: Bilder des Hofrats und des Delinquenten." *Georg Büchner Jahrbuch* 4 (1984): 317–323.
Dotzler, Bernhard. "Werthers Leser." *MLN* 114, no. 3 (1999): 445–470.
Düwell, Susanne, and Nicolas Pethes, eds. *Fall—Fallgeschichte—Fallstudie: Theorie und Geschichte einer Wissensform*. Frankfurt am Main: Campus, 2014.
Düwell, Susanne, and Nicolas Pethes. "Fall, Wissen, Repräsentation: Epistemologie und Darstellungsästhetik von Fallnarrativen in den Wissenschaften vom Menschen." In Düwell and Pethes, *Fall—Fallgeschichte—Fallstudie*, 9–33.
Dye, Robert Ellis. "Blanckenburgs *Werther*-Rezeption." In *Goethezeit: Studien zur Erkenntnis und Rezeption Goethes und seiner Zeitgenossen (Festschrift für Stuart Atkins)*, edited by Gerhart Hoffmeister, 65–79. Bern: Francke, 1981.
Eckermann, Johann Peter. *Gespräche mit Goethe*, edited by Ernst Beutler. München: dtv, 1976.
Eulenburg, Albert. "Der Marquis de Sade." *Die Zukunft* 26 (1899): 497–515.
Feuerbach, Paul Johann Anselm von. *Betrachtungen über die Öffentlichkeit und Mündlichkeit der Gerechtigkeitspflege*, 2 vols. Giessen: Georg Friedrich Heyer, 1821.
Fineman, Joel. "The History of the Anecdote: Fiction and Fiction." In *The New Historicism*, edited by Harold Aram Veeser, 49–76. New York: Routledge, 1989.
Fleming, Paul. *Exemplarity and Mediocrity: The Art of the Average from Bourgeois Tragedy to Realism*. Stanford, CA: Stanford University Press, 2009.
Fleming, Paul. "The Perfect Story: Anecdote and Exemplarity in Linnaeus and Blumenberg." *Thesis Eleven* 104, no. 1 (2011): 72–86.

Florack, Ruth. "Aggression und Lust: Anmerkungen zur Monstretragödie." In Gutjahr, *Frank Wedekind*, 163–177.
Forrester, John. "If P, Then What? Thinking in Cases." *History of the Human Sciences* 9, no. 3 (1996): 1–25.
Foucault, Michel. *Abnormal: Lectures at the Collège de France, 1974–1975.* Translated by Graham Burchell. New York: Picador, 1999.
Foucault, Michel. "About the Concept of the 'Dangerous Individual' in 19th-Century Legal Psychiatry." *International Journal of Law and Psychiatry* 1 (1978): 1–18.
Foucault, Michel. *The Birth of Biopolitics: Lectures at the Collège de France, 1978–1979.* Translated by Graham Burchell. New York: Picador, 2008.
Foucault, Michel. *The Birth of the Clinic: An Archaeology of Medical Perception.* Translated by Alan Sheridan. New York: Pantheon, 1973.
Foucault, Michel. *Discipline and Punish: The Birth of the Prison.* Translated by Alan Sheridan. New York: Vintage, 1977.
Foucault, Michel. *"Society Must Be Defended": Lectures at the Collège de France, 1975–1976.* Translated by David Macey. Picador: New York, 1997.
Foucault, Michel. "What Is an Author." In *Aesthetics, Method, and Epistemology*, edited by James D. Faubion and Paul Rabinow, 205–222. New York: New Press, 1998.
Freud, Sigmund. *Briefe an Wilhlem Fließ: 1887–1904.* Edited by Jeffrey Moussaieff Masson. Frankfurt am Main: Fischer, 1986.
Freud, Sigmund. "Creative Writers and Day-Dreaming." In *The Standard Edition of the Complete Psychological Works of Sigmund Freud*, vol. 9 (1906–1908), edited by James Strachey, 419–428. London: Hogarth Press, 2001.
Freud, Sigmund. *Dora: An Analysis of a Case of Hysteria.* Edited by Philip Rieff. New York: Touchstone, 1997.
Freud, Sigmund. "From the History of an Infantile Neurosis [The 'Wolfman']." In *The "Wolfman" and Other Cases*, translated by Louise Adey Huish. New York: Penguin, 2003.
Freud, Sigmund. "The Uncanny." In *The Standard Edition of the Complete Psychological Works of Sigmund Freud, Vol. XVII (1917–1919): An Infantile Neurosis and Other Works*, edited by James Strachey, 217–256. London: Vintage, 2001.
Freud, Sigmund, and Josef Breuer. *Studies on Hysteria.* Edited by James Strachey. New York: Basic Books, 1957.
Frey, Christiane. "Der Fall *Anton Reiser*: Vom Paratext zum Paradigma." In *Karl Philipp Moritz: Signaturen des Denkens*, edited by Anthony Krupp, 19–41. Amsterdam: Rodopi, 2010.
Frey, Christiane. "Fallgeschichte." In *Literatur und Wissen: Ein interdisziplinäres Handbuch*, edited by Roland Borgards, Harald Neumeyer, Nicolas Pethes, and Yvonne Wübben, 282–287. Stuttgart: Metzler, 2013.
Frey, Christiane. "'Ist das nicht der Fall der Krankheit?' Der literarische Fall am Beispiel von Goethes *Werther*." *Zeitschrift für Germanistik* 19 (2009): 317–329.

Frey, Christiane, and David Martyn. "Doubling Werther (1774/1787)." In Goethe, *Sufferings of Young Werther*, 217–230.
Friedrich, Peter, and Michael Niehaus. "Transparenz und Maskerade: Zur Diskussion über das öffentlich-mündliche Gerichtsverfahren um 1800 in Deutschland." In Vogl, *Poetologien des Wissens*, 163–184.
Fürnkäs, Josef. *Der Ursprung des psychologischen Romans: Karl Philipp Moritz' Anton Reiser*. Stuttgart: J. B. Metzlersche Verlagsbuchhandlung, 1977.
Gaderer, Rupert. "Michael Kohlhaas (1808/10): Schriftverkehr–Bürokratie–Querulanz." *Zeitschrift für Deutsche Philologie* 130, no. 4 (2011): 531–544.
Gailus, Andreas. "A Case of Individuality: Karl Philipp Moritz and the Magazine for Empirical Psychology." *New German Critique* 79 (2000): 67–105.
Gailus, Andreas. *Passions of the Sign: Revolution and Language in Kant, Goethe, and Kleist*. Baltimore: Johns Hopkins University Press, 2006.
Geulen, Eva. *Worthörig wider Willen: Darstellungsproblematik und Sprachreflexion in der Prosa Adalbert Stifters*. Munich: Iudicium-Verlag, 1992.
Goethe, Johann Wolfgang von. *Conversations of Goethe with Eckermann and Soret*. Translated by John Oxenford. London: George Bell, 1874.
Goethe, Johann Wolfgang von. *Elective Affinities*. Translated by R. J. Hollingdale. London: Penguin, 1971.
Goethe, Johann Wolfgang von. "From My Life: Poetry and Truth." In Goethe, *Sufferings of Young Werther*, 108–128.
Goethe, Johann Wolfgang von. *Sämtliche Werke. Briefe, Tagebücher und Gespräche*, section I, vol. 8, *Die Leiden des jungen Werther, Die Wahlverwandschaften, Kleine Prosa, Epen*, edited by Waltraut Wiethölter. Frankfurt am Main: Deutscher Klassiker Verlag, 1994.
Goethe, Johann Wolfgang von. *The Sufferings of Young Werther*. Translated and edited by Stanley Corngold. New York: W. W. Norton, 2013.
Goethe, Johann Wolfgang von. *Werke 6: Romane und Novellen I*, edited by Erich Trunz. München: C. H. Beck, 1996.
Goethe, Johann Wolfgang von. *Wilhelm Meister's Apprenticeship*. Translated and edited by Eric A. Blackwell. Princeton, NJ: Princeton University Press, 1995.
Goldmann, Stefan. "Kasus—Krankengeschichte—Novelle." In *"Fakta, und kein moralisches Geschwätz": Zu den Fallgeschichten im "Magazin zur Erfahrungsseelenkunde" (1783–1793)*, edited by Sheila Dickson, Stefan Goldmann, and Christof Wingertszahn, 33–65. Göttingen: Wallstein, 2011.
Goldmann, Stefan. "Sigmund Freud und Hermann Sudermann oder die wiedergefundene wie eine Krankengeschichte zu lesende Novelle." In *Literatur, Mythos und Freud*, edited by Helmut Peitsch and Eva Lezzi, 51–70. Potsdam: Universität Potsdam, 2009.
Gräf, Hans Gerhard. "Nachträge zu Goethes Gesprächen, 1: Johann Kaspar Lavater." *Jahrbuch der Goethe-Gesellschaft* 6 (1919): 283–285.
Gretz, Daniela. "Von 'hässlichen Tazzelwürmern' und 'heiteren Blumenketten': Adalbert Stifters *Abdias* und Gottfried Kellers *Ursula* im Spannungsfeld von

Fallgeschichte und Novelle." In Düwell and Pethes, *Fall—Fallgeschichte—Fallstudie*, 274–292.
Grosz, George. "Jugenderinnerungen." *Das Kunstblatt* 13 (1929): 166–174.
Gutjahr, Ortrud, ed. *Frank Wedekind*. Freiburger literaturpsychologische Gespräche Bd. 20. Würzburg: Königshausen & Neumann, 2001.
Hamacher, Bernd. "Geschichte und Psychologie der Moderne um 1800 (Schiller, Kleist, Goethe): 'Gegensätzische' Überlegungen zum 'Verbrecher aus Infamie' und zu 'Michael Kohlhaas.'" In Blamberger et al., *Kleist-Jahrbuch*, 60–74.
Hart, Gail K. "True Crime and Criminal Truth: Schiller's 'The Criminal of Lost Honor." In High, *Schiller's Literary Prose Works*, 222–233.
Hess, Volker. "Observation und Casus: Status und Funktion der medizinischen Fallgeschichte." In Düwell and Pethes, *Fall—Fallgeschichte—Fallstudie*, 34–59.
High, Jeffrey L., ed. *Schiller's Literary Prose Works: New Translations and Critical Essays*. Rochester, NY: Camden House, 2008.
Hirschmüller, Albrecht. *Freuds Begegnung mit der Psychiatrie*. Tübingen: Diskord, 1991.
Hitzig, Julius Eduard. *Aus Hoffmann's Leben und Nachlass. Zweiter Teil*. Berlin: Ferdinand Dümmler, 1823.
Hitzig, Julius Eduard. "Hofrath Doctor Clarus, Die Zurechnungsfähigkeit des Mörders Johann Christian Woyzeck." In Hitzig, *Zeitschrift für die Criminal-Rechts-Pflege*, 487–499.
Hitzig, Julius Eduard, ed. *Zeitschrift für die Criminal-Rechts-Pflege in den Preußischen Staaten mit Ausschluß der Rheinprovinzen*. vol. 1. Berlin: Ferdinand Dümmler, 1825.
Höcker, Arne. *Epistemologie des Extremen: Lustmord in Kriminologie und Literatur um 1900*. Munich: Wilhelm Fink, 2012.
Höcker, Arne. "Literatur durch Verfahren: Beschreibung eines Kampfes." In *Kafkas Institutionen*, edited by Arne Höcker and Oliver Simons, 235–253. Bielefeld: transcript, 2007.
Höcker, Arne, Jeannie Moser, and Philippe Weber, eds. *Wissen: Erzählen: Narrative der Humanwissenschaften*. Bielefeld: transcript, 2006.
Hoffmann, E. T. A. *The Serapion Brethren*, vol. 1. Translated by Major Alex Ewing. London: George Bell, 1908.
Hoffmann, E. T. A. "Vertheidigungsschrift in zweiter Instanz für den Tabakspinnergesellen Daniel Schmolling welcher seine Geliebte ohne erkennbare Causa facinoris ermordete (Ein Beitrag zur Lehre der Zurechnungsfähigkeit)." In *Zeitschrift für die Criminal-Rechts-Pflege in den Preußischen Staaten mit Ausschluß der Rheinprovinzen*, vol. 1, ed. Julius Eduard Hitzig, 261–376. Berlin: Ferdinand Dümmler, 1825.
Hoffmann-Curtius, Kathrin. "Frauenmord als künstlerisches Thema der Moderne." In *Serienmord. Kriminologische und kulturwissenschaftliche Skizzierungen eines ungeheuerlichen Phänomens*, edited by Frank J. Robertz and Alexandra Thomas, 282–300. Munich: Belleville, 2004.
Hückmann, Dania. "Unrechtes und Ungerechtes: Rache bei Kleist." In *Heinrich von Kleist: Konstruktive und destruktive Funktionen von Gewalt*, edited by

Ricarda Schmitt, Séan Allan, and Steven Howe, 231–246. Würzburg: Königshausen & Neumann, 2012.

Ihering, Rudolf von. *Der Kampf ums Recht.* Vienna: Propyläen, 1900.

Jacobs, Carol. *Uncontainable Romanticism: Shelley, Brontë, Kleist.* Baltimore: Johns Hopkins University Press, 1989.

Jameson, Frederic. *The Antinomies of Realism.* New York: Verso, 2015.

Japp, Uwe. "Das serapiontische Prinzip." In *E. T. A. Hoffmann: Text + Kritik: Sonderband,* edited by Heinz Ludwig Arnold, 63–75. Munich: Text + Kritik, 1992.

Japp, Uwe. "*Die Serapion-Brüder* (1819/21)." In *E. T. A. Hoffmann: Leben—Werk—Wirkung,* edited by Detlef Kremer, 257–267. Berlin: Walter de Gruyter, 2012.

Jolles, André. *Simple Forms: Legend, Saga, Myth, Riddle, Saying, Case, Memorabile, Fairytale, Joke.* Translated by Peter J. Schwartz. New York: Verso, 2017.

Jütte, Robert. "Vom medizinischen Casus zur Krankengeschichte." *Berichte zur Wissenschaftsgeschichte* 15 (1992): 50–52.

Kafka, Franz. *The Trial.* Translated by Breon Mitchell. New York: Schocken, 1999.

Kemper, Dirk. *Ineffabile: Goethe und die Individualitätsproblematik der Moderne.* Munich: Wilhelm Fink, 2004.

Kestner, Johann Christian. "Letter to Goethe Reporting on Jerusalem's Suicide." In Goethe, *Sufferings of Young Werther,* 102–104.

Kittler, Friedrich A. *Aufschreibesysteme: 1800. 1900.* Munich: Wilhelm Fink, 1985.

Kittler, Friedrich A. "Autorschaft und Liebe." In *Austreibung des Geistes aus den Geisteswissenschaften,* edited by Friedrich A. Kittler, 142–173. Paderborn: Verlag Ferdinand Schöningh, 1980.

Kittler, Friedrich A. "Über die Sozialisation Wilhelm Meisters." In *Dichtung als Sozialisationsspiel,* edited by Gerhard Kaiser and Friedrich A. Kittler, 13–124. Göttingen: Vandenhoeck & Ruprecht, 1978.

Kittler, Wolf. "Heimlichkeit und Schriftlichkeit: Das österreichische Strafprozessrecht in Franz Kafkas Roman *Der Proceß.*" *Germanic Review* 78 (2003): 194–222.

Kleist, Heinrich von. "Improbable Veracities." Translated by Carol Jacobs. *Diacritics* 9, no. 4 (Winter 1979): 45.

Kleist, Heinrich von. "Michael Kohlhaas." In *Selected Prose of Heinrich von Kleist,* translated by Peter Wortsman, 143–254. Brooklyn, NY: Archipelago, 2010.

Kleist, Heinrich von. "Michael Kohlhaas [Phöbus-Fassung]." In *Sämtliche Werke und Briefe,* vol. 2, edited by Helmut Sembdner, 292–293. Munich: dtv, 1993.

Klotz, Volker. *Geschlossene und offene Form im Drama.* Munich: Hanser, 1960.

Kolkenbrock-Netz, Jutta. "Wahnsinn der Vernunft - juristische Institution - literarische Praxis: Das Gutachten zum Fall Schmolling und die Erzählung *Der Einsiedler Serapion* von E. T. A. Hoffmann." In *Wege der Literaturwis-*

senschaft, edited by Jutta Kolkenbrock-Netz, Gerhard Plumpe, and Hans Joachim Schrimpf, 122–144. Bonn: Bouvier Verlag Herbert Grundmann, 1985.

Kosenina, Alexander. *Literarische Anthropologie: Die Neuentdeckung des Menschen.* Berlin: Akademie Verlag, 2008.

Kraepelin, Emil. "Die Abschaffung des Strafmaßes: Ein Vorschlag zur Reform der heutigen Strafrechtspflege (1880)." In Kraepelin, *Kriminologische und forensische Schriften*, edited by Wolfgang Burgmair, Eric J. Engstrom, and Paul Hoff, 13–95. Munich: Belleville, 2001.

Krafft-Ebing, Richard von. *Psychopathia sexualis: With Especial Reference to Contrary Sexual Instinct: A Medico-legal Study.* Authorized translation of the 7th enlarged and revised German edition, translated by Charles Gilbert Chaddock. Philadelphia: F. A. Davis, 1892.

Kraus, Karl. "Die Büchse der Pandora." *Die Fackel* 182 (1905): 1–14.

Krause, Marcus. "Zu einer Poetologie literarischer Fallgeschichten," 242–273.

Krupp, Anthony, ed. *Karl Philipp Moritz: Signaturen des Denkens.* Amsterdam: Rodopi, 2010.

Krupp, Anthony. "Observing Children in an Early Journal of Psychology: Karl Philipp Moritz's *Gnothi sauton (Know Thyself)*." In *Fashioning Childhood in the Eighteenth Century: Age and Identity*, edited by Anja Müller, 33–42. Aldershot: Ashgate, 2006.

Laermann, Klaus. *Eigenschaftslosigkeit: Reflexionen zu Musils Roman "Der Mann ohne Eigenschaften."* Stuttgart: Metzler, 1970.

Lau, Viktor. "'Hier muß die ganze Gegend aufgeboten werden, als wenn ein Wolf sich hätte blicken lassen': Zur Interaktion von Jurisprudenz und Literatur in der Spätaufklärung am Beispiel von Friedrich Schillers Erzählung 'Der Verbrecher aus verlorener Ehre.'" *Scientia poetica* 4 (2000): 98–107.

Lehmann, Johannes F. "Erfinden, was der Fall ist: Fallgeschichte und Rahmen bei Schiller, Büchner und Musil." *Zeitschrift für Germanistik* N. F. 19 (2009): 361–380.

Lejeune, Philippe. *On Autobiography.* Translated by Katherine Leary. Minneapolis: University of Minnesota Press, 1989.

Liebrand, Claudia. "Noch einmal: Das wilde, schöne Tier Lulu: Rezeptionsgeschichte und Text." In Gutjahr, *Frank Wedekind*, 179–194.

Lindenau, Heinrich. "Außenseiter der Gesellschaft." *Deutsche Juristen-Zeitung* 31 (1926): 1656.

Linder, Joachim. "'Sie müssen das entschuldigen, Herr Staatsanwalt, aber es ist so: wir trauen euch nicht . . .' Strafjustiz, Strafrechtsreform und Justizkritik im *März*, 1907–1911." In *Erzählte Kriminalität: Zur Typologie und Funktion von narrativen Darstellungen in Strafrechtspflege, Publizistik und Literatur zwischen 1790 und 1920*, edited by Jörg Schönert, 533–570. Tübingen: Niemeyer, 1991.

Lindner, Martin. "Der Mythos 'Lustmord': Serienmörder in der deutschen Literatur, dem Film und der bildenden Kunst zwischen 1892 und 1932." In

Verbrechen–Justiz–Medien: Konstellationen in Deutschland von 1900 bis zur Gegenwart, edited by Joachim Linder and Claus-Michael Ort, 273–305. Tübingen: Niemeyer, 1999.

Lipps, Hans. *Die Verbindlichkeit der Sprache*. Frankfurt am Main: Klostermann, 1958.

Lipps, Hans. "Instance, Example, Case, and the Relationship of the Legal Case to the Law." In Lowrie and Lüdemann, *Exemplarity and Singularity*, 16–35.

Liszt, Franz von. "Die strafrechtliche Zurechnungsfähigkeit: Vortrag, gehalten am 4. August 1896 auf dem III. Internationalen Psychologen-Kongreß." In Franz von Liszt, *Strafrechtliche Aufsätze und Vorträge*, Zweiter Band, 214–229. Berlin: J. Guttentag, 1905.

Lowrie, Michèle, and Susanne Lüdemann, eds. *Exemplarity and Singularity: Thinking in Particulars in Philosophy, Literature, and Law*. London: Routledge, 2015.

Lüdemann, Susanne. "Literarische Fallgeschichten: Schillers 'Verbrecher aus verlorener Ehre' und Kleists 'Michael Kohlhaas.'" In Ruchatz, Willer, and Pethes, *Das Beispiel*, 208–223.

Luhmann, Niklas. "Individuum, Individualität, Individualismus." In *Gesellschaftsstruktur und Semantik: Studien zur Wissenssoziologie der modernen Gesellschaft*, 149–258. Frankfurt am Main: Suhrkamp, 1993.

Lukács, Georg. *Die Theorie des Romans: Ein geschichtsphilosophischer Versuch über die Form der großen Epik*. Bielefeld: Aisthesis, 2009.

Lukács, Georg. "Erzählen oder Beschreiben?" In *Probleme des Realismus*, 101–145. Berlin: Aufbau-Verlag, 1955.

Marcus, Steven. "Freud and Dora: Story, History, Case History." In *Freud: A Collection of Critical Essays*, edited by Perry Meisel, 183–210. Englewood Cliffs, NJ: Prentice Hall, 1981.

Marcus, Steven. "Freud und Dora: Roman, Geschichte, Krankengeschichte." *Psyche* 28, no. 1 (1974): 32–79.

Martin, Ariane. "Büchner und Wedekind." In *Büchner-Rezeptionen—interkulturell und intermedial*, edited by Marco Castellari and Alessandro Costazza, 41–54. Bern: Peter Lang, 2015.

Martyn, David. "The Temper of Exemplarity: Werther's Horse." In Lowrie and Lüdemann, *Exemplarity and Singularity*, 166–180.

Maschka, Josef. "Zeichen der Jungfrauschaft und gesetzwidrige Befriedigung des Geschlechtstriebes." In *Handbuch der gerichtlichen Medicin*, 3:88–192. Tübingen: A. Hirschwald, 1882.

Meier, Albert. *Georg Büchner: Woyzeck*. Munich: Wilhelm Fink, 1980.

Meyer, Adolf-Ernst. "Nieder mit der Novelle als Psychoanalysedarstellung: Hoch lebe die Interaktionsgeschichte." In *Die Fallgeschichte: Beiträge zu ihrer Bedeutung als Forschungsinstrument*, edited by Ulrich Stuhr and Friedrich-Wilhelm Deneke, 61–84. Heidelberg: Asanger Roland Verlag, 1993.

Mittermaier, Carl Joseph Anton. "Bemerkungen über Geberdenprotokolle im Criminalprozesse." *Neues Archiv des Criminalrechts* 1, no. 3 (1816): 327–351.

Mohnkern, Ansgar. "Woran leidet Werther eigentlich? Auch ein Beitrag zur Theorie des Romans." In *Genuss und Qual: Przyjemnosc i cierpiene: Aufsätze und Aufzeichnungen*, edited by Grzegorz Jaskiewicz and Jan Wolski, 21–34. Rzeszów: Wydawnictwo Uniwersytetu Rzeszowskiego, 2014.

Moretti, Franco. "Serious Century." In *The Novel: History, Geography, and Culture*, edited by Franco Moretti, 363–400. Princeton, NJ: Princeton University Press, 2007.

Moritz, Karl Philipp. *Anton Reiser: A Psychological Novel*. Translated by Ritchie Robertson. London: Penguin, 1997.

Moritz, Karl Philipp. *Dichtungen und Schriften zur Erfahrungsseelenkunde*. Edited by Heide Hollmer and Albert Meier. Frankfurt am Main: Deutscher Klassiker Verlag, 2006.

Moritz, Karl Philipp. *Gnothi Seauton oder Magazin zur Erfahrungsseelenkunde als ein Lesebuch für Gelehrte und Ungelehrte: Mit Unterstützung mehrerer Wahrheitsfreunde herausgegeben von Karl Philipp Moritz*. Edited by Petra and Uwe Nettelbeck. Nördlingen: Franz Grelo, 1986.

Moritz, Karl Philipp. "Vorschlag zu einem Magazin einer Erfahrungs-Seelenkunde." In *Werke I: Dichtungen und Schriften zur Erfahrungsseelenkunde*. Edited by Heide Hollmer and Albert Meier, 793–905. Frankfurt am Main: Suhrkamp, 1999.

Moser-Rath, Elfriede. "Anekdote." In *Enzyklopädie des Märchens: Handwörterbuch zur historischen und vergleichenden Erzählforschung*, vol. 1, edited by Kurt Ranke, 528–542. Berlin: De Gruyter, 1999.

Mücke, Dorothea von. *The Seduction of the Occult and the Rise of the Fantastic Tale*. Stanford, CA: Stanford University Press, 2003.

Mülder-Bach, Inka, and Michael Ott, eds. "Einleitung." In *Was der Fall ist: Casus und Lapsus*, 9–31. Paderborn: Wilhelm Fink Verlag, 2014.

Müller, Lothar. *Die kranke Seele und das Licht der Erkenntnis: Karl Philipp Moritz' Anton Reiser*. Frankfurt am Main: Athenaum, 1987.

Müller Sievers, Helmut. *Desorientierung: Anatomie und Dichtung bei Georg Büchner*. Göttingen: Wallstein, 2003.

Musil, Robert. *Gesammelte Werke: Essays und Reden: Kritik*. Edited by Adolf Frisé. Reinbek bei Hamburg: Rowohlt, 1978.

Musil, Robert. *Gesammelte Werke: Prosa und Stücke, Kleine Prosa, Aphorismen, Autobiographisches*. Edited by Adolf Frisé. Reinbek bei Hamburg: Rowohlt, 1978.

Musil, Robert. *The Man without Qualities*, vol. 1. Translated by Sophie Wilkins. New York: Vintage, 1995.

Musil, Robert. *Precision and Soul: Essays and Addresses*. Translated and edited by Burton Pike and David S. Luft. Chicago: University of Chicago Press, 1990.

Nelles, Jürgen. "Werthers Herausgeber oder die Rekonstruktion der 'Geschichte des armen Werthers.'" *Jahrbuch des freien deutschen Hochstifts* (1996): 1–37.

Neumeyer, Harald. "Unkalkulierbar unbewußt: Zur Seele des Verbrechers um 1800." In *Romantische Wissenspoetik: Die Künste und die Wissenschaften um 1800*, edited by Gabriele Brandstetter and Gerhard Neumann, 151–178. Würzburg: Königshausen & Neumann, 2004.

Niehaus, Michael. *Das Verhör: Geschichte—Theorie—Fiktion*. Munich: Wilhelm Fink, 2003.

Niehaus, Michael. "Die sprechende und die stumme Anekdote." *Zeitschrift für deutsche Philologie* 133 (2013): 183–202.

Nietzsche, Friedrich. "Beyond Good and Evil." In *Basic Writings of Nietzsche*, translated and edited by Walter Kaufmann, 179–435. New York: Modern Library, 2000.

Nordau, Max. *Degeneration*. New York: D. Appleton, 1895.

Pabst, Reinhard. "Zwei unbekannte Berichte über die Hinrichtung Johann Christian Woyzecks." *Georg Büchner Jahrbuch* 7 (1988/1989): 338–350.

Pankau, Johannes G. "Prostitution, Tochtererziehung und männlicher Blick in Wedekinds Tagebüchern." In Gutjahr, *Frank Wedekind*, 19–54.

Pankau, Johannes G. *Sexualität und Modernität: Studien zum deutschen Drama des Fin de Siècle*. Würzburg: Königshausen & Neumann, 2005.

Pasquino, Pasquale. "Criminology: The Birth of a Special Knowledge." In *The Foucault Effect: Studies in Governmentality*, edited by Graham Burchell, Colin Gordon, and Peter Miller, 235–250. Chicago: University of Chicago Press, 1991.

Paulin, Roger. *Der Fall Wilhelm Jerusalem: Zum Selbstmordproblem zwischen Aufklärung und Empfindsamkeit*. Göttingen: Wallstein, 1999.

Petersdorff, Dirk von. "'I Shall Not Come to My Senses!' *Werther*, Goethe, and the Formation of Modern Subjectivity." In Goethe, *Sufferings of Young Werther*, 202–217.

Pethes, Nicolas. *Literarische Fallgeschichten: Zur Poetik einer epistemischen Schreibweise*. Konstanz: Konstanz University Press, 2016.

Pethes, Nicolas. "Telling Cases: Writing against Genre in Medicine and Literature." *Literature and Medicine* 32, no. 1 (2014): 24–45.

Pethes, Nicolas. "'Viehdummes Individuum,' 'unsterbliche Experimente': Elements for a Cultural History of Human Experimentation in Georg Büchner's Dramatic Case Study *Woyzeck*." *Monatshefte* 98, no. 1 (2006): 68–82.

Pethes, Nicolas. "Vom Einzelfall zur Menschheit: Die Fallgeschichte als Medium der Wissenspopularisierung zwischen Recht, Medizin und Literatur." In *Popularisierung und Popularität*, edited by Gereon Blaseio, Hedwig Pompe, and Nicolas Pethes, 63–92. Cologne: Dumont, 2005.

Pethes, Nicolas. *Zöglinge der Natur: Der literarische Menschenversuch des 18. Jahrhunderts*. Göttingen: Wallstein, 2007.

Pfotenhauer, Helmut. "'Die Signatur des Schönen' oder 'In wie fern Kunstwerke beschrieben werden können?': Zu Karl Philipp Moritz und seiner italienischen Ästhetik." In *Kunstliteratur als Italienerfahrung*, edited by Helmut Pfotenhauer, 67–83. Tübingen: Niemeyer, 1991.

Pikulik, Lothar. "*Die Serapions-Brüder*: Die Erzählung vom Einsiedler Serapion und das Serapion(t)ische Prinzip—E. T. A. Hoffmanns poetologische Reflexionen." In *Interpretationen: E. T. A. Hoffmann, Romane und Erzählungen*, edited by Günter Saße, 135–156. Stuttgart: Reclam, 2006.
Pomata, Gianna. "The Medical Case Narrative: Distant Reading of an Epistemic Genre." *Literature and Medicine* 32, no. 1 (2014): 1–23.
Prasse, Jutta. "Was ist wirklich geschehen?" In *Sprache und Fremdsprache: Psychoanalytische Aufsätze*, edited by Claus-Dieter Rath, 183–193. Bielefeld: transcript, 2004.
Ratmoko, David. "Das Vorbild im Nachbild des Terrors: Eine Untersuchung des gespenstischen Nachlebens von 'Michael Kohlhaas.'" In Blamberger et al., *Kleist-Jahrbuch*, 218–231.
Ruchatz, Jens, Stefan Willer, and Nicolas Pethes, eds. *Das Beispiel: Epistemologie des Exemplarischen*. Berlin: Kulturverlag Kadmos, 2007.
Rückert, Joachim. "'. . . der Welt in der Pflicht verfallen . . .' Kleists 'Kohlhaas' als moral- und rechtsphilosophische Stellungnahme." In *Kleist-Jahrbuch*, edited by Hans Joachim Kreutzer, 357–403. Berlin: Erich Schmidt Verlag, 1988/1989.
Schäffner, Wolfgang. *Die Ordnung des Wahns: Zur Poetologie psychiatrischen Wissens bei Alfred Döblin*. Munich: Wilhlem Fink, 1995.
Schäffner, Wolfgang. "Psychiatrische Erfahrung und Literatur: Antihermeneutik bei Alfred Döblin." In *Alfred Döblin-Kolloquien Münster 1989*, edited by Werner Stauffacher, 44–56. Marbach: Peter Lang, 1993.
Schiller, Friedrich. "The Criminal of Lost Honor: A True Story." In High, *Schiller's Literary Prose Works*, 39–55.
Schiller, Friedrich. *History of the Revolt of the United Netherlands*. Translated by Lieut. E. B. Eastwick and Rev. A. J. W. Morrison. London: Anthological Society, 1901.
Schiller, Friedrich. *Kritische Gesamtausgabe, Bd. 2: Schillers Briefe*, edited by Fritz Jonas. Stuttgart: DVA, 1893.
Schiller, Friedrich. "Preface to the First Part of the Celebrated Causes of Pitaval." In *Schiller's Complete Works*, vol. 2, edited by Charles J. Hempel, 458–459. Philadelphia: I. Kohler, 1861.
Schiller, Friedrich. *The Robbers*. Translated with an introduction by F. J. Lamport. London: Penguin, 1979.
Schings, Hans-Jürgen. *Melancholie und Aufklärung: Melancholiker und ihre Kritiker in Erfahrungsseelenkunde und Literatur des 18. Jahrhunderts*. Stuttgart: Metzlersche Verlagsbuchhandlung, 1977.
Schlaffer, Hannelore. "Leiden des jungen Werthers (Zweite Fassung)." In Johann Wolfgang von Goethe, *Sämtliche Werke nach Epochen seines Schaffens* (Münchner Ausgabe), Bd. 2.2., edited by Hannelore Schlaffer, Hans J. Becker, and Gerhard H. Müller. Munich: Hanser, 1987.
Schönert, Jörg, ed. *Erzählte Kriminalität: Zur Typologie und Funktion von narrativen Darstellungen in Strafrechtspflege, Publizistik und Literatur zwischen 1790 und 1920*. Tübingen: Niemeyer, 1991.

Schreiber, Elliott. "Thinking inside the Box: Moritz's Critique of the Philanthropist Project of a Non-Coercive Pedagogy." In *Signaturen des Denkens: Karl Philipp Moritz*, edited by Anthony Krupp, 103–130. Amsterdam: Rodopi, 2010.

Schreiber, Elliott. *The Topography of Modernity: Karl Philipp Moritz and the Space of Autonomy*. Ithaca, NY: Cornell University Press, 2012.

Schuller, Marianne. "Erzählen Machen: Narrative Wendungen in der Psychoanalyse nach Freud." In *Wissen: Erzählen: Narrative der Humanwissenschaften*, edited by Arne Höcker, Jeannie Moser, and Philippe Weber, 207–220. Bielefeld: transcript, 2006.

Sebald, Winfried G. "Preußische Perversionen: Anmerkungen zum Thema Literatur und Gewalt, ausgehend vom Frühwerk Alfred Döblins." In *Internationale Alfred-Döblin-Kolloquien*, Basel 1980, New York 1981; Freiburg im Breisgau 1993, edited by Werner Stauffacher, 231–238. Bern: Peter Lang, 1986.

Siebenpfeiffer, Hania. *Böse Lust: Gewaltverbrechen in Diskursen der Weimarer Republik*. Cologne: Böhlau, 2005.

Siebenpfeiffer, Hania. "Re-Writing Jack the Ripper: Zur Semiotik des Lustmords in Frank Wedekinds *Monstretragödie*." In *Lustmord: Medialisierungen eines kulturellen Phantasmas um 1900*, edited by Susanne Komfort-Heim and Susanne Scholz, 55–72. Königstein: Ulrike Helmer, 2007.

Siemsen, Hans. In *Die Weltbühne* 21, no. 1 (1925): 360–361.

Starobinski, Jean. "Psychoanalysis and Literary Understanding." In *The Living Eye*, translated by Arthur Goldhammer, 129–148. Cambridge, MA: Harvard University Press, 1989.

Stemme, Fritz. "Die Säkularisierung des Pietismus zur Erfahrungsseelenkunde." *Zeitschrift für deutsche Philologie* 72 (1953): 144–158.

Stephens, Anthony. "'Eine Träne auf den Brief': Zum Status der Ausdrucksformen in Kleists Erzählungen." In *Kleist: Sprache und Gewalt*, 178–183. Freiburg: Rombach, 1999.

Stern, Jacques. "Über den Wert der dichterischen Behandlung des Verbrechens für die Strafrechtswissenschaft." *Zeitschrift für die gesamte Strafrechtswissenschaft* 26 (1906): 145–171.

Stoker, Bram. *Dracula*. New York: W. W. Norton, 1997.

Stollberg, Michael. "Formen und Funktionen medizinischer Fallgeschichten in der Frühen Neuzeit (1500–1800)." In Süßmann, Scholz, and Engel, *Fallstudien*, 81–95.

Süßmann, Johannes. "Einleitung: Perspektiven der Fallstudienforschung." In Süßmann, Scholz, and Engel, *Fallstudien*, 7–27.

Süßmann, Johannes, Susanne Scholz, and Gisela Engel, eds. *Fallstudien: Theorie, Geschichte, Methode*. Berlin: Trafo, 2007.

Trilling, Lionel. *The Liberal Imagination*. London: Doubleday Anchor, 1951.

Türkel, Siegfried. "Der Lustmörder Christian Voigt: Ein kriminalistisch-psychiatrischer Beitrag zur Lehre vom Lustmord." *Archiv für Kriminalanthropologie und Kriminalistik* 55 (1913): 47–97.

Vischer, Friedrich Theodor. *Ästhetik oder Wissenschaft des Schönen: Zum Gebrauche der Vorlesungen: Dritter Theil, Zweiter Abschnitt.* Stuttgart: Mäcken, 1857.
Vogl, Joseph. "Einleitung." In Vogl, *Poetologien des Wissens*, 7–16.
Vogl, Joseph. "Lebende Anstalt." In *Für Alle und Keinen: Lektüre, Schrift und Leben bei Nietzsche und Kafka*, edited by Friedrich Balke, Joseph Vogl, and Benno Wagner, 21–33. Zurich: Diaphanes, 2008.
Vogl, Joseph, ed. *Poetologien des Wissens um 1800.* Munich: Wilhelm Fink, 1999.
Walkowitz, Judith. *City of Dreadful Delight: Narratives of Sexual Danger in Late-Victorian London.* Chicago: University of Chicago Press, 1992.
Wedekind, Frank. *Diary of an Erotic Life.* Translated by W. E. Yuill. Oxford: Blackwell, 1990.
Wedekind, Frank. *The First Lulu.* Translated by Eric Bentley. New York: Applause Books, 1994.
Wedekind, Frank. *Lulu: Die Büchse der Pandora: Eine Monstretragödie.* Frankfurt am Main: Suhrkamp, 1999.
Wegener, Mai. "Fälle, Ausfälle, Sündenfälle: Zu den Krankengeschichten Freuds." In Düwell and Pethes, *Fall—Fallgeschichte—Fallstudie*, 169–194.
Wellbery, David E. "Afterword to *The Sorrows of Young Werther*." In Goethe, *Sufferings of Young Werther*, 182–187.
Wellbery, David E. "Scheinvorgang: Kafkas *Das Schweigen der Sirenen*." In *Seiltänzer des Paradoxalen: Aufsätze zur ästhetischen Wissenschaft*, 177–195. Munich: Hanser, 2006.
Wetzell, Richard F. *Inventing the Criminal: A History of German Criminology 1880–1945.* Chapel Hill: University of North Carolina Press, 2000.
Wezel, Johann Karl. "Über die Erziehungsgeschichten." In *Gesamtausgabe in acht Bänden*, vol. 7, edited by Jutta Heinz and Cathrin Blöss, 429–441. Heidelberg: Mattis Verlag, 2001.
Willemsen, Roger. *Robert Musil: Vom intellektuellen Eros.* Munich: Piper, 1985.
Willer, Stefan, Jens Ruchatz, and Nicolas Pethes. "Zur Systematik des Beispiels." In Ruchatz, Willer, and Pethes, *Das Beispiel*, 7–59.
Wirth, Uwe. *Die Geburt des Autors aus dem Geist der Herausgeberfiktion: Editoriale Rahmung im Roman um 1800: Wieland, Goethe, Brentano, Jean Paul, E. T. A. Hoffmann.* Munich: Wilhelm Fink, 2008.
Wittgenstein, Ludwig. *Tractatus Logico-Philosophicus.* Translated by C. K. Ogden. New York: Dover, 1998.
Wölffel, Kurt. "Friedrich von Blanckenburgs *Versuch über den Roman*." In *Deutsche Romantheorie: Beiträge zu einer historischen Poetik des Romans in Deutschland*, edited by Reinhold Grimm, 29–60. Frankfurt am Main: Athenäum 1968.
Wübben, Yvonne. "Vom Gutachten zum Fall: Die Ordnung des Wissens in Karl-Philipp Moritz' *Magazin zur Erfahrungsseelenkunde*." In *"Fakta, und kein moralisches Geschwätz": Zu den Fallgeschichten im "Magazin zur Erfahrungsseelenkunde" (1783–1793)*, edited by Sheila Dickson, Stefan Goldmann, and Christof Wingertszahn, 140–158. Göttingen: Wallstein, 2011.

Wulffen, Erich. *Gerhard Hauptmann vor dem Forum der Kriminalpsychologie und Psychiatrie: Naturwissenschaftliche Studien.* Breslau: Langewort, 1908.

Wulffen, Erich. *Ibsens Nora vor dem Strafrichter und Psychiater.* Halle: Marhold, 1907.

Wulffen, Erich. *Psychologie des Giftmordes.* Vienna: Urania, 1917.

Index

Abel, Jacob Friedrich, 79, 90
Abel, Konrad Ludwig, 79
accountability, legal: dangerousness versus, 133n3; diminished responsibility, concept of, 196, 197; Döblin's *Two Girlfriends*, not a factor in, 183; Musil's *Man without Qualities* as critique of, 195–99; priority attributed to, 207; of Schmolling, 101–102, 107, 133–134; of Voigt, 193–194; Wedekind's *Lulu* and, 133–134; of Woyzeck, 117, 118, 119, 120, 122, 124, 129, 131, 133–134, 154
Adorno, Theodor W., "The Position of the Narrator in the Contemporary Novel," 205–206
Alexis, Willibald, and Julius Eduard Hitzig, eds., *Neue Pitaval* (1842–1890), 9–10, 142

amentia occulta, 104–105, 108
Andriopoulos, Stefan, 175
anecdotal reading of case, 140–143
Anthropology from a Pragmatic Point of View (Kant, 1785), 106
Anton Reiser (Moritz; 1785–1790). See Moritz, Karl Philipp, *Anton Reiser*
Anz, Thomas, 171
Archiv für Kriminalanthropologie und Kriminalistik, 195
Aristotle, *Poetics*, 80, 85, 89
Aufschreibesystem, 188n25

Bachofen, Johann Jakob, 146
Basedow, Johann Bernhard, 54, 59n25
Beccaria, Cesare, *On Crime and Punishment*, 116
Beobachtungen, 13, 141
Bergk, Johann Adam, 116

Berlin Alexanderplatz (Döblin, 1929), 171
Berlin Program (*To Novelists and Their Critics*; Döblin, 1913), 187–189
Beulwitz, Caroline von, 91
Bezold, Raimund, 60n27
Bilder-Lexikon der Sexualwissenschaft (1930), 178
Bildung, 15, 66, 79, 80, 173
Bildungsroman, 35, 36n23, 67, 67n43, 129n28, 173, 208
Binswanger, Otto, 194
Blanckenburg, Friedrich von: review of Goethe's *Werther* (1775), 40–43, 48, 66; *Versuch über den Roman* (1774), 40, 41, 43, 50–51, 65, 65n38, 70, 192
Bloch, Ernst, 83
Bloch, Iwan, 135–136
Bossinade, Johanna, 146
bourgeois gender/sexual norms in Wedekind's *Lulu*, 148–151, 153, 207–208
bourgeois or poetic realism, 19–21, 207–208
Bovenschen, Silvia, 148n40
Büchner, Georg: legal accountability, concept of, 19; *Lenz* (1836), 164n16; realism, problem of, 20–21
Büchner, Georg, *Woyzeck* (1837), 114–131,128n27; barber scene, 124–125, 130n30; Clarus reports and, 116–117, 121, 127, 128, 128n27, 130; decomposition of authority in, 153–154, 207; drama and case, relationship between, 120–123; Hoffmann/Schmolling case and, 112–113; *immer zu, immer zu*, 128; on making of case, 117, 130–131; staging observation in, 123–127, 154; unfinished nature of, 116–117, 121; Wedekind's *Lulu* compared, 132. *See also* Woyzeck, Johann Christian

Cameron, Deborah, 138
Campe, Joachim Heinrich, 54
Campe, Rüdiger, 36n23, 46n51, 117, 122, 128; *The Game of Probability* (2013), 84–85
case as novella, 162–167, 164n16
cases in fictional narratives, 1–23; casuistic reasoning and, 10, 18; definition and historical development of case narratives, 5–12; didacticism, literary move away from, 3–4, 40; eighteenth century psychological knowledge and, 19, 22, 93–95, 207 (*See also* Goethe; Kleist; Moritz; Schiller); as individual biographies, 13–14; interdisciplinary nature of, 94; Jerusalem case and Goethe's *Werther*, 1–5, 16; as literary case histories, 16–18, 93–95; narrative perspective of, 94–95; nineteenth century legal/medical institutions and, 19–21, 22–23, 99–100, 152–154 (*See also* Büchner; Hoffmann; sexology and sexological cases; Wedekind); scholarship on, 11–14; shift in status of literature in context of legal/psychological discourse, 100, 102–103, 112–113; three phases of, 18–23; twentieth century, realist demands of literature in, 19, 21–22, 23, 205–211 (*See also* Döblin; Freud; Kafka; Musil)
The Castle (*Das Schloss*, Kafka; 1926), 36n23
casuistry and the literary case history, 10, 18; in Döblin's *Two Girlfriends*, 180–183; Goethe's *Werther*, Blanckenburg's review of, 41–42; Hoffmann, Büchner, and Wedekind undermining casuistic displays of authority, 152–154
Cervantes, Miguel de, 164n16
Clarus, Johann Christian August, 102, 114–120, 120n11, 121, 127, 128, 128n27, 130, 154
Class, Monika, 58n19
cold narration, 71–73, 90, 189
cold observation, 56, 61, 64, 69–70, 71–73, 94

Index 231

consilia, 5
Corino, Karl, 193
"Creative Writers and Day-Dreaming" (Freud, 1906–1908), 159
The Criminal of Lost Honor (Schiller, 1786). *See* Schiller, Friedrich, *The Criminal of Lost Honor*
criminological/legal cases, 4–5, 9–10, 13. *See also* nineteenth century legal/medical institutions and cases in fictional narratives; *specific cases*

dangerousness versus accountability, concept of, 132–140, 133n3, 134n5
de Sade, Marquis, 135–136, 158
Degeneration (Nordau, 1892), 158, 159n5
Dessau school, 53, 59n25
Deutsche Allgemeine Zeitung, 178
didacticism, literary move away from, 3–4, 40
diminished responsibility, 196, 197
Dippold, Andreas, 134n5
Döblin, Alfred: *Berlin Alexanderplatz* (1929), 171; *Berlin Program* (*To Novelists and Their Critics*; 1913), 187–189; "Doctor and Poet" (1927), 189; Freud, seventieth birthday speech for, 171; *Das Leben Jacks, des Bauchaufschlitzers*, 138; legal accountability, concept of, 19; medical/psychiatric experience of, 171, 180; Musil's poetology compared to, 190–191; realism, problem of, 20–21; *Der schwarze Vorhang* (1912/1919), 202
Döblin, Alfred, *The Two Girlfriends and Their Murder by Poisoning* (1924), 174–189; accountability not a factor in, 182; casuistry in, 180–183; domestic abuse of Klein, 176–177, 180; as "fantasy of facts," 23, 184, 188, 189, 192, 208; handwriting analysis and act of letter-writing in, 183–186; homosexuality of Klein and Nebbe, 176–177, 180–182; literary agenda of, 21–22, 174–176, 186–189, 207, 208; murder of Willi Klein by Elli Klein and Grete Nebbe, 176–180; in *Outsiders of Society* series, 175
dogs, sexual relations with, 140–141
domestic abuse, in Klein/Nebbe case, 176–177, 180–181
Dora case (Freud's "Fragment of an Analysis of Hysteria"; 1905), 162, 168–170
Dörr, Volker C., 50n3, 52n9
Dracula (Stoker, 1897), 138
Droste-Hülshoff, Annette von, *Die Judenbuche* (1842), 19
Düwell, Susanne, 15

Eckermann, Johann Peter, 165–166
eighteenth century literary case histories, 19, 22, 93–95, 207. *See also* Goethe; Kleist; Moritz; Schiller
Elective Affinities (Goethe, 1809), 165–166
Ellis, Havelock, 146
Emilia Galotti (Lessing, 1772), 2, 38
Engels, Friedrich, 146
epistemic genre, 6n13
epistolary format: Döblin's *Two Girlfriends*, handwriting analysis and act of letter-writing in, 183–186; of Goethe's *Werther*, 3–4, 27–28, 52; Moritz's *Anton Reiser* and, 50, 52
Erfahrungsseelenkunde: Magazin für Erfahrungsseelenkunde, ed. Moritz (1783–1793), 9, 10, 13, 13n27, 48, 51, 51n5, 53, 57–62, 58–59n22, 63, 67–68; in Moritz's *Anton Reiser*, 22, 50–51, 53–61, 63, 64, 66–67, 68, 70; Moritz's project of, 22, 60n27, 71, 72, 80, 90, 94, 207
Eulenburg, Albert, 135–136
exemplarity and Goethe's *Werther*, 30–33, 31n10, 32n12, 40–42, 43
exordium or principium, 82

Die Fackel, 139
Der Fall Vukobrankovic (Ernst Weiß), 175

Feuerbach, Anselm Ritter von, 115; *Merkwürdige Kriminal-Rechtsfälle in aktenmäßiger Darstellung* (1808–1829), 9, 142
Fineman, Joel, 143
Fleming, Paul, 20–21n40, 32n12, 143
Fließ, Wilhelm, 164
Florack, Ruth, 139, 144, 148, 148n40, 149
Fontane, Theodor, *Unterm Birnbaum* (1885), 19
forensic narratives. *See* cases in fictional narratives
Forrester, John, 8, 14
Foucault, Michel, 8–9, 11–12, 30, 58–59n22, 99, 115, 134, 134n6; *Discipline and Punish* (1977), 11–12
Franz, Carl Wilhelm, 78
Franzos, Karl Emil, 121
Frazer, Elisabeth, 138
Freud, Sigmund, 13, 21, 157–173; on case as novella, 162–167, 164n16; "Creative Writers and Day-Dreaming" (1906–1908), 159; Dora case ("Fragment of an Analysis of Hysteria"; 1905), 162, 168–170; Elisabeth von R. case, 162–134; influence on literature, 171–173, 208; on literary fiction and psychoanalysis, 157–162; medical tradition of case history and, 163n13; reading Romantic poetry as case histories, 101; *Studies on Hysteria* (1895), 23, 162–134, 166–167, 170; "The Uncanny" (1919), 101n2, 164n16; Wedekind's *Lulu* and, 146; Wolfman case (1918), 169
Frey, Christiane, 39, 36n25, 40, 51n7
From My Life: Poetry and Truth (Goethe, 1811), 39–40
Fürnkäs, Josef, 65n38

Gailus, Andreas, 13n27, 53–54, 58–59, 83n22
gender: boyishness of Elli Klein, 181, 181n15; homosexuality and Klein/Nebbe murders, 176–177, 180–182; *Lustmord/Lustmörder*, as masculine crime, 149, 151, 178; typical female crime, Klein/Nebbe murder viewed as, 177–179; Wedekind's *Lulu* and bourgeois sexual/gender norms, 148–151, 153, 207–208
Goethe, Johann Wolfgang: acquaintance with Moritz, 48; case as novella and, 165–166; on Classicism and Romanticism, 172; *Elective Affinities* (1809), 166; as literary author, 93–94; *From My Life: Poetry and Truth* (1811), 39–40; *Wilhelm Meister's Apprenticeship* (1795–1796), 34–35, 35–36nn23–24, 39, 191
Goethe, Johann Wolfgang, *The Sufferings of Young Werther* (1774), 22, 28–48; *being away* in, 27, 28; Blanckenburg's review of (1775), 40–43, 48, 66; casuistry and, 41–42; concealed authorship of, 2n2, 3–4, 93; in development of literary case histories, 16–18; editor/Werther-as-narrator in, 30–31, 44–48, 94; epistolary format of, 3–4, 27–28, 52; exemplarity and, 30–33, 40–42, 43, 31n10, 32n12; Hoffmann's Serapiontic principle and, 153; individuality and, 28, 29–30, 37, 43; interdisciplinary nature of narrative, 94; Jerusalem case and, 1–5, 16; Kafka's *The Trial* and, 209; literature as frame of reference for, 37–40; Moritz's *Anton Reiser* and, 48, 49–53, 50n4; new form of authorship, initiating, 2n2; Nietzsche on, 37–38n27; peasant boy story in second version, 44, 46–48; public impact of, 39–40, 43; rhetoric, dismissal of, 47, 47n58; second version (1787), as psychological case history, 31–32, 44–48, 49–50, 50–51, 95; self-observation in, 28, 39; subjectivity of Werther, 27–30
Goldmann, Stefan, 163n13, 164n16, 166

Grosz, George, 138
Grundriß aller medizinischer Wissenschaften (Herz, 1782), 58

Haarmann, Fritz, 175
Hamacher, Bernd, 73n3, 76, 82n21
handwriting analysis and act of letter-writing in Döblin's *Two Girlfriends*, 183–186
Harden, Maximilian, 135
Hart, Gail K., 91
Hauptmann, Gerhard, *Lineman Thiel* (1888), 164n16
Herd, Elisabeth, 1
Herz, Marcus, 58n20; *Grundriß aller medizinischer Wissenschaften* (1782), 58
Hess, Volker, 7n16
Hirschfeld, Magnus, 176
History of the Revolt of the United Netherlands (Schiller, 1788), 88–89, 89n36
Hitzig, Julius Eduard: Hoffmann and Schmolling case and, 101n2–102n5,105–106nn6–7, 108n11, 111n16; *Neue Pitaval* (1842–1890), ed. (with Willibald Alexis), 9–10, 142; Woyzeck, review of psychiatric report on, 102
Hoche, Alfred, 180
Hoffbauer, Johann Christoff, 106
Hoffmann, E. T. A., and Schmolling case, 19, 23, 101–113; accountability of Schmolling and, 101–102, 107, 133; facts of Schmolling murder case, 103–109; Hitzig's, 101–102nn2–5,105–106nn6–7, 108n11, 111n16; literary author, Hoffmann as, 101–103, 109–112; on medical versus literary-philosophical competence for psychological evaluation in legal matters, 100–102, 106–109, 152–154; Serapiontic principle and, 23, 109–113, 137, 152–153, 154, 207
Hoffmann, E. T. A., *The Sandman* (1816), 101n2, 164n16

homosexuality and Klein/Nebbe murders, 176–178, 180–182, 187

Ihering, Rudolf von, 83
Imago (journal), 176
individuality: cases and, 13–14; in Goethe's *Werther*, 28, 29, 37, 43; modern, 89n36
insufficient cause, principle of, 190, 192

Jack the Ripper, 137–140, 144, 148–151, 153
Jacobs, Carol, 89n36
Jakob von Gunten (Walser, 1909), 36n23
Jameson, Frederic, 21
Jerusalem, Karl Wilhelm, 1–4, 16
Jolles, André, 165; *Simple Forms* (1930), 7–8, 8n17
Joyce, James, 171
Die Judenbuche (Droste-Hülshoff, 1842), 19
Juncker, Axel, 202

Kafka, Franz: *Der Proceß* (*The Trial*; 1914–1915/1925), 36n23, 209–211; *Das Schloss* (*The Castle*; 1926), 36n23; "The Silence of the Sirens" (1931), 211
Kant, Immanuel, *Anthropology from a Pragmatic Point of View* (1785), 106
Keller, Gottfried, 20
Kestner, Johann Christian, 1–3
Kinostil or kinematic style, 187
Kisch, Egon Erwin, 175
Kittler, Friedrich, 4n7, 34–35, 38–39, 188n25
Klages, Ludwig, *Handschrift und Charakter* (1917), 183
Klein, Elli, 174, 176–180, 184. See also Döblin, Alfred, *The Two Girlfriends and Their Murder by Poisoning*
Klein, Willi, 176–178
Kleist, Heinrich von, as literary author, 93–94

Kleist, Heinrich von, *Michael Kohlhaas* (1808–1810), 17, 22, 71–92; case versus history in, 86–92; Elector of Saxony passage in, 84–85; history and story, conflict between, 82–90, 83n22, 92, 93, 94–95, 207; Schiller's *Criminal of Lost Honor* and, 73n3, 76–78, 76n11, 82, 86, 87, 92; Schiller's *History of the Revolt of the United Netherlands* and, 88–89, 89n36; tear falling on letter in, 73–78, 76n11, 82–83
Kolkenbrock-Netz, Jutta, 111
Kraepelin, Emil, 133n4
Krafft-Ebing, Richard von: on literary fiction, 157–158, 161; *Psychopathia sexualis* (1886), 13, 135, 136–146, 140n23, 150, 161; Wedekind's *Lulu* and, 133–134, 140n23, 151
Kraus, Karl, 139, 148, 151, 153
Krupp, Anthony, 51n5

Lacan, Jacques, 167
Lämmert, Eberhart, 66
Lavater, Johann Kaspar, 3
Das Leben Jacks, des Bauchaufschlitzers (Döblin), 138
legal responsibility. *See* accountability, legal
legal/criminological cases, 4–5, 9–10, 13
legal/medical institutions in nineteenth century and cases in fictional narratives, 19–23. *See also* Büchner; Hoffmann; sexology and sexological cases; Wedekind
Lehmann, Johannes, 125n21
Lehne, Henriette, murder of, 103–104. *See also* Hoffmann, E. T. A., and Schmolling case
Lenz (Büchner, 1836), 164n16
Lenz, Michael Reinhold, 164n16
Leonhard, Rudolf, *Outsiders of Society* series, 175
Lessing, Gotthold Ephraim, *Emilia Galotti* (1772), 2, 38
Lessing, Theodor, 175

Letter about the Novel (Schlegel, 1799), 191
Liebrand, Claudia, 151
Lindenau, Heinrich, 175
Linder, Joachim, 175
Lineman Thiel (Hauptmann, 1888), 164n16
Lipps, Hans, 87n31, 142
Liszt, Franz von, *Die strafrechtliche Zurechnungsfähigkeit* (1896), 133n3, 196
literary case histories, 16–18, 93–95. *See also* cases in fictional narratives
literary-artistic practice: analogies drawn between sexual violence and, 144–146, 151, 153; case as novella, 162–167, 164n16; degeneracy and, 158; didacticism, move away from, 3–4, 40; Döblin's *Two Girlfriends,* literary agenda of, 21–22, 174–176, 186–189, 207, 208; Freud's influence on modernist writing, 171–173, 208; Goethe's *Werther,* literature as frame of reference for, 37–40; Kleist, Moritz, and Goethe regarded as literary authors, 93–94; medical versus literary-philosophical competence for psychological evaluation in legal matters, 100–102, 106–109, 152–153; Musil's *Man without Qualities,* literary/aesthetic agenda of, 21–22, 198–204, 206, 208; psychoanalysis and, 157–162; reality value of, 159; sexology and, 157–158, 165; shift in status of literature in context of legal/psychological discourse, 100, 103, 112–113; Wedekind's literary process and anecdotal reading of cases, 140–143
Lombroso, Cesare, 138, 158
Lüdemann, Susanne, 31n10, 73n3, 91
Luhmann, Niklas, 29, 37n26
Lukács, Georg, 19–20; *Theory of the Novel* (1914), 205
Lulu (Wedekind, 1894). *See* Wedekind, Frank, *Lulu*

Lustmord/Lustmörder, concept of, 138, 139, 149, 150, 178, 195, 197–198, 202–204

Magazin für Erfahrungsseelenkunde (ed. Moritz; 1783–1793), 9, 10, 13, 13n27, 48, 50, 51n5, 53–54, 57–61, 58–59n22, 62–63, 67–68
Maimon, Salomon, 51
The Man without Qualities (Musil, 1930–1943). See Musil, Robert, *The Man without Qualities*
manie sans délire, 105
Marcus, Steven, 168
Martyn, David, 31n10, 39, 40
Maschka, Josef, *Handbuch der gerichtlichen Medicin* (1882), 141
medical/psychiatric cases, 5–7, 10, 99. See also nineteenth century legal/medical institutions and cases in fictional narratives; sexology and sexological cases; *specific cases*
Mendelsohn, Moses, 58
Merkwürdige Kriminal-Rechtsfälle in aktenmäßiger Darstellung (Feuerbach, 1808–1829), 9, 142
Merkwürdige Rechtsfälle als ein Beitrag zur Geschichte des Menschen (ed. Schiller, 1792), 78–79, 80
Merzdorff, Dr., 104, 105–106, 105–106n7
Metzger, Johann Daniel, 106
Meynert, Theodor, 163
Michael Kohlhaas (Kleist, 1808–1810). See Kleist, Heinrich von, *Michael Kohlhaas*
Mill, John Stuart, 179
Mittermaier, Joseph Anton, 115
Moosbrugger. See Musil, Robert, *The Man without Qualities*
moral theology, cases in, 5
Moretti, Franco, 19, 20
Moritz, Karl Philipp: acquaintance with Goethe, 48; on autonomy of the artwork, 52n8; *Erfahrungs-seelenkunde* project, 22, 60n27, 71, 72, 80, 90, 94, 207; *Fakta*, call for, 189; on importance of childhood for adult development, 58n22, 59n25; on importance of self-observation, 60n27, 71; as literary author, 93–94; *Magazin für Erfahrungsseelenkunde*, ed. (1783–1793), 9, 10, 13, 13n27, 48, 51, 51n5, 53–54, 57–61, 58–59n22, 62–63, 67–68; philanthropism, critique of, 59n25; "Vorschlag für ein Magazin zur Erfahrungsseelenkunde" (1782), 54, 57–61
Moritz, Karl Philipp, *Anton Reiser* (1785–1790), 22, 49–70; childhood experiences of Moritz, based on, 62–64; cold observation/cold narration in, 56, 59–61, 64, 69–70, 71–73, 94; concealed authorship of, 93; in context of *Erfahrungsseelenkunde*, 22, 51, 53–61, 62–63, 64, 67, 68, 70; epistolary format and, 50, 52; Goethe's *Werther* and, 48, 50–52, 50n4; Hoffmann's Serapiontic principle and, 153; implementing Moritz's "Vorschlag für ein Magazin zur Erfahrungsseelenkunde," 71–72; as psychological novel, 50–53, 62–70, 207; self-observation in, 48, 51–52, 56–57, 60–61, 60n27, 69
Mücke, Dorothea von, 108
Müller, Lothar, 51n7, 58n20
Müller-Sievers, Helmut, 128
Musil, Robert: "Charakterologie und Dichtung" (1926), 198, 203; Döblin's poetology compared to, 190–191; on Döblin's *Two Girlfriends*, 179–180; on Klein/Nebbe murder, 179; legal accountability, concept of, 19; on literature and psychoanalysis, 171; "The Obscene and Pathological in Art" (1911), 201–202; "On the Essay" (1914), 200; "Possibilities of an Aesthetic" (1914), 199

Musil, Robert, *The Man without Qualities* (1930–1943), 23, 190–204; "imaginary precision" in, 21, 23, 200, 208; insufficient cause, principle of, 190, 192; legal accountability, as critique of, 195–199; literary/aesthetic agenda of, 21–22, 198–204, 206, 208; qualitativelessness, concept of, 190–193; "utopia of essayism" in, 199–202, 206, 208; Voigt case, use of, 193–195, 202–203

Nebbe, Grete, 174, 176–180, 184. See also Döblin, Alfred, *The Two Girlfriends and Their Murder by Poisoning*
Neue Pitaval (ed. Alexis and Hitzig, 1842–1890), 9–10, 142
Newes, Tilly, 151
Niehaus, Michael, 143
Niethammer, Friedrich Immanuel, 78
Nietzsche, Friedrich, 37–38n27
nineteenth century legal/medical institutions and cases in fictional narratives, 19–20, 21–23, 99–100, 152–154, 207–208. See also Büchner; Hoffmann; sexology and sexological cases; Wedekind
Nordau, Max, 138; *Degeneration* (1892), 158, 159n5
Novalis, 100
novel of the institution, 36n23
novella, case regarded as, 162–167, 164n16

observation: *Beobachtungen*, 13, 141; as cold, 56, 60–61, 61, 64, 69–70, 71–73; Schiller's poetic approach to, 80–82; staging of, in Büchner's *Woyzeck*, 122–127, 154. See also *Erfahrungsseelenkunde*; self-observation
observationes, 5, 61–62
Outsiders of Society: The Crimes of Today series, 175

Pädagogische Unterhandlungen, 54
Pankau, Johannes G., 140n23, 142
Peer, Josephine, 193, 194
Pethes, Nicolas, 14–15, 20, 122
philanthropism, 59n25
Phöbus (journal), 75
Pietism, 60n27
Pinel, Philippe, 105, 111
Pitaval, François Gayot de, ed., *Causes célèbres et interessantes* (1734–1743), 9–10, 58–59, 72, 78–80, 90, 142, 175
Platner, Ernst, 105, 105–106n7
Pockels, Karl Friedrich, 51
poetic or bourgeois realism, 19–21, 207–208
Poetics (Aristotle), 80, 85, 89
poetics of contingency, 188, 189, 195
poetology of knowledge, 15, 187
Pomata, Gianna, 6n13
Prasse, Jutta, 164
principium or exordium, 82
Der Proceß (*The Trial*, Kafka; 1914–1915/1925), 36n23
Protowsky, Ella, 194
psychiatric/medical cases, 5–7, 10, 99. See also nineteenth century legal/medical institutions and cases in fictional narratives; sexology and sexological cases; *specific cases*
Psychopathia sexualis (Krafft-Ebing, 1886), 13, 135–146, 140n23, 150, 161

Quintilian, 82

realism: poetic or bourgeois, 19–21, 207–208; problem of, 19–22; twentieth century, realist demands of literature in, 19, 21–22, 23, 205–211 (*See also* Döblin; Freud; Kafka; Musil)
reality value of literary fiction, 159
Redl, Generalstabs-Oberst, 175
Reil, Johann Christian, 106, 111
responsibility, legal. *See* accountability, legal

rhetoric: dismissal of, in Goethe's
    Werther, 47, 47n58; in Schiller's
    Criminal of Lost Honor, 82–83
Richardson, Samuel, *Pamela,* 28
Romanticism, 100–101, 137, 172
Rousseau, Jean-Jacques, *Julie,* 28
Rückert, Joachim, 74n7

Sade, Marquis de, 135–136,
    158
sadism, 135, 137
Schäffner, Wolfgang, 187
Schiller, Friedrich, 9–10; anecdotal
    reading of case and, 141; *History of
    the Revolt of the United Netherlands*
    (1788), 88–89, 89n36; in inner
    versus historical truth, 91; as literary
    author, 93–94; *Merkwürdige
    Rechtsfälle als ein Beitrag zur
    Geschichte des Menschen,* ed.
    (1792), 78, 80
Schiller, Friedrich, *The Criminal of
    Lost Honor* (1786), 22, 71–92; case
    versus history in, 86–92; cold
    observation/narration, call for,
    71–73, 90, 94, 189, 207; Goethe's
    Werther compared, 28–29; history
    and story, conflict between, 80–82,
    93; interdisciplinary nature of
    narrative, 94; Kleist's *Michael
    Kohlhaas* and, 73n3, 75–78, 76n11,
    82–84, 86, 87, 92; as literary case
    history, 17, 21, 72–73; Moritz's
    concept of self-observation and, 56;
    Pitaval, influence of, 78–80
Schlaffer, Hannelore, 44
Schlegel, Friedrich, 100; *Letter about
    the Novel* (1799), 191
Das Schloss (*The Castle,* Kafka; 1926),
    36n23
Schmolling, Daniel. *See* Hoffmann,
    E. T. A., and Schmolling case
Schneider, Marie, 133n3, 134n5
Schreiber, Elliott, 50n4
Schwan, Friedrich, 79, 90
Der schwarze Vorhang (Döblin,
    1912/1919), 202

Seelenkrankheitskunde, 58
self-observation: in Goethe's *Werther,*
    28, 39; Moritz on importance of, 71;
    in Moritz's *Anton Reiser,* 48, 50–53,
    56–57, 59–62, 60n27, 69; Pietism
    and, 60n27
Serapiontic principle, 23, 109–113,
    137, 152–153, 154, 207
sexology and sexological cases: dogs,
    sexual relations with, 140–141;
    homosexuality and Klein/Nebbe
    murders, 176–178, 180–182, 187;
    Jack the Ripper, 137–140, 144,
    148–151, 153; Klein/Nebbe murder,
    176–179; literary material and,
    157–158, 165; *Lustmord/Lust-
    mörder,* concept of, 138, 139, 149,
    150, 178, 195, 197–198, 202–204;
    Musil's "The Obscene and Patho-
    logical in Art," 201–202; nineteenth
    century medico-legal scientific
    developments and, 13–14, 99,
    112–113, 153; Voigt case, 193–195;
    Wedekind's *Lulu* and, 23, 112,
    134–141, 144–146, 148, 151, 153,
    207–208. *See also* Krafft-Ebing,
    Richard von
sexual/physical abuse, in Klein/Nebbe
    case, 176, 177, 180–181
Siebenpfeiffer, Hania, 144
Society of the Tower, in Goethe's
    Wilhelm Meister, 34–35, 39,
    36n23
Starobinski, Jean, 160n9
Stephens, Anthony, 75, 76
Stern, Jacques, 134n8
Stevenson, Robert Louis, *The Strange
    Case of Dr. Jekyll and Mr. Hyde*
    (1886), 138
Stifter, Adalbert, 20, 20–21n40
Stoker, Bram, *Dracula* (1897), 138
*The Strange Case of Dr. Jekyll and
    Mr. Hyde* (Stevenson, 1886), 138
Studies on Hysteria (Freud, 1895), 23,
    162, 166–167, 169
Sudermann, Hermann, *Der Wunsch*
    (1894), 166–167

The Sufferings of Young Werther
(Goethe, 1774). *See* Goethe, Johann
Wolfgang, *The Sufferings of Young
Werther*

The Sandman (Hoffmann, 1816),
101n2, 164n16
"thinking in cases," 8, 9, 14, 20, 34,
206
*To Novelists and Their Critics (Berlin
Program;* Döblin, 1913), 187–189
Tractatus Logico-Philosophicus
(Wittgenstein, 1921), 205
The Trial (Der Proceß, Kafka;
1914–1915/1925), 36n23
Türkel, Siegfried, 195
twentieth century, realist demands of
literature in, 19, 21–22, 23,
205–211. *See also* Döblin; Freud;
Kafka; Musil
*The Two Girlfriends and Their Murder
by Poisoning* (Döblin, 1924).
See Döblin, Alfred, *The Two
Girlfriends and Their Murder by
Poisoning*

"The Uncanny" (Freud, 1919), 101n2,
164n16
Unterm Birnbaum (Fontane, 1885), 19

Vischer, Friedrich Theodor, *Aesthetics*
(1857), 166
Vogl, Joseph, 15
Voigt, Christian, 193–195, 202.
See also Musil, Robert, *The Man
without Qualities*
Vorwärts, 178

Walkowitz, Judith, *City of Dreadful
Delight,* 138
Walser, Robert, *Jakob von Gunten*
(1909), 36n23
Weber, H. B., 104–105
Wedekind, Frank, *Lulu* (1894), 21, 23,
132–151; analogy between artistic
practice and sexual violence in,
144–146, 151, 153; anecdotal

reading of case and literary process
of, 140–143; bourgeois gender/
sexual norms in, 148–151, 153,
207–208; Büchner's *Woyzeck*
compared, 132; *Die Büchse der
Pandora (Pandora's Box),* 153,
133n2, 148n40; character of Lulu in,
147–148; classic dramatic form,
rejection of, 146–147; critical
program, absence of, 149; dangerousness versus accountability,
concept of, 132–140, 133n3, 134n5;
Doppeldrama, 148n40; *Erdgeist,*
133n2, 148n40; *The First Lulu,*
133n2, 139–140, 144–145, 148n40,
149, 149n45, 151, 153; Hoffmann/
Schmolling case and, 112–113; Jack
the Ripper in, 137–140, 144,
148–151, 153; no single historical
case model for, 132, 137; in
sexological context, 23, 112,
133–142, 144–146, 148, 151, 153,
207–208; versions of, 133n2,
148n40; Wedekind's performance of
Jack the Ripper in, 150–151, 153
Wegener, Mai, 163n13, 167
Weiß, Ernst, *Der Fall Vukobrankovic,*
175
Wellbery, David, 29, 211
Werther (Goethe, 1774). *See* Goethe,
Johann Wolfgang, *The Sufferings of
Young Werther*
Wezel, Johann Karl, 80; "Über die
Erziehungsgeschichten" (1778),
54–57, 58, 61
Wilhelm Meister's Apprenticeship
(Goethe, 1795–1796), 34, 35–
36nn23–24, 39, 191
Wirth, Uwe, 95n1
Wittgenstein, Ludwig, *Tractatus
Logico-Philosophicus* (1921), 205
Wolfman case (Freud, 1918), 169
Woost, Johanna Christiane, murder of,
114–115. *See also* Woyzeck, Johann
Christian
Woyzeck (Büchner). *See* Büchner,
Georg, *Woyzeck*

Woyzeck, Johann Christian: accountability of, determining, 117, 118, 119, 120, 122, 124, 129, 131, 133–134, 154; Clarus's psychiatric reports on, 102, 114–119, 120n11, 121, 127, 128, 130; Hitzig's review of psychiatric report on, 101–102; judicial procedure in sentencing of, 114–115
writing, act of, in Döblin's *Two Girlfriends*, 183–186

Wulffen, Erich, 159n5; *Psychology of Murder by Poisoning* (1917), 178
Der Wunsch (Sudermann, 1894), 166–167

Zeitschrift für die Criminal-Rechts-Pflege, 101, 104–105
Zeitschrift für die gesamte Strafrechtswissenschaft, 158
Zeitschrift für Staatsarzneikunde, 117
Die Zukunft, 135

CPSIA information can be obtained
at www.ICGtesting.com
Printed in the USA
LVHW051400190620
658368LV00007B/495